™

References for the Rest of Us

W9-CEN-849

COMPUTER BOOK SERIES FROM IDG

Are you intimidated and confused by computers? Do you find that traditional manuals are overloaded with technical details you'll never use? Do your friends and family always call you to fix simple problems on their PCs? Then the *". . . For Dummies"*™ computer book series from IDG is for you.

". . . For Dummies" books are written for those frustrated computer users who know they aren't really dumb but find that PC hardware, software, and indeed the unique vocabulary of computing make them feel helpless. *". . . For Dummies"* books use a lighthearted approach, a down-to-earth style, and even cartoons and humorous icons to diffuse computer novices' fears and build their confidence. Lighthearted but not lightweight, these books are a perfect survival guide to anyone forced to use a computer.

> "I like my copy so much I told friends; now they bought copies."
>
> **Irene C., Orwell, Ohio**

> "Quick, concise, nontechnical, and humorous."
>
> **Jay A., Elburn, IL**

> "Thanks, I needed this book. Now I can sleep at night."
>
> **Robin F., British Columbia, Canada**

Already, hundreds of thousands of satisfied readers agree. They have made *". . . For Dummies"* books the #1 introductory level computer book series and have written asking for more. So if you're looking for the most fun and easy way to learn about computers look to *". . . For Dummies"* books to give you a helping hand.

IDG BOOKS

PCs
FOR
DUMMIES™
2ND EDITION

PCs FOR DUMMIES™
2ND EDITION

by **Dan Gookin,**
author of bestselling
DOS For Dummies and *WordPerfect For Dummies*

and **Andy Rathbone**
author of bestselling
Windows For Dummies and
Upgrading and Fixing PCs For Dummies

IDG
BOOKS

IDG Books Worldwide, Inc.
An International Data Group Company

San Mateo, California ◆ Indianapolis, Indiana ◆ Boston, Massachusetts

PCs For Dummies, 2nd Edition

Published by
IDG Books Worldwide, Inc.
An International Data Group Company
155 Bovet Road, Suite 310
San Mateo, CA 94402

Library of Congress Catalog Card No.: 94-75045

ISBN 1-56884-078-0

Printed in the United States of America

10 9 8 7 6 5 4 3 2 1

Distributed in the United States by IDG Books Worldwide, Inc.

Distributed in Canada by Macmillan of Canada, a Division of Canada Publishing Corporation; by Computer and Technical Books in Miami, Florida, for South America and the Caribbean; by Longman Singapore in Singapore, Malaysia, Thailand, and Korea; by Toppan Co. Ltd. in Japan; by Asia Computerworld in Hong Kong; by Woodslane Pty. Ltd. in Australia and New Zealand; and by Transword Publishers Ltd. in the U.K. and Europe.

For information on where to purchase IDG Books outside the U.S., contact Christina Turner at 415-312-0633.

For information on translations, contact Marc Jeffrey Mikulich, Foreign Rights Manager, at IDG Books Worldwide; FAX NUMBER 415-358-1260.

For sales inquiries and special prices for bulk quantities, write to the address above or call IDG Books Worldwide at (415) 312-0600.

 is a trademark of IDG Books Worldwide, Inc.

About the Authors

Dan Gookin got started with computers back in the post slide rule age of computing: 1982. His first intention was to buy a computer to replace his aged and constantly breaking typewriter. Working as slave labor in a restaurant, however, Gookin was unable to afford the full "word processor" setup and settled on a computer that had a monitor, keyboard, and little else. Soon his writing career was underway with several submissions to fiction magazines and lots of rejections.

The big break came in 1984 when he began writing about computers. Applying his flair for fiction with a self-taught knowledge of computers, Gookin was able to demystify the subject and explain technology in a relaxed and understandable voice. He even dared to add humor, which eventually won him a column in a local computer magazine.

Eventually Gookin's talents came to roost as a ghostwriter at a computer book publishing house. That was followed by an editing position at a San Diego computer magazine. During this time, he also regularly participated on a radio talk show about computers. In addition, Gookin kept writing books about computers, some of which became minor bestsellers.

In 1990, Gookin came to IDG Books with a book proposal. From that initial meeting unfolded an idea for an outrageous book: a long overdue and original idea for the computer book for the rest of us. What became *DOS For Dummies* blossomed into an international bestseller with hundreds of thousands of copies in print and many translations.

Today, Gookin still considers himself a writer and computer "guru" whose job it is to remind everyone that computers are not to be taken too seriously. His approach to computers is light and humorous yet very informative. He knows the complex beasts are important and can help people become productive and successful. Gookin mixes his knowledge of computers with a unique, dry sense of humor that keeps everyone informed — and awake. His favorite quote is "Computers are a notoriously dull subject, but that doesn't mean I have to write about them that way."

Gookin's titles for IDG Books include the bestselling *DOS For Dummies, More DOS For Dummies, WordPerfect For Dummies, WordPerfect 6 For Dummies, PCs For Dummies, Word For Windows For Dummies,* and the *Illustrated Computer Dictionary For Dummies.* All told, he's written over 30 books on computers and contributes regularly to *DOS Resource Guide, InfoWorld,* and *PC Computing Magazine.* Gookin holds a degree in Communications from the University of California, San Diego, and currently lives with his wife and boys in the as-yet-untamed state of Idaho.

About the Authors

Andy Rathbone started geeking around with computers in 1985 when he bought a boxy CP/M Kaypro 2X with lime-green letters. Like other budding nerds, he soon began playing with null-modem adapters, dialing up computer bulletin boards, and working part time at Radio Shack.

In between playing computer games, he served as editor of the *Daily Aztec* newspaper at San Diego State University. After graduating with a comparative literature degree, he went to work for a bizarre underground coffee-table magazine that sort of disappeared.

Andy began combining his two interests, words and computers, by selling articles to a local computer magazine. During the next few years, Rathbone started ghostwriting computer books for more-famous computer authors, as well as writing several hundred articles about computers for technoid publications like *Supercomputing Review*, *CompuServe*, *ID Systems*, *DataPro,* and *Shareware*.

In 1992, Andy and *DOS For Dummies* author/legend Dan Gookin teamed up to write *PCs For Dummies*, which was a runner-up in the Computer Press Association's 1993 awards. Andy subsequently wrote *Windows For Dummies, More Windows For Dummies, OS/2 For Dummies*, and *Upgrading and Fixing PCs For Dummies.*

Andy is currently writing *Multimedia For Dummies*, as well as contributing regularly to *CompuServe*, a magazine mailed monthly to CompuServe members. (Feel free to drop him a line at 75300,1565.)

Andy lives with his most-excellent wife, Tina, and their cat in San Diego, California. When not writing, Rathbone fiddles with his MIDI synthesizer and tries to keep the cat off both keyboards.

About IDG Books Worldwide

Welcome to the world of IDG Books Worldwide.

IDG Books Worldwide, Inc., is a division of International Data Group, the world's largest publisher of computer-related information and the leading global provider of information services on information technology. IDG publishes over 194 computer publications in 62 countries. Forty million people read one or more IDG publications each month.

If you use personal computers, IDG Books is committed to publishing quality books that meet your needs. We rely on our extensive network of publications, including such leading periodicals as *Macworld, InfoWorld, PC World, Computerworld, Publish, Network World,* and *SunWorld,* to help us make informed and timely decisions in creating useful computer books that meet your needs.

Every IDG book strives to bring extra value and skill-building instruction to the reader. Our books are written by experts, with the backing of IDG periodicals, and with careful thought devoted to issues such as audience, interior design, use of icons, and illustrations. Our editorial staff is a careful mix of high-tech journalists and experienced book people. Our close contact with the makers of computer products helps ensure accuracy and thorough coverage. Our heavy use of personal computers at every step in production means we can deliver books in the most timely manner.

We are delivering books of high quality at competitive prices on topics customers want. At IDG, we believe in quality, and we have been delivering quality for over 25 years. You'll find no better book on a subject than an IDG book.

John Kilcullen
President and C.E.O.
IDG Books Worldwide, Inc.

IDG Books Worldwide, Inc. is a division of International Data Group. The officers are Patrick J. McGovern, Founder and Board Chairman; Walter Boyd, President. International Data Group's publications include: **ARGENTINA's** Computerworld Argentina, InfoWorld Argentina; **ASIA's** Computerworld Hong Kong, PC World Hong Kong, Computerworld Southeast Asia, PC World Singapore, Computerworld Malaysia, PC World Malaysia; **AUSTRALIA's** Computerworld Australia, Australian PC World, Australian Macworld, Network World, Reseller, IDG Sources; **AUSTRIA's** Computerwelt Oesterreich, PC Test; **BRAZIL's** Computerworld, Mundo IBM, Mundo Unix, PC World, Publish; **BULGARIA's** Computerworld Bulgaria, Ediworld, PC & Mac World Bulgaria; **CANADA's** Direct Access, Graduate Computerworld, InfoCanada, Network World Canada; **CHILE's** Computerworld, Informatica; **COLOMBIA's** Computerworld Columbia; **CZECH REPUBLIC's** Computerworld, Elektronika, PC World; **DENMARK's** CAD/CAM WORLD, Communications World, Computerworld Danmark, LOTUS World, Macintosh Produktkatalog, Macworld Danmark, PC World Danmark, PC World Produktguide, Windows World; **ECUADOR's** PC World; **EGYPT's** Computerworld (CW) Middle East, PC World Middle East; **FINLAND's** MikroPC, Tietoviikko, Tietoverkko; **FRANCE's** Distributique, GOLDEN MAC, InfoPC, Languages & Systems, Le Guide du Monde Informatique, Le Monde Informatique, Telecoms & Reseaux; **GERMANY's** Computerwoche, Computerwoche Focus, Computerwoche Extra, Computerwoche Karriere, Information Management, Macwelt, Netzwelt, PC Welt, PC Woche, Publish, Unit; **HUNGARY's** Alaplap, Computerworld SZT, PC World; **INDIA's** Computers & Communications; **ISRAEL's** Computerworld Israel, PC World Israel; **ITALY's** Computerworld Italia, Lotus Magazine, Macworld Italia, Networking Italia, PC World Italia; **JAPAN's** Computerworld Japan, Macworld Japan, SunWorld Japan, Windows World; **KENYA's** East African Computer News; **KOREA's** Computerworld Korea, Macworld Korea, PC World Korea; **MEXICO's** Compu Edicion, Compu Manufactura, Computacion/Punto de Venta, Computerworld Mexico, MacWorld, Mundo Unix, PC World, Windows; **THE NETHERLAND'S** Computer! Totaal, LAN Magazine, MacWorld; **NEW ZEALAND's** Computer Listings, Computerworld New Zealand, New Zealand PC World; **NIGERIA's** PC World Africa; **NORWAY's** Computerworld Norge, C/World, Lotusworld Norge, Macworld Norge, Networld, PC World Ekspress, PC World Norge, PC World's Product Guide, Publish World, Student Data, Unix World, Windowsworld, IDG Direct Response; **PANAMA's** PC World; **PERU's** Computerworld Peru, PC World; **PEOPLE'S REPUBLIC OF CHINA's** China Computerworld, PC World China, Electronics International, China Network World; **IDG HIGH TECH BEIJING's** New Product World; **IDG SHENZHEN's** Computer News Digest; **PHILIPPINES'** Computerworld, PC World; **POLAND's** Computerworld Poland, PC World/Komputer; **PORTUGAL's** Cerebro/PC World, Correio Informatico/Computerworld, MacIn; **ROMANIA's** PC World; **RUSSIA's** Computerworld-Moscow, Mir-PC, Sety; **SLOVENIA's** Monitor Magazine; **SOUTH AFRICA's** Computing S.A.; **SPAIN's** Amiga World, Computerworld Espana, Communicaciones World, Macworld Espana, NeXTWORLD, PC World Espana, Publish, Sunworld; **SWEDEN's** Attack, ComputerSweden, Corporate Computing, Lokala Natverk/LAN, Lotus World, MAC&PC, Macworld, Mikrodatorn, PC World, Publishing & Design (CAP), Datalngenjoren, Maxi Data, Windows World; **SWITZERLAND's** Computerworld Schweiz, Macworld Schweiz, PC & Workstation; **TAIWAN's** Computerworld Taiwan, Global Computer Express, PC World Taiwan; **THAILAND's** Thai Computerworld; **TURKEY's** Computerworld Monitor, Macworld Turkiye, PC World Turkiye; **UNITED KINGDOM's** Lotus Magazine, Macworld, Sunworld; **UNITED STATES'** AmigaWorld, Cable in the Classroom, CD Review, CIO, Computerworld, Desktop Video World, DOS Resource Guide, Electronic News, Federal Computer Week, Federal Integrator, GamePro, IDG Books, InfoWorld, InfoWorld Direct, Laser Event, Macworld, Multimedia World, Network World, NeXTWORLD, PC Games, PC Letter, PC World Publish, Sumeria, SunWorld, SWATPro, Video Event; **VENEZUELA's** Computerworld Venezuela, MicroComputerworld Venezuela; **VIETNAM's** PC World Vietnam

Credits

Publisher
David Solomon

Managing Editor
Mary Bednarek

Acquisitions Editor
Terrie Lynn Solomon

Production Director
Beth Jenkins

Senior Editors
Tracy Barr
Sandra Blackthorn
Diane Graves Steele

Production Coordinator
Cindy L. Phipps

Acquisitions Assistant
Megg Bonar

Editorial Assistant
Darlene Cunningham

Project Editor
H. Leigh Davis

Copy Editors
Julie King
Patricia Seiler
Rebecca Whitney

Technical Reviewer
Ron Dippold, Senior Engineer
Qualcomm Incorporated

Production Staff
Tony Augsburger
Valery Bourke
Mary Breidenbach
Sherry Gomoll
Drew R. Moore
Gina Scott

Proofreader
Chuck A. Hutchinson

Indexer
Steve Rath

Book Design
University Graphics

Acknowledgments

The publisher would like to give special thanks to Patrick J. McGovern, without whom this book would not have been possible.

Say What You Think!

Listen up, all you readers of IDG's international bestsellers: the one — the only — absolutely world famous ...*For Dummies* books! It's time for you to take advantage of a new, direct pipeline to the authors and editors of IDG Books Worldwide. In between putting the finishing touches on the next round of ...*For Dummies* books, the authors and editors of IDG Books Worldwide like to sit around and mull over what their readers have to say. And we know that you readers always say what you think. So here's your chance. We'd really like your input for future printings and editions of this book — and ideas for future ...*For Dummies* titles as well. Tell us what you liked (and didn't like) about this book. How about the chapters you found most useful — or most funny? And since we know you're not a bit shy, what about the chapters you think can be improved?

Just to show you how much we appreciate your input, we'll add you to our Dummies Database/Fan Club and keep you up to date on the latest ...*For Dummies* books, news, cartoons, calendars, and more! Please send your name, address, and phone number, as well as your comments, questions, and suggestions, to our very own ...*For Dummies* coordinator at the following address:

...*For Dummies* Coordinator
IDG Books Worldwide
3250 North Post Road, Suite 140
Indianapolis, IN 46226

(Yes, Virginia, there really is a
. . . *For Dummies* coordinator:
We are not making this up.)

Please mention the name of
this book in your comments.

Thanks for your input!

**Don't forget to fill out the Reader Response
Card in the back of this book and send it in!**

**IDG
BOOKS**

Contents at a Glance

Cartoons at a Glance

By Rich Tennant

page 345

page 351

page 73

page 79

page 10

page 289

page 197

page 7

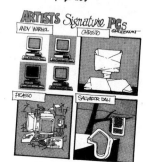

page 240

page 87

page 161

page 156

Table of Contents

Introduction

*W*elcome to *PCs For Dummies,* 2nd Edition, the book that answers the question "How does a computer turn a smart person like you into a dummy?" Computers are useful, yes. And a fair number of people — heaven help them — fall in love with computers. But the rest of us are left sitting dumb and numb in front of the box. It's not that using a computer is beyond the range of our IQs; it's that no one has ever bothered to sit down and explain things in human terms. Until now.

This book talks about using a computer in friendly, human — and often irreverent — terms. Nothing is sacred here. Electronics can be praised by others. This book focuses on you and your needs. In this book, you'll discover everything you need to know about your computer without painful jargon or the prerequisite master's degree in engineering. And you'll have fun.

About This Book

This book is designed so that you can pick it up at any point and start reading — like a reference. There are 27 chapters, and each one covers a specific aspect of the computer — turning it on, using a printer, using software, kicking it, and so on. Each chapter is divided into self-contained nuggets of information, all relating to the major theme of the chapter. The chapter on setting up your system, for example, contains self-contained information like this:

✔ Examining what to turn on first

✔ Booting your computer — where to kick it

✔ Learning which buttons you can ignore

✔ Examining what happens when the computer finds itself

✔ Knowing what to do when you're dumped at the DOS prompt

✔ Making the computer do something

✔ Exiting a program

✔ Turning off the computer

You don't have to memorize anything in this book. Nothing about a computer is memorable. Each section is designed so you can read the information quickly, digest what you've read, and then put down the book and get on with using the computer. If anything technical crops up, you'll be alerted to its presence so you can cleanly avoid it.

How to Use This Book

This book works like a reference. Start with the topic you want more information about; look for it in the table of contents or in the index. The table of contents gives chapter and section titles and page numbers. The index gives topics and page numbers. Turn to the area of interest and read the information you need. Then, with the information in your head, you can quickly close the book and freely perform whatever task you need — without learning anything else. Of course, if you want to learn additional information about the topic or learn something else, you can check many of the cross-references used throughout this book or just continue reading.

When you need to type something, you'll see the text you need to type as follows:

```
C:\> TYPE ME IN
```

In this example, you type **TYPE ME IN** after the C:\> and then press the Enter key. Because typing stuff can be confounding, we usually also describe in detail what you need to type. (By the way, this book does explain what that C:\> thing is.)

Whenever we describe a message or information that you'll see on the screen, we present it as follows:

```
This is a message on-screen.
```

This book rarely suggests that you look elsewhere for information. Everything you need to know about your PC is covered here — except information on using the software you own and using DOS. For using DOS, you can refer to *DOS For Dummies,* published by IDG Books Worldwide. For specific programs, you can look for other . . .*For Dummies* books as well. Even so, information is provided here for getting help when you need it.

If you really want to learn about your computer, you need to buy a computer tutorial. Or go hard-core and visit a university bookstore; buy a thick book without illustrations. Some good tutorials exist, as well as books and magazine articles that will further your knowledge. We can't recommend anything offhand because no one's paying us a kickback here.

What You Don't Need to Read

A lot of technical information is involved with using a computer. To better insulate you from it, we've enclosed such material in sidebars that are clearly marked as technical information. You don't have to read that stuff. Often, it's just a complex explanation of information already discussed in the chapter. Reading that information will only teach you something substantial about your computer, which is not the goal here.

And Just Who Are You?

We're going to make some admittedly foolish assumptions about you: You have a computer, and you use it somehow to do something. You know what you need to do, and you're fully able to do it, probably with some instruction from a more knowledgeable computer user. Hopefully, this book will decrease your reliance on that person. But don't be too quick to burn bridges.

How This Book Is Organized

This book has four major parts, each of which is divided into several chapters. Each chapter covers a major topic and is divided into sections, which address issues or concerns about the topic. That's how this book is organized, but how you read it is up to you. Pick a topic, a chapter, a section — whatever — and just start reading. Any related information is cross-referenced in the text.

Here are the parts and what they contain:

Part I: Introducing Your Computer

This part contains basic computer stuff. It introduces you to the computer and its parts and provides descriptions. This part contains information on setting up a computer, getting help, and understanding common computer phrases.

Part II: Intimidating, Cold, and Impersonal: The Computer

The chapters in this part discuss the cold, hard electronic truth about the computer. Each chapter covers a specific part of the computer — inside and out — and how it fits into the big picture. We also offer a special chapter on *laptop* computers (those portable computers small enough to fling out a window with one arm) for those of you unfortunate enough to have a laptop thrust your way.

Part III: Working with a Computer

We toyed with the idea of calling this part "Working against a Computer" but thought twice about it. Working with a computer involves using DOS (yech!), software, Windows, networks, and a host of other interesting hurdles and speed bumps. These chapters offer advice for you and ridicule for the computer — all in one sane package.

Part IV: The Part of Tens

As is becoming a tradition in these . . .*For Dummies* books, the last part contains lists of information — mostly unnecessary — plus tips and suggestions, all organized into convenient chapters. This supplemental information is included at no extra cost to you.

Icons Used in This Book

 This icon alerts you to needless technical information — drivel we add because we just feel like explaining something totally unnecessary (a hard habit to break). Feel free to skip over anything tagged with this little picture.

 This icon usually indicates helpful advice or an insight that makes using the computer interesting. For example, when pouring acid over your computer, be sure to wear protective gloves and goggles.

 Ummm, we forgot what this one means.

 This icon indicates that you need to be careful with the information presented; usually, it's a reminder for you *not* to do something.

Where to Go from Here

With this book in hand, you're now ready to go out and conquer your PC. Start by looking through the table of contents or the index. Find a topic, turn to the page indicated, and you're ready to go. Also, feel free to write in this book, fill in the blanks, dog-ear the pages, and do anything that would make a librarian blanch. Enjoy.

Part I
Introducing Your Computer

The 5th Wave By Rich Tennant

"COMPATIBILITY? NO PROBLEM. THIS BABY COMES IN OVER A DOZEN DESIGNER COLORS."

In this part...

You can get acquainted with your PC. We present the basics here — important stuff like letting you know that your computer won't explode. This part also includes information on how to set up your system, what to do the first time you turn on and use the computer, computer terms no one has ever bothered to explain, and who to scream at for help.

We present each chapter's material in small, easy-to-understand sections. And, if information is technical (mostly worth skipping, in other words), it is clearly marked.

Chapter 1

Your Computer Will Not Explode (Basic Stuff You Should Know)

• •

In This Chapter

▶ What is a computer, a PC, a clone, and a compatible?

▶ The computer as just another electronic gadget

▶ What is hardware and what is software?

▶ What is DOS?

▶ A tour of the typical PC

▶ A tour of the console

▶ Special types of computers

▶ What is a peripheral?

▶ Programs and applications

• •

*T*he last thing you should be concerned about is that your *PC* — your *personal computer* — will blow up. It'll never happen. No sparks. No flash. No boom. In many science fiction movies, computers blow up and spew fire and rocks, but in reality, it won't happen. Computers are just too dull.

The idea that computers may explode stems from the 1960s. Back when Irwin Allen produced some of the most interesting TV science fiction and filled everyone with the fear that any computer or technical device could spurt flames during times of high drama. Back when *Star Trek*'s Mr. Spock pointed at an alien computer and said, in his Vulcan way, things like "Destroy this chip and the entire planet will become molten rubble." These are not very encouraging concepts for the late 20th-century spreadsheet user.

But now that you are safe with the idea that PCs won't explode, you can relax and enjoy this chapter, which provides you with a gentle introduction to computers. You learn basic ideas here. This chapter is kind of like a primer for the rest of the book. In fact, most of the concepts covered here are discussed later in full, boring, technical detail.

What Is a Computer or PC?

What is this thing everyone is nuts about? Is it a computer or is it a PC? What is a PC? What is a clone? What is a compatible? These and other seemingly silly terms are all legitimate replacement words for *computer*. So what is a computer?

A computer is that thing on your desk that looks like a TV set illegally parked by a typewriter. Call it whatever you like, but it's basically a computer. But, because you may also have a computer on your wrist, in your car, or in the toaster, we need to be more specific. What you have on your desk is really a PC.

PC is a term IBM devised to describe its first desk-sized computer. PC stands for *personal computer*. The IBM PC is the model for some 60 million similar units sold since its introduction. The IBM PC is like the Model-T Ford; it's the first one of its kind. The first IBM PC was like the first car ever made, and all computers produced since its introduction look and behave similarly (but without the crank to start them up).

The 5th Wave   By Rich Tennant

"ALRIGHT, STEADY EVERYONE. MARGO, GO OVER TO TOM'S PC AND PRESS 'ESCAPE',...VERY CAREFULLY."

- ✔ The word *computer* is a general term applied to the entire spectrum of computing devices. Basically, a computer is like a super calculator with a really big display. In addition to adding and subtracting numbers, the calculator also displays and manipulates text. This is what makes the computer useful to us nonmath types.

- ✔ Computers range in variety and size, from the simple game-playing computers like Nintendo's GameBoy to advanced hand-held computers, larger portable computers, desk-sized models, and free-standing units that pull down more power than the Hoover Dam puts out during any given hour. Any of these things can be called a computer.

- ✔ Since about 1981, the time that the first IBM PC was introduced, the term *PC* has been used to refer to anyone's personal computer — whether it's the original IBM equipment, a Macintosh, or some inexpensive toy you bought at Kmart. Because you're a person and you use the computer, it's your personal computer — your PC.

- ✔ Because the term *PC* is strongly associated with IBM types of equipment, Macintosh owners like to disassociate themselves from it. They call their computers *Mac*s even though Macintosh computers are just another type of PC.

- ✔ After the first IBM unit, no other computer has ever been officially called "the PC." IBM actually copyrighted the term, but it is in wide use and even shows up in the dictionary (the last stop on the road from being copyrightable).

Skip this technical background material if you want

The second IBM PC was called the IBM PC XT. XT stands for eXtended Technology. Basically, the XT was a PC with a 10MB *hard drive* in it. (We talk about hard drives in Chapter 8.) A later model, the IBM PC AT, had a larger hard drive and a faster, better design. AT stands for Advanced Technology. Actually, most of today's computers are modeled after the IBM PC AT.

In 1987, IBM introduced its next generation of personal computers: the PS/2 series. PS stands for Personal System, and /2 means second generation. Unlike the term *PC*, the term *PS/2* is highly copyrighted. You don't see any other PS types of systems, and no one calls his or her computer "my PS."

What Is a Clone and What Is a Compatible?

Only IBM could make the IBM PC. Every other computer that looks and acts like that original model is referred to as a *clone*. Unless you have the original IBM equipment, you have a clone.

Compatible is another term like *clone*. Compatible refers to any similar type of computer that doesn't have the IBM label. However, a compatible is considered to have a bit more status than a run-of-the-mill clone. Clones are regarded as cheap — usually assembled by someone who works in the back of the local computer store. A compatible, on the other hand, is made by a national electronics firm and widely supported. You pay more for a compatible PC than for a clone.

- ✔ The clone label has waned during the past few years as the number of clone PCs has far exceeded the number of original PCs sold and in existence. Quite frankly, if it doesn't say *IBM* on it anywhere, it's a clone.

- ✔ In addition to describing a type of clone, compatible means that you can run the same software as the IBM equipment. You can also use the same *hardware* — printers, memory, and other stuff — as the original IBM equipment. Today, the compatibility issue surrounds DOS more than IBM. PCs are said to be DOS compatible rather than IBM compatible (see the section "What Is DOS?" later in this chapter for more information).

- ✔ Some computers are referred to by cute names or marketing terms. IBM computers have the names IBM PC, IBM AT, and IBM PS/2, for example. These are actually attempts at clever names, but it looks like some marketing droid thought of them.

Some history you don't have to read

Not long ago personal computers were referred to as *microcomputers*. This term came from the *microprocessor*, the computer's main chip, or the computer's "brain." The big "I want to control the world and foul up your phone bill" computers were called *mainframes*. Smaller, corporate- and college-sized computers (that only fouled up grades or paychecks) were called *minicomputers*.

According to the geeks who ran the mainframes and minicomputers, microcomputers were hobbyists' playthings—toys. However, the features available on the personal computer—the microcomputer—you can have on your desk today exceed many of the features of the early mainframes. So there.

> ✔ Gone are the days of cute names for PCs. Sniff, sniff. (Only a nerd would reminisce.) Most computers today are named after their manufacturer plus some vague number — the Mondo PC Mach 5, the SmartFast i486, and the Testosterone 486/33, for example. You get the idea. These things are all still computers, PCs, clones, or compatibles.

The Computer: Just Another Electronic Gadget

You may need a computer for various reasons — to perform a task, to get the job done, to educate, or to entertain, for example. Computers make doing anything easier. Because they lack a specific purpose, it's hard to say exactly what a computer can do for you. Unlike other electronic gadgets you may have, the computer is special. But it's still no different from your television, stereo, copy machine, or microwave oven. Because those devices don't intimidate you, the computer shouldn't either. (Notice how the VCR isn't included in the list?)

As an example, consider the typical VCR. (Sorry.) Next to the computer, it's probably the most feared device in the home. Few people can program a VCR. Ask your friends to record a program next Sunday at 9 p.m., and they'll get the shakes. Or try to get some friends to record something on one channel while watching another; they may spontaneously combust. Still, many folks (some who even work for the government) use their VCRs just to view movies and record TV shows. That's OK. You don't need to program the thing to get the most from it. The same holds true with a computer.

Technical drivel on the BIOS

One term you may hear is *BIOS compatible*. BIOS is an acronym for *basic input/output system*. It refers to the way the computer behaves — the way it interacts with the software and DOS. The instructions — the BIOS — are saved on a special chip or *ROM (read-only memory)* inside the computer, which is the reason that some computer nerds refer to the BIOS as the *ROM BIOS* just to confuse you.

In order to be fully IBM compatible, your PC must have a compatible BIOS, which means that your computer must behave the same way as the IBM equipment internally. Prior to about 1987, this was a major issue. It isn't anymore, but you still see the term BIOS tossed around. Think of BIOS as an internal list of rules for how the computer behaves — like the rules Miss Bradshaw imposed on you in the second grade.

It's entirely possible to be a very bright person yet not know a thing about how to use a computer. True, you should know what you want to do and be able to get that done. Yet, although the device is capable of much more, don't worry about mastering it. Those who feel the desire will. The rest of us can just use the beast and quickly turn it off when we're done. No problem.

Computers are actually very friendly. Because you can read information on-screen, many computers give you a list of options, provide suggestions, or tell you what to do next. The microwave oven can't do that.

What Is Hardware and What Is Software?

There are two parts to every computer system. You need to know about both parts and the technical terms they go by: *hardware* and *software*. Yech! Put down the book and count to ten. Think: Calm blue waters, calm blue waters. . . .

To put this discussion in a different light, think of your stereo system as *hardware*. It includes the stereo itself, the speakers, the amplifier, the turntable, and your old 8-track. The stereo hardware is really nothing without the music you get from your CDs, records, and AM/FM receiver. All the music is *software*.

With a computer, software is more important than hardware. You buy a computer to do, say, word processing or something enriching like, say, accounting. The computer itself — the hardware — knows nothing about those things. Instead, you need software to tell the computer "OK, I will now process words" or "I will now try to embezzle $40,000 from my boss."

- Computer hardware isn't anything you'll find in your local True Value store. With a computer, hardware is the physical part — the stuff you can touch, feel in your hand, drop on the floor, lug through an airport, toss out a window, and so on.

- Computer software is the brains of the operation — the instructions that tell the computer what to do, how to act, when to lose your monthly report, and so on.

- Computer software is more important than computer hardware. The software tells the hardware what to do.

- Note that although computer software comes on floppy disks, the disks aren't the software. Software is stored on disks just as music is stored on records and CDs.

- Without the proper software, your computer is a seriously heavy paperweight.

What Is DOS?

Congratulations to DOS, the first three-letter acronym (or TLA) discussed in detail in this book. It's important, too, because DOS is the main piece of software in the computer. DOS controls everything — even other software or computer programs you have in your computer. It's the master, the head honcho, *el queso grande,* and so on.

- ✔ DOS stands for *Disk Operating System. Operating system* is a fancy term for the program that operates a computer, controlling everything and making it all useful (just as *digestive system* refers to the thing in your body that mushes up food and makes it useful).
- ✔ You need DOS to run your computer.
- ✔ If a computer uses DOS as its main control program, the computer is called a DOS computer, which is the same thing as a PC, clone, or compatible, as described earlier in this chapter.
- ✔ Chapter 13 provides more information about DOS. If you're really desperate, consider running to your bookstore right now and buying *DOS For Dummies,* published by IDG Books Worldwide.

DOS is the boss. Remember that rhyme, and you'll never suffer the embarrassment of mispronouncing DOS again. (**Hint:** It's not pronounced *dose.* Call it *dose* in front of computer nerds, and they'll laugh so big you'll be able to see the bits of Cheetos wedged between their teeth. Be safe. It's pronounced *doss,* like *boss.*)

Some unavoidable legal issues regarding DOS (don't bother reading)

When we use the term DOS in this book, we're referring to *MS-DOS,* the *Microsoft Disk Operating System.* Other brands of DOS exist as well: PC DOS, COMPAQ DOS, Tandy DOS, and so on. Mostly, these DOSs are copies of MS-DOS, repackaged and relabeled by your computer's manufacturer. They're still DOS as far as this book is concerned.

What isn't DOS here is DR DOS, another PC operating system from Digital Research/Novell.

This book does not cover DR DOS specifically, but it does cover all the computers that run DR DOS.

If you are a DR DOS user, remember that our DOS refers to MS-DOS — not your DOS. If you're not a DR DOS user, this discussion is just confusing you. Please nod your head and quietly return to the text.

And if you're *really* curious about DR DOS, quietly page ahead to Chapter 14.

The Typical PC

Now take a look at Figure 1-1, which shows a typical personal computer — a generic PC if there ever was one. Familiarize yourself with all the parts and the ugly terms used to describe them. This is required knowledge for all of us.

Here's what all the parts do:

Console: The boxy thing, the main part of the computer. It's also called the *system unit,* which should be consoling. This part of the computer houses its secret, internal components — electronics and stuff like that. Keeping that junk inside the console prevents you from staring at it in awe rather than doing your work, and it also keeps your cat from sleeping on it and being electrocuted. (The console's innards are mulled over in Chapter 6.)

Keyboard: The combination typewriter-calculator thing you use to tell the computer what to do. The keyboard has keys like a typewriter, special cryptic computer keys, and a numeric keypad like you find on an adding machine. Today's computer keyboards have 101 keys: 26 are alphabetic keys, 10 have numbers and punctuation symbols on them, 10 are for control, and the rest will confuse you.

Disk drive: The computer's information storage device. The computer stores information on disks like a VCR records TV shows on videotape; the disk is the videotape, and the disk drive is your computer's VCR. The disk drive is an important part of your computer — so much so, in fact, that Chapter 8 is completely devoted to the subject.

Printer: The thing that sits to one side of the computer and prints information on paper, which is the reason that it's called the printer. We mention it here because some people think that the printer is a kindly old gent wearing an ink-stained apron who runs an offset press for a living. Printers are a popular part of computers, rich in diversity and thick with confusion. They're addressed in Chapter 10.

Monitor: The TV-like display typically sitting on top of the system unit. It's referred to by a number of interesting terms only a nerd would love: *display, CRT (cathode ray tube), VDT (video display terminal),* and *screen* (although *screen* usually refers to the thing you see on the monitor — not the monitor itself). Monitors are covered in Chapter 9.

Network: Not a device you can see as much as something you must contend with. Your only sign of a network is going to be a thick cable hanging out the back of your computer — something to curl your toe around while you're awaiting the muse of electronic inspiration.

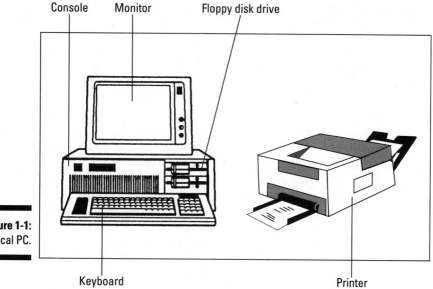

Console   Monitor   Floppy disk drive

Figure 1-1:
A typical PC.

Keyboard   Printer

✔ These parts are all important. Make sure that you know where the console, keyboard, disk drive, monitor, and printer are in your own system. If the printer isn't present, it's probably a network printer sitting in some other room.

✔ Laptop computers have most of the same pieces, but they're contained in a single compact case. For more information on laptops, refer to Chapter 12, which covers the subject in friendly detail.

✔ You need to know nothing about networks. Basically, this book's attitude toward networking is *let someone else do it.* Chapter 17 hammers out the subject for you (if you care).

A Console Tour

The console is the centerpiece of the computer system. It's the thing — the hardware — you'll be working with most often. The most important part of the console is the disk drive, into which you insert floppy disks. You may have one or two disk drives, each with its own opening.

Somewhere on the console you'll find the computer's main on/off switch. It may be smack dab in front, on the right rear side, or on the back. Look for and identify this switch.

Behind the console you'll find a number of interesting things. Primarily, the back of the console is where you connect various cables, cords, and wires that hook the computer to all its external parts, or *peripherals.* This area is where the keyboard, monitor, printer, and so on, are all connected. The main power cord between the computer and the wall also gets plugged in back there.

✔ Chapter 8 provides additional information on disk drives and how to use them.

✔ If your PC is plugged into a power strip or surge protector, and that's how you turn everything on, then the console's power switch always needs to be turned on. (It makes sense when you think about it.) You can find information on power strips and surge protectors in the section "What about Those Surge Protectors?" in Chapter 2.

✔ The section "Setting up the console" in Chapter 2 provides information on hooking up various devices to the console; other sections in that chapter provide information on setting up the monitor and printer. Additional information on hooking up other gadgets is provided in Part II of this book.

FCC class A and B ratings, what they mean, and why bother

Computers are rated by the Federal Communications Commission (FCC). That's the same agency that supervises your local TV and radio stations. Why? Because the FCC controls the air hovering over the United States — specifically, any information sent electronically through the air, such as TV or radio signals.

You can't hear radio signals or see a TV transmission without a radio or television set. Likewise, you can't hear all the electronic noise your computer is putting out. If you could, you'd probably go deaf. (For an experiment, set a radio or television close to a computer and watch what happens to reception.)

Because computers generate electronic emissions, they're regulated by the FCC. This regulation prevents them from interfering with other radio waves, such as your neighbor's television or radio. (Ever see what happens to the television when the blender runs? The same thing happens when you have a noisy computer.)

The FCC has devised two class ratings for computers: Class A computers are the most noisy, and class B computers are the least noisy. Class A computing devices are designed for use in office environments, where there is little chance that they'll interfere with the Jones' TV set. Class B computing devices are designed for the home environment. This certification must be stamped on the back of every PC sold in the United States.

Computer stores may sell both class A and class B equipment. Class B is more expensive because the case has to be carefully designed so it doesn't allow too much electronic noise to seep out. If you're buying for the home, buy class B. However — nudge, nudge — the store will sell you either type. To be nice to your neighbors, however, get class B for the den.

Special Types of Computers

Nothing is stable or sane in the world of personal computers. Just when you think every PC looks like an old Philco television, someone else out there designs a new box. The majority of PCs look like their IBM ancestors: a monitor sitting on a boxy system unit with a keyboard in front (see "The Typical PC" earlier in this chapter for descriptions of these items and Figure 1-1 for a look at them).

Another variety of computer is the *tower model,* shown in Figure 1-2. It began its life as a desktop unit turned over on its side. This setup enables you to conveniently store the bulky PC under a desk while still having access to the keyboard and monitor on top of the desk. Computers work fine in that position, so some genius decided to design a case that had feet on the side rather than on the bottom. Lo, the tower-model PC was born. (PCs work great in any orientation; in Australia, for example, all people use their computers upside down.)

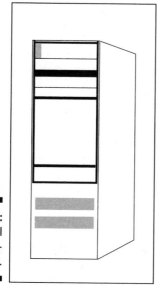

Figure 1-2:
A typical
tower-
model PC.

Smaller computers with carrying handles are called *portables* or *laptops*. With this style of PC, everything is in one handy — although often heavy — case. The monitor is attached on a hinged lid, and the keyboard is a smaller, more compact version of the full-sized, "aircraft carrier" keyboard on desktop models.

- ✔ Not all desktop or tower units are alike. Small footprint desktop units and minitower models are available. Incidentally, a computer's *footprint* is the amount of space it occupies on the desktop.

- ✔ Some users put the monitor and keyboard to the side of the system unit. This setup gives them a better viewing angle for the screen but can only be done if you have enough desk space to "spread out" the PC.

- ✔ Chapter 12 gives details on using laptop computers and computing on the road.

What Is a Peripheral?

Peripheral refers to anything outside of the main. For example, the *peripheral nervous system* is all the nerves in your body outside of your brain (which is called the *central nervous system*). *Peripheral vision* includes things you can see without looking directly at them. And *peripheral nervous vision* is what first-time computer buyers get when they enter the store. With a computer, however, a *peripheral* is any accessory or auxiliary equipment you may buy and connect to the computer.

Peripherals enable you to expand your computer system without having to buy a totally new computer. You can add these extra hardware devices yourself or have a guru, computer consultant, or some other high-paid individual do it for you. (Chapter 5 discusses how to find a guru.)

Peripheralitis: Something you'll probably never get

A disease many computer owners get is *peripheralitis.* That's the overwhelming desire to spend more and more money on your computer, typically by buying peripherals. PC beginners are relatively immune to this disease; most prefer to just use the darn thing and then quickly shut it off. Still, it's amazing what computers can do, provided that users have the cash or VISA balance to pay for it all.

The variety of peripherals you can buy for your computer is endless. Common peripheral items include the computer's printer, although this peripheral is more or less considered part of any standard computer; a *modem,* for calling up other computers or the Pentagon by using a standard telephone; a *scanner,* for reading text or graphics images; a special computer fax machine; a device for making the computer play music; and numerous other fancy — and expensive — items.

- If you were a computer, your arms and legs would be considered peripherals. However, you're restricted by design to only two arms and legs each, so your upgrade options are limited.

- All peripherals are hardware.

- Although the word peripheral refers to things outside of a computer, you can also add peripherals internally — inside the PC's system unit. (In a way, peripheral refers to anything beyond what comes standard in the computer.)

- Part II of this book provides detailed information on all the stuff you can attach to a PC. Several chapters are devoted to the major types of peripherals attached to most PCs. Chapter 11 is specific to adding peripherals.

Programs and Applications

To get work done on any computer, you're going to need software. Software goes by a number of names and aliases: programs, applications, and so on. Basically, anything in a computer that's not hardware is software, so it's a general term for a lot of things. (Refer to the section "What Is Hardware and What Is Software?" earlier in this chapter for details.)

- Major categories of software are referred to as *applications.* For example, word processing is an application. If you want to do accounting on a computer, you look for an accounting application. All applications are software.

- Computer programs are also software, but the term *program* is specific. Microsoft Word, for example, is a program. It's also a word processing application. All programs are software.

- Everything you do on a computer requires software. Different categories or applications exist, and within those categories are different programs you can select from. Some programs are well suited to some tasks, some are advanced, and some are generalized.

- Chapter 15 goes into the gory details on computer software — what's available and what you can do with it.

● ●

Summary

This chapter provided an introduction to PCs. You examined the following points:

▶ You learned what the terms *computer*, *PC*, *clone*, and *compatible* actually mean.

▶ You learned that the computer is just another electronic gadget like a television, stereo, copy machine, or microwave oven.

▶ You examined the difference between hardware and software.

▶ You learned about DOS, the Disk Operating System.

▶ You examined a typical PC and took a tour of the console.

▶ You learned about special types of computers.

▶ You learned about peripherals, programs, and applications.

In the next chapter, you learn how to set up your system, if you haven't done so already.

● ●

Chapter 2
Setting Up Your System (If You Haven't Already)

*P*art of the joy of buying a computer is setting it up. This task is about as endearing as wiring together a stereo, and yet it is somehow closer to marrying your VCR and television so you can watch cable and record HBO at the same time. (There's a whole wing at the local sanitarium devoted to those who have tried.) In short, setting up a PC can be complicated. Fortunately, it's something you need to do only once, if at all.

This chapter is about setting up a PC for the first time.

If you've already set up your PC, you may want to go through the checklist in the "Summary" section to make sure that you've done everything correctly.

Opening the Big Boxes and Unpacking Everything

Setting up a computer starts with opening big boxes — typically, two to three. You should start by locating a packing list, which should be attached to the outside of one of the boxes. Make sure that you have everything you paid for.

✔ Sometimes packing lists come separately, or you may have an invoice. Either way, make sure that you have all the boxes you need.

✔ If you got the computer through the mail, check to be sure that all the pieces have arrived together. The same rule applies if your computer arrived at your office from the computer or MIS department. If not, contact the delivery people.

✔ If you brought the computer from the store, check your order form to verify that you have everything you paid for. If not, get on the phone immediately.

 Always keep the phone numbers of your dealer and computer manufacturer handy. Also, look out for special support numbers; some manufacturers offer 24-hour, toll-free support via an 800 number. Jot it down someplace safe where you won't lose it. Then put it on a sticky note along the top of your monitor — at least until you have the number committed to memory or just haven't called in a while.

To open your computer boxes, take the same approach any kid takes at a birthday party. The biggest box must contain the best stuff, so start unpacking with the biggest box first. It contains the computer system unit, or *console*. The next biggest box may contain the monitor or display. Any other boxes contain the manuals, the keyboard, and extra goodies. If you bought a printer, it comes in its own box as well. And, of course, all the software you bought comes in more boxes. (The computer industry is a gold mine for the cardboard box industry.)

The console

Start with the console, which is probably in the largest box. The console itself is the least mobile of the units you'll unpack, so setting it up first gives you a good starting base.

Remember to open the console box (and all the other boxes) carefully. They're often sealed shut with large, ugly staples that can fly up and into your eyeball if you're in too much of a hurry (or at least that's what my mom says).

Remove any packing material, such as nonbiodegradable foam or polystyrene. Lift the console out of the box and carefully set it on the table top. If it comes in a plastic bag, remove the bag as well.

The monitor

The monitor comes in its own box, separate from the console. Remove the packing foam and set it aside. Then carefully lift out the monitor. It's OK to cut the monitor free from its plastic bag; keeping the bag on makes the screen difficult to see.

Set the monitor aside for the meantime. You need to dink with the console before you can proudly set the monitor on top of it.

The keyboard

Sometimes a third (or fourth) box is included with your computer — in addition to any software and manuals you may get. This box may contain the keyboard, the mouse, other interesting hardware, or just the manuals that attempt to tell you all about your computer.

The printer

Carefully remove the printer from its box. It has its own manual plus any cables and connectors that are necessary. If you don't feel like setting up the printer just now, that's OK. There's no sense in overwhelming yourself.

> ✔ The section "Setting up the printer" later in this chapter goes into detail on setting up your printer for the first time.

> ✔ If you bought any paper for the printer, cables, and so on, set them aside with the printer stuff.

Miscellaneous material

Various goodies may also be contained in the console box; be sure to look out for them. Computers often come with boxes inside of boxes, like the old Chinese "magic box." Sometimes the keyboard, manuals, and various cables are lurking inside the console box. Check for them before you toss out the boxes.

> ✔ Try to find a packing list inside one of the boxes. Confirm that you have everything mentioned in the packing list. If not, call the manufacturer.

> ✔ If a box says "open me first," then start there.

✔ Look inside each box for a "read me first" booklet. Follow the instructions there for setting up your PC. Or keep reading here if you don't understand the translation.

✔ Double-check all your boxes for extra goodies: cables, manuals, power cords, and so on. I once rescued my keyboard from the trash can because it was hidden in a box within the box my console came in.

✔ Chapter 10 provides additional information on setting up your computer printer.

Should I toss out the boxes?

Computers are shipped with a lot of packing material, plastic bags, twist ties, and rubber bands. You can throw out everything you think is trash if you want. Or, to be good to the environment, you can recycle everything. However, if the computer ends up being a lemon, you may need to ship it back in the original containers or lose your warranty.

Our advice is save all the boxes and packing foam for at least a month, which should give you time to see whether the computer needs to be returned. After that, feel free to toss out the boxes.

I keep all my computer boxes and the packing material (except for the annoying foam peanuts). Heck, I have boxes from 1984. The reason? When I move — although it's not that often — I prefer to pack the computers in their original cases. Many moving companies won't insure your computers unless they're in the original cases with the original packing foam, so I never toss out my computer boxes. That's why God invented attics anyway.

Putting It Together

Assembling a computer is something better left to a technical person. Remind your office computer gurus that they should be assembling your office system. At home, invite your computer-knowledgeable friends over to see the new PC. But don't tell them it's sitting on the floor suffocating in a bag. Surprise them. Computer people are often delighted to assemble a PC. It's like delivering a calf but without the mess.

If you're stuck and have to assemble your own PC, here's what you need:

✔ A medium-sized Phillips or standard screwdriver (we don't know — get both)

✔ A tiny, flat-head screwdriver — one designed for teensy, tiny screws

   ✔ About an hour of your time

   ✔ Plenty of patience

Figure 2-1 shows where everything goes in a traditional computer setup. Figure 2-2 shows various cables you plug into the back of a typical PC. These figures show generalities; your computer may be slightly different.

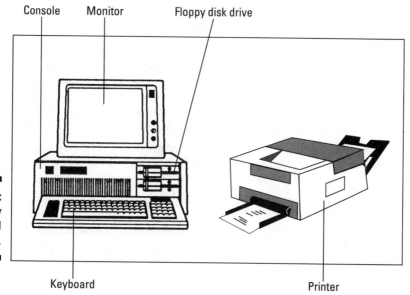

Console   Monitor   Floppy disk drive

Figure 2-1:
A fully
assembled
computer.

Keyboard   Printer

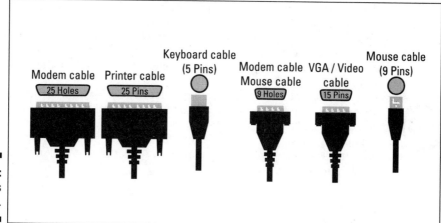

Modem cable Printer cable Keyboard cable (5 Pins) Modem cable Mouse cable VGA / Video cable Mouse cable (9 Pins)

25 Holes   25 Pins   9 Holes   15 Pins

Figure 2-2:
Various
cables.

✔ You probably don't need two screwdrivers but gather up a few anyway. It looks impressive.

✔ Keep pets and small children at a distance when you set up your PC. If you keep a cold beverage handy, put it in a safe spot where spilling it won't be a problem (like in another room).

✔ You may also need a flashlight to see behind your computer.

Setting up the console

Start by setting the console where you want it. The pretty side, usually containing the company label and computer model name and number, goes toward you. Remove the system unit from its plastic bag if you haven't already done so.

✔ Give the console plenty of room to breathe. Don't put it in a cabinet or against a wall where its internal fan won't allow air to circulate.

✔ Avoid putting the computer by a window. Sunlight heats up the computer and makes the monitor harder to see. It also invites society's criminal element to liberate your computer via the old smash and grab.

✔ Give yourself some working room behind the console for now. You need to weasel your way back there to attach some wires and cables. After that's done, you can shove the console to its final resting position.

✔ If you have a tower-model PC, the console will sit flat on the floor, usually under a desk. Pull it out away from the desk for now so you can connect the cables described later in this section.

Removing the disk drive tongue depressors

The disk drives may contain paper or plastic doohickeys. Look for the disk drive slots on the front of the console. A square piece of cardboard is stuck in larger-sized drives. Gently flip open the latch, pinch the cardboard, and yank it straight out. For the smaller drives, press the button underneath the slot, and the plastic holder is ejected part way; pinch it and pull it all the way out.

You can toss out the disk drive tongue depressors if you want. I keep mine for the same reason I keep the boxes: just in case I need to move the computer. You don't need to stick the depressors in the drive when the PC is turned off. But putting them there whenever you haul the computer long distances prevents something from happening to the disk drives. We don't know what exactly, but we bet it's nasty.

Connecting cables to the console

The console is the main computer unit. As such, its duty is to have as many unsightly cables hanging out of it as possible. These cables connect around the back, where they're most inconvenient to access. Figure 2-2, shown a little earlier, displays the back of a system unit and the locations of various connectors.

You must connect three important items when first setting up your PC:

✔ The keyboard cable

✔ The power cord

✔ The printer cable

The keyboard cable

The keyboard connector is a hole about as big as your thumb. It's located in the bottom center of the back of the PC. You need to carefully insert the keyboard cable into the hole.

✔ Look into the hole first and make sure that the pins in the cable are all lined up with the tiny holes inside the keyboard connector hole. A notch on one side of the hole and cable needs to be lined up.

✔ You then need to wrap the keyboard cable around the side of the computer to the keyboard in front. (Why the keyboard connector is on the back of the PC rather than on the front remains a mystery for modern times.)

✔ A few PCs may have keyboard connectors in the front. If your PC does, you probably paid extra for it.

✔ The original IBM PC and perhaps a few other computers have what appears to be two keyboard connectors. Only one of them is, in fact, a keyboard connector. The other is used for a cassette tape player, which is the most primitive storage device ever on a PC. Which is which? On the older PCs, the connector on the left (as you're facing the back of the PC) is for the keyboard.

✔ Some computers may have permanent keyboards that don't disconnect. For example, some COMPAQ PCs have a keyboard cable that snakes out the front of the console.

Never plug in the keyboard while the computer is turned on. You won't get electrocuted (although we're not certain), but you may damage either the computer or the keyboard. Always wait until the computer is turned off before plugging in your keyboard cable.

The power cord

The power cord plugs into both the back of the PC and a socket in the wall. The connector is usually on the left side of the computer as you're facing the back. It's kind of obvious which end of the cable plugs into the PC and which end plugs into the wall — provided that you've been around major appliances all your life and not stuck in the White House.

- ✔ Make sure that the computer's power switch is in the "Off" or "O" position when you plug in the power cord.

- ✔ Some computers have a second power connector — an "outtie" — next to the real power cable. That connector is used for the monitor's power cable. Most monitors never take advantage of it, however. Go figure.

- ✔ There's nothing special about a PC's power cable. If you lose it, you can replace it with a similar cable supplied to a wide variety of devices.

The printer cable

One end of the printer cable plugs into the computer, and the other end plugs into the printer. Thankfully, both ends are different. Plug the smaller of the two ends into the printer connector in the back of the console. You'll have to look awhile, but most printer connectors are shaped like a D and have 25 holes in them. (Don't bother counting; there are 25 holes.)

If you see more than one printer connector, plug the cable into the connector labeled LPT1 or PRN or First Printer — something like that. If the connectors aren't labeled, just stick the cable into any old connector. In Chapter 10, you'll figure out whether it's the right connector.

Never plug in the printer cable while the computer is turned on. You should always attach printer cables while the computer is turned off. Otherwise, you may fry your PC's insides, and there will be much gnashing of teeth.

A technical definition you don't have to read

The thing you plug the printer cable into — that connector on the back of the console — is called a *printer port*. Yes, port, like the place a ship goes to unload its cargo. You'll often hear the term *port* used in computing. It's simply a fancy term for the hole on the back of the computer to which some interesting device is attached.

Setting up the monitor

After attaching all the cables and whatnot to the console, you're ready to set up the monitor. There are two schools of thought here. The traditionalist school of thought is that you should set the monitor on top of the console. The keyboard then goes in front of everything, giving you the standard, acceptable PC configuration. OK.

The radical, liberal-arts school of thought is that you should put the monitor and keyboard to one side of the console. This setup is entirely possible, depending on the length of the various keyboard and monitor cables and the amount of room on your desk.

- ✔ Decide where you want your keyboard and monitor. Remember that you still need access to the console to turn it on, swap disks, and stare at the pretty glowing lights when you're bored.

- ✔ If there isn't enough cable to put the keyboard and monitor to one side, you can buy extension cables at your favorite computer store. Make sure that you get the proper cable for your monitor and keyboard; count the little holes or pins in the connector, write the number down, and then show up at the computer store and beg someone to help you.

- ✔ Dan Gookin puts his monitor and keyboard to one side of the console. Andy Rathbone puts his monitor and keyboard on top of his desk; his console sits on a box under his desk. (C'mon Andy, train your computer so it doesn't need a box anymore.)

- ✔ Chapter 9 provides more information on monitors, including how to work the various knobs.

Connecting the cables

The monitor has two cables. One goes into the console, which is how the computer displays information on-screen. Call that cable the *video cable*. The second cable is plugged into a wall socket. Plug them both in now.

- ✔ If the power cable has a weird-looking connector on it, don't think that you've purchased a European monitor. That connector plugs into the back of the console, next to the console's power cable connector thingy.

- ✔ The video cable fits into only one connector on the console. *But be careful.* There may be other connectors of the same size that will deceive you. They do so on purpose. If they're marked "Video" or "VGA," that's what you want. And by all means, never force in the connector. If it doesn't fit, it doesn't go there.

- ✔ You may want to tighten the video cable by using a small screwdriver. Doing so permanently attaches the cable to the console but makes unscrewing it later more difficult. Our advice is don't screw in the video cable. It won't suddenly fall out. If for some reason it does, you can just tighten the screws.

Exploring other monitor stuff

Some monitors come with a tilt-and-swivel base, which enables you to move the monitor to various orientations, albeit stiffly. This type of base is also an option you can buy for the monitor if it's not already built in.

As with the console, the monitor needs to breathe. Don't set anything on top of the monitor or cover its air vents in any way.

You don't want to read this bothersome explanation

Most of today's computers are sold with a *VGA graphics system.* That's a fancy term that describes how the monitor's and computer's insides are trained to produce some of the most impressive computer graphics in the world — without busting your budget. On that system, the video cable has 15 wires in it. Likewise, the connector on the console has 15 holes. To deceive you, another connector of the same size appears on the back of many consoles. But that connector has only 9 holes.

The 9-hole connector is a *serial port,* to which you may connect a mouse, a modem, or some other interesting gizmo. It's not where you plug in the monitor. The VGA monitor plugs into a 15-hole connector.

Older PC graphics systems have a different number of holes in the connector. You can usually spot them by a single-hole RF jack connector just to the side of the video connector. If you find the RF jack, you're very close to where you plug in the monitor.

Setting up the printer

The printer is a device separate and unique from the computer. We have several interesting things to say about printers, but we put most of them off until Chapter 10. (OK, *we* think that they're interesting. You may not.)

You set up the printer similarly to the way you set up everything else. Take it out of the box, unpack it, and then set it where you want it. Put the printer near the computer — the nearer the better — but it doesn't need to be too close. You need to connect two cables, which you read about shortly.

- ✔ Keeping the printer at arm's length can come in handy.

- ✔ Be sure to look through the box for manuals, font cartridges, and other stuff you'll need for the printer.

- ✔ Printers don't come with cables — for a reason. Not every printer will be hooked up to an IBM type of computer. Therefore, you need to buy an IBM printer cable separately.

- ✔ Laser printers require *toner cartridges,* which must be purchased separately. Other types of printers usually come with their own ribbons, inkwells, carbon paper, and so on.

Putting the printer together

Printers come in many pieces. There's the printer itself, the ribbon or toner cartridge, and the thing that holds the paper. An instruction sheet that comes with the printer explains what goes where. Find that sheet and then follow its instructions.

Basic printer setup requires yanking a few shipping items from the printer's insides, installing the ribbon/toner cartridge, setting up the paper-feeding mechanism or paper tray, adding any font cards, and plugging in the cables.

- ✔ If the instruction sheet reads like it's written in German, it probably is. Most instruction sheets list instructions in several languages. Look for the English version.

- ✔ Laser printers require a detailed internal setup, which usually requires that you yank out several plastic doohickeys. Other types of printers may require similar removal of parts. Those parts hold the printer's insides in during shipment. You don't need to keep them; freely toss them out (even if you plan on moving the printer later).

- ✔ If you have a font cartridge, it goes into the special font slot hidden somewhere on the computer. An instruction sheet should tell you where it goes. Make sure that the printer is turned off when you plug in the font cartridge.

Connecting the cables

Printers have two required cables: the power cable, which plugs into a wall socket, and the printer cable, which plugs into the computer. How to connect the power cable is obvious, but you may want to consider plugging it into a power strip, as described in the section "What about Those Surge Protectors?" later in this chapter.

The printer cable should already be connected to the PC's console, as described earlier in this chapter. The other end of that cable plugs into the printer. This is the fun part. The connector is big and has two clips on it. There's no way to plug it in wrong, and little guesswork is involved as to where to put it.

- ✔ The majority of printers plug into the computer's printer port. We're glad that makes sense. A few, however, plug into the PC's serial port, which causes a major headache — one that's postponed until Chapter 10 (see the section on using a serial printer).

- ✔ You don't need to use the printer right away. We recommend that you get to know the PC first. Then worry about the printer.

Printer tips

Here are some handy computer printer tips you don't have to commit to memory (they're repeated in Chapter 10 anyway, for good measure):

- ✔ Printers need paper. Laser printers can print on any copy machine paper, but they also accept letterhead and plain typewriter paper. Avoid bond paper that may have dust or powder on it; that stuff clogs up the printer. Also avoid erasable typing paper.

Trivial printer cable information

The printer can only be a maximum of 20 feet from the computer. That's the longest a printer cable can be before information is lost. Cables longer than 20 feet just can't carry the signal from the computer, and nothing (or random information) is printed.

The typical printer cable is 6 feet long — good enough for setting the printer nearby but not necessarily next to the computer. Longer cables are available, and you can always daisy-chain cables. But keep in mind the 20-foot limit.

✔ Nonlaser printers can use *fanfold* paper. This paper comes with dozens (or hundreds) of sheets connected together. Detachable dots on the sides of the paper enable it to be pulled or pushed through the printer. Insert the paper by using the dots and guides. Some printers automatically line up the paper and are ready to print when you turn them on.

✔ You don't need to have the same printer model as your computer. For example, *any* model of printer — not just an IBM printer — works with an IBM computer (although IBM salespersons may claim differently).

✔ You don't need to have the printer turned on unless you're printing something. Leaving laser printers turned on wastes up to 1,000 watts of electricity per hour. That makes for a big electricity bill when you're not printing anything.

✔ The printer does not print unless it's *on-line,* or *selected.* A button on the printer somewhere enables you to activate the printer, bringing it on-line or making it selected. No, it's not enough just to turn on the printer.

What about Those Surge Protectors?

Computers make you realize something about modern living: There aren't enough power sockets to plug everything in. The standard computer requires two power sockets: one for the console and another for the monitor. Extra devices, fax machines, modems, scanners, printers, and so on, all require their own power sockets. As usual, there are right and wrong ways to deal with this situation.

The wrong ways follow:

✔ Never use an extension cord to meet your power needs. People trip over extension cords and unplug them routinely.

✔ Don't use any power splitters or those octopus-like things that turn one socket into three. Computers need grounded sockets, which must have three prongs in them.

The right ways follow:

✔ Buy a power strip. This device plugs into a single socket and contains up to six additional sockets. Everything associated with the PC — even the lamp on your desk — can plug into the power strip.

✔ Buy one of those Power Director things. They usually sit below the monitor and have a row of switches: for the computer, monitor, printer, and other items. A single master switch enables you to turn on everything at once.

What's Next?

With the computer all set up and ready to roll, you're probably tempted to turn it on. But wait. You should look for a few things before you steamroll ahead:

- ✔ Find any manuals that came with your computer. Look for the ones that contain directions and troubleshooting help. Keep these manuals handy.

- ✔ Keep the DOS manual that came with your computer plus any software manuals. Keep any disks and their software manuals together.

- ✔ You can throw away most of the little scraps of paper. Don't throw away anything that has a phone number on it until you've written the number down.

- ✔ Mail in your registration or warranty card. Make a note of the computer's serial number and file it away as well. In an office situation, you should keep track of all your equipment's serial numbers.

- ✔ Make sure that you have a legitimate copy of DOS. You should have DOS on your disk and a copy of the DOS manual. If you don't have a manual, or if you have only photocopied pages, your dealer has sold you a bootlegged version of DOS. Do the right thing: Rush to the software store and buy a copy of MS-DOS for your computer. (Don't worry about reporting the dealer; he or she will pay in the long run.)

You may skip this stuff on surge protectors, but only if you're foolish

A special type of power strip is the *surge protector,* which has protection against power surges and other nasty electrical things that can fry the computer. But *caveat emptor* here: There are varying degrees of surge protectors.

The simplest form of electronic protection is the line filter. It sifts out noise from the power lines, giving you cleaner power. Surge protectors are more expensive. They protect against power surges, which happen when the electricity company puts out a greater amount of juice over a long period of time. Spike protection is the highest, and most expensive, type of protection. A *spike* is a single, high-voltage charge — usually caused by a lightning strike. Only special spike protectors can guard against them and save your computer's life.

How serious is all this? Not very. Unless the power in your area is highly unstable and lightning strikes often, don't worry. A power strip with a noise filter, however, is a good investment.

Dealing with software

You may have purchased some software with your computer. If so, great. However, leave all those boxes alone for now. One of the mistakes many beginners make is overwhelming themselves with computer software. Although it's OK to buy lots of software (and if you haven't, you'll probably buy more later), it's counterproductive to use it all right away.

- DOS is the most important piece of software you have. Locate its disks and put them on top of the pile.

- If you have anything you must do — a priority project, for example — set the software you need aside from the rest of the stuff. For example, if learning 1-2-3, WordPerfect, or Windows is your top priority, set the software aside and get ready to learn and use it first. Everything else can wait.

- Remember that no job can be done immediately. No matter how much of an annoying person your boss is, you must learn software before you can be productive with it. Give yourself at least two weeks before you squeeze something from a computer.

Dealing with other hardware

You may have purchased other hardware goodies, each waiting for setup. Put them on hold for now. Later chapters go into detail on using devices like a mouse, modem, fax, or scanner. The idea here is not to overwhelm you with too much computer stuff right away. Learning what you have set up already will take time enough.

- Hardware is added either internally or externally to the computer.

- Installing internal hardware requires some type of computer nerd. True, you can do it yourself. Many books and magazine articles go into the details if you want to bother with installing internal hardware. Our advice is force someone else to do it.

- External hardware requires a power cable and some type of cable to connect it with the PC. A few devices don't use a power cable. Also, you need special software to run the external hardware. A mouse requires a mouse *device driver;* a modem requires *communications software.* These and even more baffling concepts are covered in Part III of this book.

Setting up DOS

No way. Setting up DOS is a complex and involved process. You shouldn't be bothered with it — for two reasons. The first reason is that most computers come from the factory with DOS installed for you. The factory may have already set up other software, too, so that you're ready to roll. This book assumes that this is the case.

The second reason is that others are more adept at setting up computers — especially those who love and enjoy using them. If your office has a computer manager, he or she should set up the computer just the way it should be set up. For the home computer, you can have that knowledgeable friend of yours do it. Or call up the store for some of that service you paid for and make the store people do it. Either way, setting up DOS is something you shouldn't mess with.

> ✔ Setting up software isn't all that terrible. This book discusses it in Chapter 15.

> ✔ No matter what anyone tells you, you don't need to learn DOS to use your computer. Knowing a few terms is OK, and having a reference such as *DOS For Dummies*, published by IDG Books Worldwide, helps. But leave learning DOS up to those with ambition. The rest of us need only worry about getting our work done.

Summary

Setting up a computer isn't that difficult, provided that you don't get distracted by such things as nuts and bolts, screwdrivers, and modern technology. Here is a brief list of what you need to do:

1. Unpack the boxes and remove the console, keyboard, monitor, and so on. Check for cables and manuals hidden within other boxes.

2. Set up the console where you want it.

3. Connect the keyboard, printer, and power cord to the console.

4. Set up the monitor where you want it.

5. Plug the monitor's video cable into the console and power cable into the wall or power strip.

6. Set up the printer where you want it and then plug in the printer cable and power cable.

7. Set aside your software and other goodies to work with later.

Check over these items before continuing with the next chapter. In Chapter 3, you learn how to turn on the computer, do something, and then turn it off. Quick, safe, no mess, and no pain. Promise.

Chapter 3
Taming the Beast

· ·

In This Chapter

▶ Examining what to turn on first

▶ Booting your computer — where to kick it

▶ Learning which buttons you can ignore

▶ Examining what happens when the computer finds itself (understanding the BIOS nonsense, the memory check, and the noise that occurs while the computer looks for DOS)

▶ Knowing what to do when you're dumped at the DOS prompt

▶ Making the computer do something

▶ Exiting a program

▶ Turning off the computer

· ·

*W*hen you borrow a friend's car for the first time, it's normal for you to be frustrated while you grope around for the ignition switch. The frustration often increases when you try to locate the reverse gear, the trunk release, and the seat adjustment lever. Trying to use a computer for the first time can be just as frustrating. (If only computers had turn-signal-shaped "on" switches . . .)

This chapter alleviates some of the confusion users often feel the first time they turn on a computer. You learn about those loud grinding noises (which are not your fault) and why all those weird characters scroll by your screen too quickly to read. And you learn about people who leave their computers turned on all the time. Scandalous!

Deciding What to Turn On First

Turning on a computer should be as simple as flipping a switch. But, because the system is computerized, turning on the computer is much more complicated. Does it matter whether you turn on the computer before the monitor? Do you turn on the printer first? What about those other computer gadgets?

Actually, it doesn't really matter which item is turned on first. Most people turn on the monitor first, however, so they can watch what happens when they turn on the computer.

Turning on the monitor

So, where did they hide the switch?

It's usually somewhere along the front of the monitor, just underneath the screen. Common hiding spots include under the front rim, along the right edge, or near the back. On older monitors, look for the place with the most finger smudges. (To keep the switch clean, some manufacturers cover it with a fancy fold-down plastic lid. That means the lid is usually the area with the most finger smudges.)

Flip the switch, and the monitor should make a slight squeaking noise as it is turned on, just like your TV set does. In fact, a monitor is really just an expensive, modified TV set with only one channel, as you learn about in Chapter 9.

Turning on the computer

After turning on the monitor, turn on the computer. Where's the computer's switch? Depending on the model, it can be anywhere.

In the grand ol' days of computing, technoweenies wormed their skinny arms through the cables behind their computer and pulled up a big red lever to turn it on. Modern convenience now dictates that the switch be mounted somewhere along the front. It's usually a fashionable push-button switch — the biggest one. If you're lucky, it will be labeled "Power."

- ✔ The power switch is usually the largest switch on the computer. It's sometimes hidden on older machines; look for the thumbprints.

- ✔ Traditionally, on most desktop PCs, the power switch is near the back on the right-hand side. It's on the right-hand side because most people are right-handed. And it's near the back because putting it on the front didn't occur to IBM.

- ✔ If you've just set up the computer, make sure that it's plugged in; then flip the power switch to turn on the computer. (Make sure that you first remove the cardboard inserts, or tongue depressors, from the disk drives.)

Switches aren't labeled with "off" or "on" anymore. Instead, you often see two symbols: a horizontal line and a circle. The line means "on," and the circle means "off." These symbols often appear on other gadgets, like printers, monitors, and imported blenders. You don't need to remember these symbols, however. Just place your ear next to the case. All computing machinery hums when it's turned on. If it's silent, flip the switch in the other direction. Known as *international symbols,* the line and the circle were designed to confuse all cultures equally.

Turning on everything at once

Some people don't hassle with the switches on the computer, monitor, printer, and other computing doodads. They just flip one master switch, and *all* the components jump into action. These people use an item known as a Power Director thing; it looks like a thin box with a row of small switches across the front.

The computer, monitor, printer, and other doodads plug into the Power Director, which plugs into the wall or surge protector. By flipping one switch on the Power Director, you can turn on all your computer stuff at the same time.

- ✔ The best power directors have a bunch of switches, one for each component, positioned in a row next to the master switch. That way you can still control each device separately. You can turn off the printer when you're not using it, for example.

- ✔ Remember to keep the switches of all your equipment turned on and then rely on the master switch to power them up and down again. Turn on the console, monitor, printer, and so on, and then switch them on and off by using the Power Director.

- ✔ *Power Director* is a brand name for the on/off control center distributed by Computer Accessories. Other brands exist; check your local computer store.

The evolution of the power switch

The design of the power switch has evolved through the years:

1. The big red lever on the back of the computer, halfway hidden by protruding cables (circa 1981–1985)

2. The big red lever on the side of the computer, near the back (circa 1985–1989)

3. The reduced-sized red lever on the front of the computer (circa 1989–1991)

4. The fashionably styled push-button switch mounted on the front of the computer—usually square, round, or hexagonal (circa 1991–present)

5. The Frankenstein-style lever marked "Dead" and "Alive" (circa 1892–present)

The Manual Tells Me to Boot My Computer: Where Do I Kick It?

Booting a computer has nothing to do with kicking it. Instead, *booting* simply refers to turning on a computer. "To boot a computer" means to turn it on. Rebooting a computer is the same as pressing the Reset button.

Make sure that there isn't a disk in drive A when you start the computer. If a disk is in floppy disk drive A, the computer won't start from the hard drive like it's supposed to. Keep drive A empty. (Some people keep a disk in drive A because it looks cool; don't be a fool. Just say "no" to disks in drive A when you boot the computer.)

Examining Various Buttons to Ignore

Several smaller buttons and levers usually appear near the power switch; they're described here so you can ignore them.

The key lock

Some PCs sport a keyhole with a key. No, this key doesn't start the computer. You may find the word "Lock" or some padlock-like symbol near the keyhole. No, it doesn't lock up the computer, either. The key lock is used for locking up the keyboard. Turn the key and the keyboard is deaf to anything you type.

Skippable information about booting your computer

Nerdy computer types think the phrase "booting your computer" is cute, but it's getting kind of dated. Here's the scoop:

When your computer is turned on, it starts by looking for instructions hidden in a tiny chip. Those simple instructions tell it to move on to slightly more important instructions, which lead to bigger and more important instructions. Finally, after starting with that tiny wisp of an instruction, the computer becomes a full-functioned being, ready to go to work. Because the computer accomplished something major by first grabbing something small, somebody said it was "pulling itself up by its bootstraps."

Doesn't this information leave you with a numbing cold? No surprise, inner chuckle, or introspective reflection? Welcome to the world of computer talk.

Why have a lock? Probably because IBM put one in its old PC AT computer. Everyone else followed suit and — get this — some of the locks are only for show. They don't lock up anything.

- ✔ The lock is mainly for computer salespeople so they can keep kids from turning off the flashy showroom demos and trying to play computer games.

- ✔ Normal people don't need the key lock. Luckily, most people lose their keys early on, before they have a chance to accidentally lock themselves out of their own computer.

- ✔ If you don't lose your key, just leave it hanging in the lock, which gives the computer that much desired Alfa Romeo look.

The Reset button

Sooner or later, your computer will freeze up cold. You'll see your work on-screen, but the computer won't respond to any of your commands. You'll poke frantically at the keys, and the computer will only mock you by making funny beeping noises. Nothing else will happen. *This* is why you bought a computer?

These freeze ups can happen when you've done something wrong. They can also happen when you've done nothing wrong. In any event, by pressing the Reset button, you are telling the computer to give up and start over.

- ✔ The Reset button is a panic button, but only use it when nothing else works. When you press this button, you're destroying all the work you haven't saved during the day. If you haven't saved your work all day, you lose both your morning *and* prelunch energy bursts.

- ✔ Before pressing the panic, er, Reset button, check Chapter 20 for less violent disciplinary procedures.

- ✔ Do not use the Reset button to quit one program and start the next. There are proper ways to quit programs, as discussed in the section "Exiting a Program" later in this chapter.

Skip this technical background material if you want

What's the Turbo switch for? It enables the computer to run either fast or slow. Normal people leave the Turbo switch on all the time so the computer always runs quickly. After paying extra money for a zippy, slick computer, who'd want to slow it down? Computer nerds, of course.

Years ago, when computers first began to speed up in power, some technoweenies were afraid

that their games would run too fast. By moving the Turbo switch to the slow position, they still had a fighting chance against Targulz and the Destroyers. With today's software, there's rarely a need for the Turbo switch anymore, but it's still there, just like the dopey SysRq key on the keyboard. But that's another story, described in Chapter 7.

The Turbo button

Leave the Turbo button in the "on" position. What is the Turbo button? Although it sounds cool, the Turbo button is a harmless eccentricity, so ignore it and don't bother reading the technical sidebar about it.

The Computer Finds Itself (The Turn-On)

Humans become contemplative when alone in elevators. Computers look deep within themselves when first starting in the morning. Immediately after you turn on the computer, it makes warming-up noises. Usually, you hear a beep, a scuttling sound, a second beep, a bunch of clicks, and a whirring noise. Eventually, a rabbit pops out of the disk drive, mutters something about being late, and scurries out of the room.

As your computer wakes up, it looks inside itself to see what it is, what it's connected to, and how much power it has been given. As it tries to understand itself, the computer informs you of its progress by sending a stream of numbers and code words across the screen.

Computer repair people watch all those words and numbers scroll by so they know when the computer's having trouble. All other people twiddle their thumbs, wishing the computer would hurry up and get to the good stuff.

- ✔ Just kidding about the rabbit part.
- ✔ You just flip the "on" switch; the computer does the hard part of checking its internal components and making sure that it still has the same parts it went to sleep with. The results of these tests appear on-screen. Ignore them.

What's this BIOS nonsense?

Humans grab for their cup of coffee in the morning; computers look for their BIOS (pronounced like the tongue-twisted equivalent of "Hi, boss!") and CMOS (pronounced "see moss"). BIOS and CMOS sound too complicated to describe here, so we save their surprisingly simple explanations for the sidebar that follows.

About the only time you should care about BIOS is when the computer first starts. Sometimes you see a BIOS copyright notice, like this one, for example:

```
Copyright 1990-91 Phoenix Systems
```

The memory check

In addition to checking in with the BIOS and CMOS in the morning, the computer takes inventory of its memory. As the computer tests its memory chips, one by one, it displays the results of the tally on-screen.

TECHNICAL STUFF

Don't bother reading this stuff about BIOS or CMOS

BIOS sounds like a flammable gas caused by fast food. But it's just a computer chip with grade-school-level instructions for the computer. Called the *basic input/output system,* BIOS tells the computer to check out its basic hardware before going any further. Nobody really has to mess around with a computer's BIOS. It's "burned" into a computer chip at the factory, and it never changes.

Another chip, known as *CMOS,* stores even more information for the computer. (CMOS stands for *complementary metal-oxide semiconductor,* by the way.) The CMOS instructions change when-

ever somebody adds stuff to the computer. It keeps track of the size and type of the hard drive, for example, as well as the current time and date. CMOS. See moss. See moss run. Run, moss, run.

When you turn on the computer, the BIOS rubs elbows with the CMOS, and they share data to make sure that they're working with the same set of numbers. Normally, you never have to mess with either of them. You just see the word BIOS flashed on-screen when you first turn on the computer. That's the only reason BIOS is mentioned here. See? You really *didn't* have to bother reading this stuff.

- Computers love memory, stored on *RAM (random-access memory)* chips. They use it as a scratching pad. The more memory computers have, the more room they have to take notes, and the quicker they can work.

- Chapter 4 provides more information than you want to know about RAM and memory. The subject of memory itself is covered in Chapter 6.

- Some older computers take a long time to test all their RAM chips. If you get tired of waiting, try pressing the Esc key. This action tells the computer to assume that the chips are OK and move on to the next step.

- When it is first turned on, the computer reads information from its BIOS and CMOS chips. Everybody else ignores these things, unless they wonder what BIOS means when it appears on-screen each morning.

More noise as DOS is loaded

Ever hear that terrible grinding sound when your PC starts? It's like a chunky carrot top dropped into a garbage disposal. That noise is the computer looking for a disk with DOS on it. The computer must have DOS, or it just won't start.

If the computer doesn't find DOS in its floppy disk drive, the computer looks on the hard drive. That's where DOS is stored on most computers. If the computer *still* doesn't find DOS, it panics, leaving you with something called an *error message,* like this:

```
Non-System Disk or Disk Error
```

This message means that you probably left the wrong disk in the floppy drive. Remove the disk and press the spacebar. If the computer still doesn't work, turn to Chapter 20.

Optional information, secluded to make avoiding it easier

The computer looks at several important files when it's first turned on. Two of them, MSDOS.SYS and IO.SYS, are almost always *hidden*; they're invisible and you can't see them. This setup is great for PC beginners because we don't want to mess with them anyway.

Three other important files, COMMAND.COM, CONFIG.SYS, and AUTOEXEC.BAT, are easier to find.

Don't delete any of these files. Sometimes you may be using a program or shell (such as PC Tools), in which deleting these files is made easier. Avoid the temptation. Never delete an unknown file on a PC. It's better to leave it hanging around than suffer the horrid consequences of deleting it.

✔ Your computer is supposed to make anguished noises when it's first
turned on.

✔ The PC starts looking for DOS in floppy disk drive A due to tradition.
The first computers lacked hard drives, so floppy drives are always
checked first.

✔ The process of loading DOS is the reason that most of the cryptic messages
appear on-screen when the computer starts.

✔ If you see the words `Non-System Disk` or `Disk Error` when you first
turn on the computer, remove the disk you inadvertently left in the floppy
drive.

✔ After a minute or so, most of the noises stop and the screen stops displaying new information. Congratulations. You've reached the second step,
and you didn't have to do anything but flip a switch.

Being Dumped at the DOS Prompt

Depending on how your computer has been set up, it leaves you at one of two
places when it's first turned on. (This isn't your fault; blame the person who set
up your computer.)

Friendly computers go straight to the program you normally use and gently
leave you there so you can get right to work. For example, the PC starts and, lo,
you're suddenly in the happy, friendly Windows environment, ready to play
Solitaire for 45 minutes before starting any serious work. Or you may find
yourself at a cheery menu prompt or automatically in WordPerfect. Cool. No
DOS prompt. No mess.

Unfriendly computers leave you with what's known as the *DOS prompt.* Run for
your life.

The DOS prompt usually looks something like this:

```
C:\>
```

✔ The DOS prompt may also look like `C>` — a C with a greater-than sign.
Other letters may be used, and you may see the date or time or a number
of other weird things. In any case, this place is where you type in commands that direct the PC to do something.

✔ DOS was written by nerd programmers for other nerd programmers.
Nobody expected normal people to use it, much less understand it.

✔ It's possible to make any computer start the friendly way (by running a program or a happy, friendly thing like Windows). Refer to your personal computer guru (check out Chapter 5) for assistance.

✔ If you'd like tourist information about navigating the land of DOS, check out Chapter 13.

Making the Computer Do Something

If you see the DOS prompt, it means that the computer is waiting for you to tell it what to do. (It's *prompting* you for information. Get it?) What you type and what you do are up to you. Typically, you'll want to run a program so you can get work done. (Although the temptation to sit and stare at the DOS prompt exists, avoid it if you can.)

To start your favorite program, type its name at the DOS prompt and press the Enter key. To start WordPerfect, for example, type its name, WP, and then press Enter, like this:

```
C:\> WP
```

By typing **WP** at the DOS prompt (and then pressing Enter), you're telling the computer to find the program named WP and begin running it.

✔ If you normally select from several program names listed on-screen, you're probably using a *menu* (it looks like the one found in restaurants). To start the menu, try typing **MENU** and then pressing the Enter key, like this:

```
C:\> MENU
```

In the preceding line, the word MENU is typed after the DOS prompt. After typing **MENU,** remember to press Enter.

If you want to run Windows, you type **WIN** and press Enter:

```
C:\> WIN
```

In the preceding line, the word WIN is typed after the DOS prompt. After you press Enter, the computer starts running Windows.

✔ The computer handles the basic computer start-up chores when you first turn it on; the computer then hands you the reins. At that point, you start working with software, the real brains of the computer (see Chapter 15 for more information on software).

✔ When faced with the DOS prompt, you must tell the computer to load your software before you can do anything constructive. Usually, you type the program's name.

✔ If you make a mistake when typing, press the Backspace key and the incorrect character disappears. (The Backspace key is near the top right side of the keyboard; the key cap has a left-pointing arrow on it.)

Exiting a Program

Proper computer etiquette requires that you quit a program and return to the ugly DOS prompt before turning off the computer. If you're not sure how to exit the program, check the manual or call over the office computer guru.

Before quitting the program, however, you must save your work. Here's why: When you type words and they appear on-screen, that's the only place you'll find them — on the screen. You must tell the software to *save* those words to a file. Otherwise, you lose all your work when you turn off the computer. You should try to save your work every five minutes (or at least whenever you think about it).

✔ Don't turn off the computer while the program still appears on-screen.

✔ Most programs display a warning message if you try to exit without saving your work. Old versions of some programs, like Lotus 1-2-3, do not. If you haven't saved your spreadsheet and try to exit, the program merely waves good-bye. You can wave good-bye to your spreadsheet, too.

✔ After you exit the program, the screen looks like it did before you started the program. You see the DOS prompt or the menu. Exit the menu, too.

✔ Never use the Reset button to quit a program.

Turning Off the Computer

When you're through computing for the day, you turn off the computer. Doing so is probably the most pleasing thing you'll ever do with it. Such satisfaction comes from turning off the beast that you may be tempted to do it several times a day. (Don't. Computers don't like being turned off a lot.)

As with many other computer-oriented activities, there's a catch to turning off the computer. You can't just flip the switch to the off position. You must follow these steps in the following order:

1. Save your work.

Programs are stupid. If you don't specifically tell them to save your work, they assume that you've only been playing around for the past four hours. They won't save the results of your efforts automatically. Check the manual for the program's Save command or raise your hand to alert the office computer guru.

2. Exit the program.

After saving your work, quit the program and return to the DOS prompt. If you're running Windows or a menu program, select the option that quits it as well.

3. Wait for all drives to stop spinning.

4. Remove the floppy disk.

If you've left a floppy disk in a drive, remove it, put it back in its protective paper sleeve, and store it with the other disks.

5. Do the network stuff, if applicable.

If you're going to turn off the computer, make sure that you log off the network — provided that you're connected to a network. How do you know? Ask someone who does know. Mutter the word *network* and see who blanches. That's probably your network administrator. Discuss *logging off* with the network administrator before you do so.

6. Turn off the computer.

Find the switch you used to turn on the computer and flip it in the other direction (or push it in). Turn off the monitor, too. Or just turn off the whole thing with your Power Director's master switch.

7. Argue.

Argue with other computer users about whether computers should be left on all the time or turned off at the end of each day. Actually, don't argue. Just leave it turned on, without a dust cover, and with the monitor turned off. Turning it on and off sends jolts of electricity through its sensitive parts; you wouldn't want that to happen to you, would you?

Deciding whether to leave the PC turned on all the time

Computer users belong to one of two schools: those who leave their computers turned on all the time and those who turn them off at the end of the day. Users of both schools turn off their monitor at the end of the day — no doubt about that. But the computer angle is subject to debate.

The always-on school teaches the following:

Each time you turn on the computer, the internal components heat up. When you turn off the PC, the internal components cool. This fluctuation in temperature makes the circuit boards expand and contract, which wears out the solder joints.

The off-at-the-end-of-the-day school teaches the following:

When your computer's turned on 24 hours a day, the motors in the hard drive and fan work con-

stantly, leading to premature wear and tear in the bearings.

Leaving the computer turned on all the time means that it will *always* be subject to damaging power surges and harmful fluctuations in electricity.

Your computer probably draws more than 200 watts of power, which can subtly increase the electricity bill.

So which method works best?

Who knows? Dan Gookin leaves his computers on 24 hours a day, unless he's off on a three-day weekend. For a year, Andy Rathbone turned off his computer at the end of each day because the noisy fan kept him awake. Now he keeps it in the garage, and he leaves it turned on all the time.

Summary

This chapter's purpose was to alleviate some of the confusion users often feel the first time they turn on a computer. You examined the following points:

▶ You learned that it doesn't really matter which item is turned on first. Some people turn everything on at once by using a Power Director.

▶ You learned what the term "boot your computer" means.

▶ You examined various buttons near the power switch and learned that you don't have to worry about them.

▶ You examined what happens when the computer is first started in the morning. You learned that the computer looks for its BIOS, checks its memory, and makes noise as it looks for DOS.

▶ You learned what to do when you're dumped at the DOS prompt and how to make the computer do something.

▶ You learned how to exit a program and turn off the computer.

In the following chapter, you examine some common computer stuff that no one else will ever explain to you.

Chapter 4
Common Computer Stuff
(No One Will Ever Tell You About)

• •

In This Chapter

▶ An alphabetic list of various computer terms that computer nerds think everybody already knows

▶ Simple explanations for each of the terms

• •

*H*undreds of computer terms fill the indexes of boring manuals and pop up in the conversations of computer geeks. It's kind of like how doctors say "lacerated basal phalanx" rather than severed toe. Luckily, there's no reason to bother learning most of these computer terms. In fact, many of the terms are just replacement names for existing terms. (That way, computer geeks can confuse more people with less effort.)

This chapter provides simple explanations for terms that the boneheads think everybody else already knows.

ASCII (and How to Pronounce It)

ASCII is an acronym. This one has been elevated to the point where it's also a word. ASCII is pronounced *ask-ee* (similar to *nasty*). It's not pronounced *ask-2*.

ASCII stands for the *American Standard Code for Information Interchange*. It's a set of numbers (0 through 127), each of which is assigned to a letter of the alphabet (both upper- and lowercase), the numbers 0 through 9, punctuation symbols, other weird characters, and 32 special *control codes* that represent keys on the keyboard, such as Enter, Backspace, Tab, Esc, and so on.

Where did ASCII come from?

In the mid-60s, programmer types created ASCII to be a universal language, like Esperanto, but with a big-business-sized marketing budget. The programmers decided to limit the number of ASCII characters to 128. At the time, this was a good-sized number (huge, in fact) that most computers could handle (even though today's PCs can handle 256 and sometimes up to 32,000 codes for different characters).

The idea was that any computer that was ASCII compatible could exchange files and information with other ASCII-compatible computers, even if the two computers came from different home planets. This idea still works today. You can take an ASCII file from an IBM type of computer and magically beam it into a Macintosh, and the file still looks more or less the same. (Nothing is perfect, however, and the end result always requires additional work; don't get your hopes up.)

✔ An ASCII file contains pure text, numbers, and common punctuation symbols. It doesn't contain italics, fancy headlines, or pictures of clowns.

✔ Most word processors and other programs enable you to save a file in ASCII format. Because ASCII means that the text is stripped down to its bare essentials, an ASCII file can be read by most other programs and computers.

✔ Why not save *all* data files in ASCII format? Because ASCII is too limiting. Word processors stick their own special codes into ASCII files to simplify formatting and other chores. Plus, ASCII only applies to text and numbers. It's useless for graphics and similar data.

Command Line

The *command line* is the stuff you type at the DOS prompt when you want the computer to do something. A command line can be one of three things: the name of a program, a DOS command, or a rapidly typed insult at the computer and its questionable heritage. Here is a typical command line:

```
C:\> FORMAT A:
```

The text FORMAT A: is the command line. When you press Enter, you send that text off to DOS for processing. If DOS can carry out your request, the computer does what the command line instructs. If not, the computer says Bad command or file name, which is the computer equivalent of "Huh?"

You don't send your command to the computer until you press Enter. If you change your mind before you press Enter, use the Backspace key to erase your command, one character at a time. Or press the Esc key to escape and start over.

Default

Finally — a term that you're *supposed* to ignore. (Stomp your feet, clap your hands, and throw floppy disks in the air!) Here's the scoop: Sometimes a program presents you with a somber list of choices and casually suggests that you choose the only option that's not listed: the *default* option.

Don't bother looking for it. Just press the Enter key.

Those crafty programmers already figured out which option works best for 99 percent of the people using the program. So, if you just press Enter instead of fiddling around, the program automatically makes the right choice.

- ✔ The "default" option is similar to the "any" key in that neither of them appears on the keyboard.
- ✔ Default can also mean "standard option" or "what to select when you don't have a clue." For example, small children pinch each other *by default*.
- ✔ Pick up the floppy disks when you're through throwing them.

DOS Prompt

The DOS prompt consists of the strange and confusing characters you see at the beginning of each line while you're working with DOS. It's the computer's way of *prompt*ing you to tell it what to do.

The DOS prompt usually looks like this:

```
C:\>
```

Or it can look like this:

```
C>
```

- ✔ You type commands at the DOS prompt to make the computer do something useful.
- ✔ The letter in the prompt usually tells you what disk drive you're currently raiding.
- ✔ For more information about DOS, refer to Chapter 13.

DOS Version

On the surface, there's not much difference between versions of DOS. They all have that C:\> thing, and they all make you type strings of nonsensical nouns and occasional verbs.

However, Microsoft has released six major versions of DOS. It has also fixed some of those versions when they didn't work right. Version 3.0, for example, was patched up and rereleased as Version 3.1.

DOS 6.2 is the current version. How can you find out? Type **VER** at any command prompt, like this:

```
C:\> VER
```

Then press Enter, and DOS reveals its version heritage.

Who cares? Well, each version of DOS adds new features or gets rid of the old ones that didn't work. That means that some picky pieces of software demand certain versions of DOS in order to work.

Most of those picky pieces of software want the most current version of DOS. In fact, keeping the current version of DOS on your computer is one of the best ways to make sure that your computer can run the latest, greatest programs.

Microsoft often added new commands to new versions of DOS. If you try to run the DOS Shell on a computer using DOS Version 3.3, for example, DOS just says something rude. The reason is that Microsoft didn't think about adding the DOS Shell until Version 4.0. (And that particular DOS Shell looks different from the one in Version 5.0 too.)

FCC Class A and B

The Federal Communications Commission (FCC) checks to see what sort of electronic noise the computer creates. This invisible noise can interfere with radio and TV reception, like when your next-door neighbor's saber saw sends bad vibes through your TV set.

The FCC labels the electronic noise level as either class A or class B. Class B equipment is better shielded, emits less noise, and usually costs more. Class A standards aren't as stringent because class A equipment is meant for office use, where nobody's supposed to be watching TV anyway.

✔ Home buyers should purchase class B equipment — especially if they want to compute and mix drinks in the blender at the same time.

✔ In keeping with the government tradition of general obfuscation, class B is the better shielded product, not class A.

Files

A *file* is a collection of information stored by the computer. *Program files* contain instructions for the computer to do something useful, like balance a checkbook. *Data files* contain the stuff you create, like a letter to Ms. Manners.

When computer nerds created computers, they looked for some metaphor to describe what they were doing. Because computers perform mostly office work, it seemed natural for computer nerds to swipe common office terms. For example, a file in a file cabinet contains information; so does a computer file.

✔ Files are ethereal. You can't pick up and hold a file. You can hold the disk that contains the file (or files). And you can print a file and then hold the sheaf of papers.

✔ Computer software comes in the form of files — specifically, program files that tell the computer what to do. Other files, those that are not program files, are not really software because they don't tell the computer to do anything.

✔ The name given to a file is referred to as the *filename*.

✔ Program files come with a predetermined name when you buy them.

✔ You must come up with your own names for the data files you create. If DOS or the program refuses to accept your creative filename, you're probably in or treading dangerously close to the Forbidden Filenames Zone. Turn to Chapter 13 quickly, before the beating of the drums reaches fever pitch.

GUI

Acronym alert: GUI is yet another computer acronym. It's pronounced *gooey*, as in "ooey GUI rich and chewy." *GUI* stands for *graphical user interface* and means that you control the computer through pictures and symbols on the computer's screen. For example, the Travel Kiosks at airports use a GUI. There, you can select a button right on the screen to see information about the golf courses at expensive hotels.

With a GUI on a personal computer, you don't have to touch the screen. Instead, you use the arrow keys or a plastic robot called a *mouse* to move a tiny on-screen arrow. When the arrow points at the symbol you want (a picture of a fountain pen, for example), you press Enter or a button on the mouse. Because the fountain pen represents your word processing program, that program comes to the screen, ready for work.

Some people prefer dealing with pictures rather than typing weird language at the DOS prompt.

Where did GUI come from? Who knows. Read the mountains of legal paperwork or take a software attorney to lunch.

- ✔ After you pronounce *GUI* as *gooey* a few times, you'll be able to stifle the urge to giggle. That urge will return when you pronounce the plural, *gooeys.*

- ✔ Some popular GUIs are Windows, OS/2, and NeXTStep.

- ✔ Because computer geeks often name everything twice, the symbols in a GUI are also called *icons.* These icons have nothing to do with icons you may see hanging in a Greek Orthodox church. (There's a big difference between Greeks and geeks.)

- ✔ For more information on GUIs, refer to Chapter 16.

Hard Copy (or to Get Hard Copy)

Hard copy is information printed on a piece of paper; "to get hard copy" means to print information. When someone tells you to "get a hard copy of it," that person means for you to print it. The reason is obvious. No one wants to lug around the computer to people so they can see what's on the screen.

The term *hard copy* has been commonplace in newspaper offices since the late 1800s. When the Morse code operator heard something juicy coming over the wire, the operator told the editor, who whirled around and barked, "Get me a hard copy of that, Jones, pronto!" Jones then handed the editor a printed copy of the information he previously heard as dashes and dots. The term's association with the tabloid journalism of the 1890s gives it a somewhat steamy connotation, leading to dumb TV shows.

- ✔ Some people make a hard copy of anything they create on the computer. That way, when the computer dies unexpectedly, they still have something to show for their efforts.

- ✔ Hard copy can be anything from a single page to an entire book or anything that spews from the printer.

- ✔ For more information about hard copies, refer to Chapter 10.

Hardware

A computer's *hardware* is the part of the PC you can actually touch: the console, printer, floppy disks, and monitor (which leaves fingerprints).

Coined in the 1500s by burly blacksmiths, *hardware* refers to any physical tool. In the '60s, nerd programmers decided to call programs *software* (the opposite of hardware).

- ✔ Hardware either lives inside the computer or comes with a cord that plugs into the computer — unless you're trendy enough to have a cordless mouse, which deserves an extra explanation (see Chapter 11).

- ✔ By itself, hardware does nothing but drive up the electricity bill. Hardware needs software to tell it what to do.

IBM

IBM stands for *International Business Machines,* the huge company that specialized in making huge computers for other huge companies. When IBM saw how much money others were making with a tiny Apple computer in the mid-70s, IBM wanted a cut of that market, too.

So IBM hired a bunch of engineers and told them to make a small personal-sized computer and aim it at the small-business market. The engineers created the personal computer and released the specs to the public so that everybody would develop software for it.

Everybody did. Everybody copied the computer, too.

- ✔ The term IBM also refers to any type of computer that mimics the original personal computer or other IBM equipment.

- ✔ IBM dominated the computer market until about 1985. Ever since then, IBM's slice of the pie has been small. However, 80 percent of all computers sold are IBM compatible.

Read this stuff only if you want to be precise

OK, confession time. One kilobyte does not equal 1,000 bytes or characters. It's really 1,024 bytes. The extra 24 bytes are actually a tax levied by Congress. Seriously, 1,024 is the number 2 raised to the 10th power — 2^{10}. Computers just *love* the number 2, and 1,024 is the closest power of 2 to 1,000. It's OK for us to think that 1K = 1,000. The extra change does, however, add up over time.

Likewise, 1MB equals 1,048,576 bytes, not an even million. One megabyte is actually 1,024K, which means that you have 1,024 multiplied by 1,024 to give you one mega of bytes. This stuff, like the concept of a million dollars, is all trivial.

Kilobyte and Megabyte

Conceptually speaking, a *byte* is equal to a single letter or character in a computer file. The term *kilo* means 1,000, so one *kilobyte* is roughly 1,000 bytes, about 1,000 characters, or a little less than half of a page of text.

The term *mega* means 1,000,000. One *megabyte* is 1,000 kilobytes, so it is about 1,000,000 characters or somewhere close to 500 pages.

- ✔ Kilobyte is commonly abbreviated as K.
- ✔ Megabyte is commonly abbreviated as MB.

Loading a Program or File

Just as files are plucked from the file cabinet and spread across your desk, files are *loaded* from a disk inside the computer. "To load" means to transfer something from disk to the computer's memory. Only after something has been loaded into memory can you work with it.

- ✔ You load programs by typing a command line at the DOS prompt or by selecting their names from a menu or shell.
- ✔ You load data files by using special commands in your program. For example, in Windows, you *load* files. In WordPerfect and 1-2-3, you *retrieve* files. In some programs, you may *transfer-load* files. Weird.

The following expressions mean exactly the same thing as loading a program:

- ✔ Executing a program
- ✔ Running a program
- ✔ Loading up a program
- ✔ Booting up a program
- ✔ Launching a program

Macintosh

The computer people who antagonized their significant others by staying up all night to create the Apple computer made a lot of money. After buying roses for their significant others to apologize, they stayed up all night again to create another computer: the Macintosh.

It was a tiny thing that everybody said looked like a toaster. Repair shops had to open them repeatedly to vacuum out the dried bread crumbs. The computers were so cute and friendly that people called them Macs rather than Macintoshes. Figure 4-1 shows a typical Macintosh.

Figure 4-1:
A typical
Macintosh.

The Mac uses a fun GUI (see the section "GUI" earlier in this chapter) rather than a hard-to-learn DOS prompt. Just about everything about Macs breathes "Hi, there — come play!" Macs even smile when you first turn them on. And, when the computer crashes and dies, there's no arms-folded, foot-tapping error message. There's a cool picture of a bomb on-screen.

Also, the out-of-the-box PC can only beep rudely. The Mac can giggle, burp, or even talk sexy.

- The IBM-compatible computer was created by and for computer nerds. In contrast, the creators of the Macintosh computer made a real effort to create a computer that *humans* can use. A Mac is often easier to use than an IBM compatible and almost always more fun (and a heck of a lot slower).

- Because Macintosh computers use pictures a lot, Macs appeal more to people with graphics-based careers. You'll find them in the art departments of magazine companies, for example, and in other noisy, creative departments down the hall from the accounting office.

- Unlike IBM, Apple kept the Macintosh's innards a secret. Nobody could rip off the design to create compatibles or clones. Because there's no competition, Macintosh computers cost a lot more than most IBM-compatible computers.

- Macintosh computers popularized the *mouse,* which is a small, palm-sized plastic device that sits on a roller. By pushing the mouse across your desk, you move a corresponding arrow on-screen. You press a button on the mouse to activate the object that the arrow's currently pointing at. For more information, refer to Chapter 11.

Multitasking

The big computing buzzword of the '90s is *multitasking.* It means forcing the computer to accomplish more than one task at the same time. For example, when you're on the phone, cooking dinner, looking at the TV, and fending off a small child, you're multitasking; you're doing four — or more — things at once. The same idea applies to the computer.

Multitasking computers can do more than one thing at a time. Where the typical computer can do only one thing at once, a multitasking PC can do two or more things at once. Granted, you don't have two heads or more than one set of hands. Still, you don't have to watch many things a computer does. The idea is that you can move on and do something else while the computer toils at some task by itself.

✔ For the DOS nerd, multitasking presents a cornucopia of opportunities. For the PC beginner, it opens a confusing can of worms. Imagine being buffaloed by DOS four ways at once rather than one way at a time. Sheesh.

✔ Three popular programs enable some of the more powerful IBM-compatible computers to multitask: Windows, OS/2, and DESQview. Pray that you have to use Windows. It has the best version of Solitaire.

✔ When you're not working on a particular program, it's said to be *in the background,* which is similar to putting something on the back burner. It continues to burn, but you don't need to pay attention to it.

✔ You can find more information about Windows in Chapter 16. OS/2 is covered — or uncovered — in Chapter 14.

Network

A network enables computer nerds to connect computers with extra cables and software so *all* the machines stop working when one of them does. Seriously, networked computers can share information. They can all use one printer, for example, and employees can send messages back and forth asking each other where to have lunch that day.

Here are three ways to tell whether you're on a network:

1. **Your coworkers and you can share a printer, files, or messages without getting out of your chairs.**

2. **You must *log in* or *log out* when using the computer.**

3. **The computer stops working or "goes down" a lot.**

✔ If you're not on a network, ignore it.

✔ If you're on a network, ignore it. Networks come with a human attendant, right out of the box (see Chapter 17).

On the Screen/Monitor

The *monitor* is the big bulky thing that looks like a TV set. The *screen* is the glassy area you look at to see stuff displayed. What you see is said to be "on the monitor." Please, don't look on top of the monitor; look at the glassy part.

✔ The sticky notes on the monitor are not "on the monitor."

✔ Monitors attract a thin layer of dust, which you can call *pixel dust*. Don't spray glass cleaner on the screen to get rid of that yucky dust film. Spray the glass cleaner on a rag and apply the rag to the screen.

Programs and Data Files

Files contain information in a form that the computer can manipulate. Program files and data files differ in several areas:

Program files: The expensive files you have to get from somebody else. They contain instructions that tell the computer what to do — process your words, for example, or balance your checkbook. WordPerfect, dBASE, and 1-2-3 are all programs.

Data files: The files *you* create. They contain the information you created on the computer by using a program. A love letter written with WordPerfect is stored in a data file, as is an inventory of your comic book collection in dBASE.

Documents: Special types of files created by word processors. They're written things — stuff you can print and send to people: memos, letters, chapters from a book, reports, essays, and so on. Anything a word processor produces is a document kind of file.

Worksheets: The files produced by spreadsheets. A worksheet is like a giant grid that contains numbers and mathematical formulas and stuff that makes accountants go *schwing*.

Graphics files: The files produced by special graphics software. They contain images, pictures, or other stuff you want to display or toss on an overhead projector for that big presentation others will doubtlessly sleep through.

✔ Anything that isn't a program file is a data file. Documents, worksheets, graphics files, and any other files on disk that aren't programs are data files.

✔ Chapter 15 goes into full detail on different types of programs. Refer to Chapter 13 for information on DOS and files.

Pull a Directory

To pull a directory is to list the files that are on a disk. "Pull" means to list. With DOS, it means to use the DIR command. You type **DIR** at the DOS prompt and then press Enter to see the list of files on disk (you are pulling a directory):

```
C:\> DIR
```

In the preceding line, the DIR command is typed at the DOS prompt to pull a directory. Yank, yank, yank. You soon see a list of files and other stuff on-screen.

- ✔ In a file cabinet, files are stored in a drawer. In a computer, files are stored in a directory.

- ✔ There is no corresponding term for you to *push* a directory.

Quit, Exit, and Return to DOS

Just as programs can be started up, they can be turned off. But you don't do so by flipping the computer's power switch, no matter how tempting this idea may be. Instead, you must find the way the program meant for you to quit.

The manual helps. If you have one, look in the index for the word *exit*. Or, if you have a computer guru nearby, you can slowly wave the manual high above your head.

- ✔ When the program leaves the screen, it leaves you at the same point where it started. If you were at the DOS prompt, for example, the program leaves you there. Or you may return to a menu or a shell, depending on how your computer was set up.

- ✔ Remember to save your work before exiting a program.

The following phrases all describe leaving a program:

- ✔ Exiting a program
- ✔ Quitting a program
- ✔ Getting out of a program
- ✔ Returning to DOS
- ✔ Bag this junk and let's get a pizza

RAM or Memory

RAM and memory are two exchangeable terms. They both refer to storage inside the computer. Regardless of whatever it is technically, you should know that the more RAM or memory you have, the more the computer can do. More RAM is better than less RAM. More memory means that you can do more than with less memory.

- *RAM* stands for *random-access memory*. Specially, it refers to the type of chips inside the computer where information is stored.

- *Memory* is the friendly term for temporary storage inside the computer. (Long-term storage is provided by the disk drives.)

- Computers use their memory differently from humans. People use *brains* to think — not memory. Computers, however, use their RAM as a scratching pad of sorts. The bigger the scratching pad, the more space the computer has to make its calculations. That's why lots of RAM is good.

Run, Execute, and Launch

"Running a program" means working with it so you can do something useful. You can *run* 1-2-3, you can *execute* 1-2-3, and you can *launch* 1-2-3. These are three confusing terms for the same thing.

- You run a program by typing its name at the DOS prompt.

- If you're using a menu or shell, you run (execute, launch, and so on) a program by selecting the proper menu item, pressing a key, or muttering the correct chant.

- *Run* is the most common term, but some manual writers say *execute* because they want this idea to be confused with 18th century scientists who liked to make sparks when they threw switches.

A military view of RAM — reading optional, safety's on

A tank's firing power is measured in kilotons of TNT. The computer's explosive power is measured in kilobytes of RAM. Each successive *kilobyte* of RAM can bore through another sheet of drywall. A *megabyte* of RAM can blast through 1,000 sheets of drywall — enough to knock free soft drink cans from all vending machines within a three-block radius.

Most computer industry officials deny this fact, however, saying that RAM enables a computer to store *information* — not firepower.

Save

Saving is the process of telling the computer to transfer the information you just created to a disk for storage and safekeeping. Therefore, "save your data" has nothing to do with religious conviction.

Computers can't tell whether you're working or just fiddling around. So, after you create something (a report that took five hours, for example), the computer doesn't know that you intend to keep it. You must specifically tell the program to save the information.

✔ You can save information by getting a hard copy of it (see the section "Hard Copy (or to Get Hard Copy)" earlier in this chapter). Most likely, *saving* means saving something to disk — either a floppy disk, a hard disk, or a network disk on another computer.

✔ If you don't tell the computer to save your work, it won't do so automatically. If you try to leave a program without saving your work, some programs take pity and flash a message warning that you haven't saved your work. Other programs don't. And, if you turn off your computer in the middle of a program, your program won't have a chance to tell you anything at all.

✔ After you learn how to save your work, try to save it every five minutes or whenever you remember. Some programs even offer an autosave feature that automatically saves your work every few minutes.

Send to the Printer

This term means telling the program to send the results of your work through a cable to a *printer,* the mechanical thing nearby that always runs out of paper. "Send to the printer" is another confusing term that means the same thing as "get hard copy."

✔ When you send something to the printer, you don't take it to the shop down the street. You tell the computer to transfer the information from its screen to its own printer, usually sitting no more than 20 feet away.

✔ A program's command to print something almost always has a P in it. Don't bank on it, though. With WordPerfect, you press Shift-F7 to print. There's no P there.

✔ Printers never waste paper until you turn them on.

✔ Printers connect to something called a *port* on the back of the computer. Or, if you don't see a wire running from the back of the computer to the printer (or you don't see the printer, for that matter), you're probably on a network system.

> ✔ For some reason, a printer's port is called a *parallel port*.
>
> ✔ If you send something to the printer and the printer just sits there, wait a few moments. Then try turning the printer on.
>
> ✔ Refer to Chapter 10 for more information on printers.

Software

Software is a set of instructions that tells the computer how to do things. It's intangible; you can't see it. You can only see where it's stored or its results.

> ✔ Software comes on a disk, but the disk itself isn't the software. The software is the information stored on the disk.
>
> ✔ The computer's software controls the computer's *hardware* — physical things (like the printer) that you can actually touch and smell.

Windows

Written by a company called Microsoft, *Windows* is a popular system for IBM-compatible computers that replaces the DOS prompt with pictures and graphics.

It's called Windows because it fills the screen with overlapping *windows* — box-like areas containing their own programs. Your word processor can be in one window, for example, and a spreadsheet can be in a window sticking out from underneath. When you move to the spreadsheet window, it leaps to the forefront, slightly hiding the word processor window beneath it.

Technical tidbits I'd skip if I were you

Actually, the *software* is the instructions stored on the disk, the *medium* is the floppy disk, and the *hardware* is the floppy disk drive. With a record album, the *software* is the music itself, the *medium* is the record, and the *hardware* is the turn-table. With a radio, the *software* is the sound, the *medium* is the airwaves, and the *hardware* is the radio itself. With a VCR, the *software* is the movie, the *medium* is the — well, you get the idea.

This method of hopping from window to window makes transferring information easier; you can copy information from the spreadsheet and put it into your word processor. It also enables you to quickly hide that game of PC Solitaire when the boss comes strolling into the room.

- ✔ Windows works best with a fast computer, a huge hard drive, and great gobs of memory.

- ✔ Windows, with an initial capital letter, refers to the Windows program itself. The lowercase version, windows, refers to the box-like areas on-screen.

- ✔ Microsoft also released DOS; it's trying to make amends with Windows.

- ✔ Windows is a GUI (see the section "GUI" earlier in this chapter).

- ✔ A special jumbo version of Windows, *Windows NT*, works for big companies with big computers and big networks. Another special version of Windows, *Windows for Workgroups*, works for smaller companies with smaller computers and small networks. They all look and feel pretty much the same.

Workstation/Work Station

Computer marketing people really like to run words together (or runwordstogether). When run together, the words usually mean something different from when the words are separated. Take workstation and work station.

A *workstation* is a special breed of high-powered computer. It doesn't use DOS as an operating system; it uses something even more complicated.

A *work station* sometimes describes the area where you do your computing — the place with the mess. It was invented by the old computer overlords who rejected the idea that one person should have his or her own computer.

- ✔ Workstations are often used for heavy-duty graphics: charting the flow of air over an airplane wing, for example.

- ✔ As PCs have become more powerful, they've become capable of running programs that previously required a workstation.

- ✔ Some offices have word processing work stations set up. The PCs are raring to go with some word processor. There's no need to run any software; just sit down and type.

. . . .

Summary

This chapter provided simple explanations for various computer terms:

▶ You were presented with an alphabetic list of various computer terms.

▶ You examined simple explanations for each of the terms and received some extra tidbits of information about various concepts related to those terms.

In the following chapter, you examine how to scream for help and learn who to scream at.

. . . .

Chapter 5
How to Scream for Help (and Who to Scream At)

*Y*ou may be a major executive, a teacher, a mad scientist, or any smart, talented, gifted individual. But this computer thing makes you feel like a dummy. No problem. That's why this book was written. We're not going to argue against computer literacy; everyone should know how to use an automated teller machine, and not being afraid of a computer is important. But should you memorize everything about a computer? *Naaaaa.* There's no need to. Plenty of other people have already done that. Your task as a PC beginner is to use those people's skills, thank them profusely, and then get on with your work.

This chapter discusses how to get help from PC-knowledgeable friends and office comrades. Regardless of whom you decide to ask for help, call that person your *computer guru.* And remember that a certain amount of finesse is involved; a line must be drawn between getting occasional help and taxing your guru's patience. This chapter also discusses the differences between major problems that require assistance and things you can quickly remedy yourself.

Who Is Your Guru?

Your personal computer guru is going to be someone who loves computers and knows enough about them to offer help when you need it. Your guru is an important person to know and respect. Everyone has one — even the gurus themselves! If you don't have one, you'll need one.

At the office, the guru is probably the computer manager, but you should ask around to see whether anyone else can do the job. Quite a few computer zanies may be lurking around the office. If you find one, he or she may be able to offer help, suggestions, and advice more quickly than the computer manager (who goes by a schedule). Especially for help on particular types of software, turn to people who use the programs regularly; they may discover tricks that they can pass along.

For the home, finding a guru can be more difficult. Usually a neighbor, friend, or relative will know enough about computers to help you install hardware or software, or at least give you advice about some program.

Whatever your situation, identify your guru and keep that person in mind for troubled times or for extracting advice and tips. It's like having a good mechanic handy or knowing a friendly doctor. You may not use your guru all the time, but knowing he or she is there makes computing easier.

- Don't forget the gurus you've already paid for: the technical-support people at your computer store or the telephone support you get with every piece of software you buy. Everything comes with support; it's part of the purchase price. Especially for software, call the support department if you're having trouble. (But don't abuse phone support; it's not an excuse for not reading the manual.)

- Some computer stores may offer classes or have coffee groups where you can ask questions. But keep in mind that this is a limited source of information. If you continue to ask a computer dealer for help, the dealer may become annoyed or start charging you for information. Better ways exist.

- Local computer clubs dot the nation. Don't be afraid to show up at one and ask a few questions. You may even adopt a guru there or learn about special sessions for beginners. Many computer clubs or special interest groups (SIGs) are designed specifically for questions and answers. Check the local paper or computer flier at the store for more information.

- Community colleges offer introductory courses on computers and some software programs. Come armed with your questions.

- Check your bookstore or newsstand. Although this and other . . .*For Dummies* books may be all you need, other self-help texts exist. We're personal fans of *PC Novice* magazine, which always has plenty of tips and questions and answers for new computer owners. Other magazines have similar features, but keep in mind that most are very technical in nature.

- If these traditional avenues fail, consider the unconventional. If you're a member of the Prodigy on-line service, try there for help. Or try one of the other numerous on-line services, such as CompuServe and GEnie. (Of course, this advice assumes that you know how to wrestle with a modem in the first place.)

The 5th Wave   **By Rich Tennant**

"HERE'S YOUR PROBLEM. SOME BOZO JAMMED YOUR KEYBOARD WITH A 4-LEAF CLOVER."

A *computer consultant* is someone who likes computers and charges you a fee because of it. Computer consultants help you get out of any circumstance, offer suggestions, buy things for you, set up your system, train you about software, and create custom programs — all for a fee. Having a consultant can be worth the cost. We should warn you, however, that most of these "gurus for hire" do no more than the free, bribable gurus.

Is Something Really Wrong?

There are two circumstances in which you'll need to call someone else for help. The first circumstance is when you want to do something and need to know how it's done. For example, you want to use columns in WordPerfect but don't have a clue how to do it. That's when you need a true guru — someone who has mastered the PC or its software and, if he or she doesn't know the answer, can sift through the manuals and discover it quickly.

The second circumstance is when something runs amok in a computer. This situation happens all the time, even to the gurus. Computers are like garden hoses in a way; they can tie themselves up into twisty tangled knots with little or no effort on your behalf. Because learning about a PC or knowing the innards of DOS or some piece of software is beyond a normal person's abilities, it's time to call for help.

✔ Before calling your guru for assistance, try working through the problem again. For example, if you're trying to print and it just doesn't work, try again after a few moments. Working out a problem ahead of time lets your gurus know that you're not abusing their help.

✔ Many computer applications have *help functions*. A help function is a feature — relatively new to computer software — that offers suggestions, advice, and hints about using the program. The big-selling programs offer more help than no-name (or *el cheapo*) programs. Try this method of getting help first before calling someone else. If this method doesn't work, you could try the manual. (Yeah, right.)

✔ The typical help key for most programs is F1. Press the key labeled F1 to use the help function.

✔ Don't be too quick to blame yourself if you can't do something. If you've done it the way the manual says and it still doesn't work, either the manual or the computer program is wrong. What you have is a genuine *bug,* and your guru — or the software manufacturer — should be made aware of it.

✔ Chapter 20 covers many types of computer glitches and how to remedy them. Also, Part II of this book contains several chapters devoted to individual parts of the PC. Check there for problems and solutions before you scream for help.

✔ Some computer gurus operate for free. Never take advantage of their generosity. Refer to the section "Common Bribes for Computer People," later in this chapter if you want to thank them in an appropriate way (well, appropriate for them).

How to Scream for Help

Approaching your guru with a problem requires skill. You don't just say "It doesn't work" and toss up your hands. Unless you're a soap opera star or royalty, don't expect much help from that approach. Instead, try the following:

1. **Relax.**

   Everyone has things to do and deadlines to meet. Don't dump any of your stress on the computer guru. If that's a problem for you, then arrange to have your guru look at the PC when you're not there. No guru will help a rude user. (Who would want to?)

2. Document what's going on.

When something doesn't work, write it down or be very detailed when you recite the problem. For example, don't just say, "I tried to start my computer, and it won't boot." Instead, write down any messages you see, such as Not a DOS disk. Or, if the computer beeps, write that down. If the printer doesn't print, yet the light is flashing, make a note of it. This kind of information helps the guru determine the problem (and it also shows that you care).

3. Demonstrate the problem.

If you happen to be with your guru, show what the computer does. Your guru may want to sit in your chair. That's OK. Just tell your guru what you wanted to do and demonstrate how it didn't work. For example, print your spreadsheet and show your guru the odd characters that appear.

When the guru can't be there, try to be near your computer when you're on the phone. Type in commands as the guru instructs you. Try to be accurate about describing your situation or what appears on-screen.

4. Offer a suggestion.

This step is optional. Obviously, you don't know how to fix the problem. But, by offering a suggestion, you're showing the guru that you care. If you can't think of anything to say, make something up: "The disk drive needs a new steering wheel" or "The printer is in Italian mode" or "I think it needs to be plugged into a 220-volt socket." The best suggestion to make is "Something needs replacing."

✔ Nobody will help you if you ask the same questions over and over again. After telling you three times how to print sideways in your spreadsheet, your guru may become understandably rude and uncooperative. Instead of letting that happen, write down the answer and keep a log book handy if you need to.

✔ You don't really want to learn anything about a computer. Even so, some gurus may try to teach you something. If so, grab the old yellow pad and write down everything your guru says. True, you may never use those instructions. But writing them down makes the gurus happy.

Common Bribes for Computer People

Those who love diddling with computers are an odd lot. In addition to thanking them when they help you, consider offering a treat every so often. That way, you dupe them into believing that they're not being used.

If you don't read your manuals, you probably won't read this stuff either

Why are computer manuals so bad? And why are some books on using computers so atrocious? Stand back for a shock: There are legitimate reasons.

The number one reason computer manuals are so bad is that they're written by people who are all too familiar with the programs. I remember reading the following in a computer manual: "The function of this key should be obvious." The manual never told what the key did because the function was obvious to the person who wrote the manual. That person didn't consider the PC beginner's needs.

Another problem with the manuals is that they must often be completed weeks before the software is done. Manuals must be bound and printed, which takes a lot longer than copying several hundred disks. Therefore, errors creep into the manuals unintentionally because the manuals are etched in stone and the programs are still changing.

Computer manuals are interesting to read through after you've been using the program. Most users start with a manual, take a legitimately good stab at it, and then toss it in frustration. A few weeks later, though, they thumb through the manual and can grasp some small piece of information in it.

Computer books are generally bad because they either are rushed through the publishing process, are not properly checked, or offer no insights aside from what's already in the manuals. There is hope, however. Generally, an index leads you to information you need. But don't expect the information to be overtly obvious. Computer-book authors suffer the same fate as the manual writers; they become too familiar with the subject matter to consider a PC beginner's needs. (Needless to say, you won't find that problem here.)

Forget about giving your computer gurus money or software programs for their favors. Instead, consider the following foodstuffs:

- ✔ Doritos — preferably nacho-cheese flavored or something with a nearly all-red thermometer on the side of the package.

- ✔ Anything made by Hostess — Twinkies, Ding Dongs, Fruit Pies (especially the ones with pudding in them), and so on. The Dolly Madison line of snack cakes is also OK.

- ✔ M&Ms — the two-pound package. You'll get bonus points if you pick out all the blacks and browns.

- ✔ Oreos with Double Stuff. More stuff. More cholesterol. Computer people like that.

- ✔ Cheetos. This prize is the primary reason that computer nerds have yellow stuff between their teeth.

✔ Doughnuts. Don't be afraid to offer a computer person a stale doughnut. In fact, banging a doughnut on a table is one of the ways most computer people wake each other up in the afternoon.

✔ Ritz crackers and peanut butter. Sometimes, just giving computer people a four-pound tub of generic peanut butter is best. Hand it to them along with a butter knife — but don't look.

✔ Jolt Cola — all the caffeine and twice the sugar. (Another favorite beverage is Diet Coke; for the most part, computer zanies don't drink much beer.)

✔ Pizza — perhaps the ultimate choice. You don't even need to enter the house for this one. Slide a pizza under your guru's door if you're afraid to venture inside.

Avoid giving healthy food, although all-natural potato chips are OK. Steer clear of vegetables or anything green (except for M&Ms). Meat is OK, if you want to fix dinner for your gurus. But don't ask them how they want it (the answer is usually "raw").

The authors of this book will not be held responsible for any health conditions that may result from this diet. Further, if you decide to throw a party and serve this junk, please display this book proudly or at least mention it in a favorable way.

Summary

This chapter discussed how to get help from knowledgeable friends and office associates. You examined the following points:

▶ At the office, the computer guru is probably the computer manager. Or you can request help from someone who uses a particular program regularly.

▶ At home, you can usually find a computer-knowledgeable neighbor, friend, or relative.

▶ Before calling a guru for assistance, try working through the problem again. Check the program's help feature or even the manual.

▶ When approaching the guru for help, be sure that you have documented the problem. Demonstrate the problem and offer suggestions if you can.

▶ Remember to offer your guru treats as a special thank you. High-fat, high-cholesterol junk food works best.

You have now completed Part I of this book, an introduction to your computer. In the following part, you examine all the basic parts of the PC and some other interesting items that you may encounter while computing.

Part II
Intimidating, Cold, and Impersonal: The Computer

The 5th Wave   **By Rich Tennant**

"OH NO — PC KRISHNAS."

In this part...

You learn about PC hardware, which includes all the basic parts of the computer — anything large enough to drop on the floor and hurt an ingrown toenail. The idea is to get you familiar with the various pieces of your system and introduce you to some other interesting — or dreadful — items you may encounter while computing.

As usual, everything here is presented in small, easily digestible chunks. Items worth skipping are clearly marked. But, although you can read only what concerns you, don't put the blinders on too tight; a better way to do something is always lurking out there. Hopefully, you can find it in one of the following chapters.

Chapter 6
Inside the Bowels of the Beast (What Is All That Stuff?)

In This Chapter

▶ A layman's guide to motherboards, microprocessors, and math coprocessors

▶ An introduction to memory and memory management

▶ The BIOS — what it is and why you can't compute without it

▶ What you can do with expansion slots and cards

▶ A look at your computer's power supply

*T*he *console* or *system unit* (that ugly beige box) is an intimidating thing. Those few tiny lights and an annoying hum are the only clues that anything's going on in there. Still, lurking inside the box is an engineer's dream of electronic parts, doodads, and other stuff that makes the computer work. Because the only way to familiarize yourself with this junk is to pull apart your PC and look at it, you can freely ignore it as a PC beginner.

On the downside, you need to familiarize yourself with some terms, and you may need to know about some other items "in the box" from time to time. This chapter chews over the terms and topics one by one like a mama bird, enabling you to swallow them with ease. Consider this the predigestion approach to computer technology.

The Motherboard

The *motherboard* is the main piece of circuitry inside your PC. Like the downtown of a big city, it's where everything happens.

The motherboard is important because the most important things inside your PC cling to it. In fact, for the most part, the console is simply a housing for the motherboard. (Disk drives used to be separate on some systems.) You'll find the following electronic goodies on the motherboard. There's no need to memorize this list:

✔ The microprocessor — the computer's "brain"

✔ The computer's memory

✔ Expansion slots and the special expansion cards that plug into them

✔ Special chips called ROM chips

✔ The BIOS

✔ Other support circuitry

Each of these items is discussed in detail later in this chapter.

✔ Although the motherboard contains a lot of items, it's essentially one unit and is referred to as such.

✔ You can only add or remove two things on the motherboard: extra memory and expansion cards (which plug into the expansion slots). This chore, referred to as *upgrading,* is best left to the gurus.

✔ The term *motherboard* is as cute as it sounds. "Mother" implies that it's the main circuitry board in the computer. Hanging off Mother are various daughterboards that add more functions to the basic motherboard. Believe it or not.

A more technical description, if you care

The motherboard is a piece of fiberglass, usually dark green in color because computer scientists are a macho bunch, and pink or powder blue is definitely out. Chips and whatnot are soldered to the motherboard and then connected by tiny copper wires, or *traces,* which look like little roads all over the motherboard. This is how the various chips, resistors, and capacitors chat with each other.

Electricity is supplied to everything via a thin metal sheet sandwiched in the middle of the motherboard itself. Somehow, through the miracle of electronics, everything works and the end result is a working computer. Of course, to make it practical, you need a power supply, monitor, keyboard, disk drives, and so on.

The Microprocessor (or It Has a Brain)

The computer's brain is called the *microprocessor*. That's the main chip in a computer that does all the work. It's also the center of activity on the motherboard.

The microprocessor is essentially a small calculator. It does basic calculator-like things — adding, subtracting, multiplying, and dividing values stored in the computer's memory. Computer programs tell the microprocessor what to do, which is how everything works inside a PC.

Physically speaking, the microprocessor resembles a square after-dinner mint — or sometimes a small, flat bug — with metal legs. It's identified by the number printed on top, which tells you a lot about the microprocessor's power (and therefore the power of the computer). Significant microprocessor numbers are listed in Table 6-1, if you're curious.

✔ Other ungainly terms for the microprocessor include the *processor*; the *central processing unit* (*CPU*); and the number of the microprocessor, such as *8088, 80286, 80386,* and so on. (Note that although there are many numbers/names for a microprocessor, the three above are the most common.)

✔ There are three main varieties of microprocessors for PCs: the 8088/8086; the 80286, or *AT* microprocessor; and the 386 family of microprocessors. We elaborate on these in the following three sections of this chapter.

✔ In addition to the numbers assigned to them, microprocessors are also gauged by how fast they can think. This value is given in *megahertz*, abbreviated *MHz*. The bigger the MHz number, the faster the microprocessor, which is about all you need to know.

✔ It's the *micro* part of microprocessor that led old-time computer users to call PCs microcomputers. This may have applied to the first microprocessor, but today's powerhouse PCs are anything but micro.

✔ How can you tell which microprocessor your PC has? The best way is to look at the label, which probably has a microprocessor number in it: 386 and 486 are common. If that fails, your bill of sale may list the microprocessor type. And, as a last resort, you can use *PC diagnostic software* to figure out which microprocessor you have.

✔ Many microprocessors can benefit from a companion chip, the *math coprocessor*. This is covered later in this chapter, in the section "The math coprocessor."

Table 6-1 lists the popular numbers assigned to microprocessors, along with other technical drivel associated with them.

Table 6-1   Microprocessor Number Quiz (Extra Credit Only)

Microprocessor	Relative Power (Bits)	Type of PC and Observations
8088	8/16	Early PCs, the PC XT, and some laptops. This was a veritable slug.
8086	16/16	The first COMPAQ. The 8086 was faster than the 8088 but more expensive.
V20	8/16	Early PC clones. The V20 was an 8088 clone made by NEC. It ran 5 percent faster. Wow.
V30	16/16	Early PC clones and some laptops. The V30 was an 8086 clone.
80286	16/16	AT types of PCs and compatibles and some laptops. Much faster than the 8088/8086, this microprocessor first appeared in the IBM PC AT.
80386	32/32	The father of the 386 family of computers. This is also called the 80386DX or just a 386.
80386SLI	16/32	Designed for laptops, its power-saving features let laptops run longer on battery power.
80386SX (386SX)	16/32	Laptops and inexpensive systems. These are slightly slower than the full 80386DX but cheaper.
80486	32/32	Expensive. This type is also called the i486 or the 486DX.
80486SX	32/32	Not quite as expensive as the preceding one. This is a cheaper version of the full-blown 80486.
80486DX2	32/32	A slightly cheaper alternative to the normal 486DX, this chip can "think" twice as fast as it can talk to its neighboring computer parts. After all, the parts don't always need to know everything that's going on, so why slow things down?
586/Pentium	32/64	Mega-expensive. Intel grew tired of other companies copying its "86" series of chips, so it named its 586 chip a "Pentium." (It's easier to trademark a trendy name than a number.)
Power PC	64/64	Apple, IBM, and Motorola developed this chip as an alternative to Intel's processors. It's mega fast but unproven in the marketplace.

The 8088/8086

The first PCs used the old and slow 8088, 8086, V20, or V30 microprocessors. All of these microprocessors are lumped into one category, which you'll see referred to as *8088/8086* or the *PC XT* level of computer.

These processors are rarely used today. You find them in some laptop computers, some cheap stores, mail-order and clearance-house offers, and older clones in garage sales. Today's PCs use faster microprocessors because they're more powerful and just as cheap as the 8088/8086 microprocessors.

✔ The labels *8088/8086* and *PC XT* refer to the type of microprocessor in the computer; they're not brand names.

✔ These types of computers are incapable of running the latest software, such as Windows. They are, however, still useful as learning tools and as stand-alone word processing and data entry computers. However, we recommend that individual users buy something else.

The AT system

IBM's second-generation PC was knighted the *PC AT,* with AT standing for Advanced Technology. The new computer had an 80286 microprocessor — the second generation 8088. So much for technical history.

All PCs that have an 80286 for a brain are generally referred to as *AT-class* systems. Although faster than the old, clunky 8088/8086 or PC XT systems, they've been surpassed by the newer 386 family of personal computers.

✔ A PC AT is an IBM computer. Computers made by other manufacturers are said to be *AT compatible,* but only those with an 80286 for a brain are true AT systems. This is confusing because it's possible for your computer to be AT compatible and not have an 80286 microprocessor. That's because IBM wasn't the first to come out with 80386 computers, so there is no cute moniker for them.

✔ AT systems with the 80286 microprocessor are faster than the earlier models but still are outdated by the 386 family of computers. For a simple word processing tool or learning system — or even for a laptop computer — an 80286 processor is great. But for demanding modern software such as Windows and for future programs, this microprocessor falls short.

The 386 family

If you bought your computer in the past few years, odds are pretty good that you have a *386 family* microprocessor. Good for you. This is the best possible system for taking advantage of today's computing needs, as well as those of the near future.

The term *386 family* refers to a whole bunch of computers that are compatible with the basic 80386 microprocessor. As far as your PC's software is concerned, all these computers fit into one big family. The real differences between them are technical features and price.

The 386 family includes all the following microprocessors:

- 80386, 386DX, 386SX, and all varieties of the 80386
- 80486, i486DX, i486SX, and all varieties of the 80486
- All the latest, greatest microprocessors — the Pentium (the 80586) and so on

If you have one of the preceding microprocessors in your PC, you're in the 386 family and can use software that takes advantage of that microprocessor.

- The differences between the various members of the 386 family are related only to hardware. As far as your software is concerned, the 80386SX and the 80486 are equally capable of executing the programs.
- There are differences in power and price among the microprocessors in the 386 family, however. This means that some computers do the job *faster* than others. But that's only a hardware issue. For your software, any 386 family microprocessor will do the job.
- Windows 386 Enhanced mode operates on all PCs with a 386 family microprocessor. The same holds true for the bizarre issue of *memory management,* where you need a 386 family microprocessor to work the memory magic. (Memory management is covered later in this chapter.)

The "and later" syndrome

You may be thrown the following common curve ball: "This software works only with 80386 and later microprocessors." It's the "later" part that gets you. How do you know what is later than an 80386, especially if you don't have a PC microprocessor time line in front of you? The following should help:

- Earliest: 8088, 8086, V20, and V30
- Middle ages: 80286
- Latest: 80386, 386SX, and so on
- Extremely tardy: 80486, 486SX, and Pentium

The latest microprocessors are at the bottom of the list. They can run any and all software written for microprocessors listed above them.

The 5th Wave   By Rich Tennant

"IT'S AMAZING HOW MUCH MORE SOME PEOPLE CAN GET OUT OF A PC THAN OTHERS."

✔ Some descriptions may say "greater" rather than "later." Later refers to the point in history when the microprocessor was introduced.

✔ All microprocessors are said to be *backward compatible*. That means that software written for an earlier microprocessor works on a later model.

OverDrive

Overdrive — Vrrroooommmm!

Intel, the company that sells the most microprocessors, had a problem. People weren't buying new microprocessors just to give their computers a boost — they were buying whole new computers to go with them.

So Intel came up with an "OverDrive" microprocessor. People who plugged this single OverDrive chip into their computers could make their old computer work as much as 70 percent faster.

The hard part? People had to open up their computers, find the special spot where the new chip plugged in, and push the chip into the socket — all before the trolls got out.

OverDrive chips can "think" twice as fast as they can share the *results* of those thoughts. Engineers like the concept because microprocessors often have to "think" for a long time before sharing their results anyway. Everybody else likes OverDrive chips because they're cheaper than buying a new computer. And because the chips don't talk *too* fast, they also work in older motherboards, in which all the parts still talk slowly.

Some 486 motherboards come with a special socket. The folks at the shop can plug in an OverDrive chip, and the computer starts chewing data more quickly.

No special socket? Then let the folks at the shop yank out the motherboard's old 486 chip, drop in the new OverDrive chip, and let you speed on down the highway. (Those old 486 chips are tough to yank out yourself.)

The math coprocessor

A special companion to the microprocessor is the *coprocessor.* The type of coprocessor you can get for most PCs is a *math coprocessor.* Acting like a handy calculator for the microprocessor, this chip enables the microprocessor to do math much faster. Basically, the coprocessor knows all the shortcuts for calculations the microprocessor would have to do longhand.

Don't read this PowerPC stuff for two years

Microsoft and Intel have become bullies on the PC playground. No matter what happens with PCs, Microsoft cashes in on the software and Intel makes money by selling the chip that makes the computer scoot.

So IBM, Apple, and a chip maker called Motorola put their heads together, grunted, and created a new chip called the *PowerPC.* The idea behind the PowerPC sounds great: Software written for the PowerPC chip can run on both IBM's *and* Apple's version of the PowerPC. And the PowerPC is much cheaper than what Intel has to offer.

Don't grab your credit cards yet, though. Any groundbreaking technology is bound to hit a few large rocks. First, IBM and Apple are having trouble building a PowerPC computer that can run each other's software. It's happening—but slowly.

Second, hardly anybody's writing any software specifically to take advantage of the PowerPC. That means that early PowerPC buyers will have to stick with their regular old DOS or Macintosh software until the PowerPC software comes along.

Third, that regular old DOS or Macintosh software runs much more slowly on a PowerPC than it does on their regular old computers.

The verdict? Give the PowerPC some time; it still needs an operating system. After all, Microsoft has spent ten years getting MS-DOS right, and IBM has been trying to fix OS/2 since 1987.

The PowerPC might be the next big thing down the road. But don't let that stop you from buying a computer today.

A math coprocessor is helpful only if you're doing intensive math operations. These include graphics, scientific applications, and some spreadsheet problems. If that's you, you could benefit from a math coprocessor. If you don't use your PC that way, you probably don't need a math coprocessor.

✔ All math coprocessors have famous numbers, just like microprocessors. But the final digit in a math coprocessor number is a 7. Therefore, the 8088 and 8086 have the 8087 math coprocessor, the 80286 has the 80287, and the 80386 has the 80387.

✔ The 80486 or i486DX does not require a math coprocessor; it's built in.

✔ The 80486SX does require a math coprocessor, aptly named the 80487. Note that purchasing a full 80486DX PC is cheaper than buying an 80486SX and upgrading it with the 80487 chip.

✔ You can add a math coprocessor to most PCs as an option after purchase. The math chip must be plugged into your PC's motherboard — a task best suited to those nerdy enough to handle such things.

✔ Windows runs slightly faster when you add a math coprocessor.

✔ Some people refer to the math coprocessor as a *floating point coprocessor* or *floating point unit.* This comes from doing too many math operations, after which your mind starts to drift and you become lightheaded, bobbing about like an olive in a martini glass.

What Is Memory?

Memory contains the instructions that the microprocessor steps through to execute a program. The microprocessor in turn stores in memory the information that it develops while executing the program. You can think of memory as a collection of storage bins from which the microprocessor pulls an instruction of the next step in a job sequence, and, after performing some calculation, it stores the result of the calculation for later use. This concept can be applied to your using a "things to do" list where each line on the list is a memory location, and as you step through the things to do, you scribble notes on the list. Of course, the technical details of computer operation are far more complicated than this simple analogy, but the analogy gives you some idea of memory's job.

✔ The more memory you have, the better. With more memory, you can work on larger documents and spreadsheets, and enjoy applications that use graphics and sound. That isn't possible when memory is limited.

- ✔ All computers have a limited amount of memory, which means that some day you may run short. When that happens, you'll see an error message shouting, "Out of memory!" Don't panic. The computer can handle the situation. You can add more memory to your system if you like. Consult your favorite computer guru.

- ✔ When you *load* something from disk, the computer copies that information from disk to the computer's memory. Only in memory can that information be examined or changed. When you *save* information back to disk, the computer copies it from memory to the disk.

- ✔ The term *RAM* is used interchangeably with the word *memory*. They're the same thing. (In fact, RAM stands for random-access memory.)

- ✔ There are four types of memory in a PC: *conventional, upper, extended,* and *expanded.* These will confuse you to no end, so ignore them if you want. Those daring enough can read through the section called "Memory terms to drive you insane" for detailed and long-winded explanations.

- ✔ Memory is a component of the motherboard, sitting very close to the microprocessor. It exists as a series of tiny chips called *RAM chips.* You can add more memory to the computer by plugging in more RAM chips, either on the motherboard itself or via some cutesy memory expansion card. Again, leave this job to the pros.

Memory terms to drive you insane

The following four sections refer to different types of memory in a PC. This is definitely optional reading. Believe us when we tell you that these terms are for diehards only. No PC beginner will ever be grilled for the following knowledge. Feel free to skip this section. Just gingerly walk out of the casino now, while you still have some chips.

Boring technical details on the differences between RAM and ROM

RAM stands for *random-access memory.* It refers to memory that the microprocessor can read from and write to. When you create something in memory, it's done in RAM.

ROM stands for *read-only memory.* The microprocessor can read from ROM, but it cannot write to it or modify it. ROM is permanent. Often, ROM chips contain special instructions for the computer — important stuff that will never change. Because that information is stored on a memory chip, the microprocessor can access it. The instructions will always be there because they are unerasable.

Note that these terms are used primarily by DOS programmers and technoid types. To the microprocessor, everything is the same in your computer; there are no different types of memory at all — just endless expanses of RAM.

Conventional memory

The basic memory in all PCs is called *conventional memory,* although some may call it *DOS memory* and others may even call it *low DOS memory.* This memory is the first 640K of RAM in your PC.

Conventional memory is important because that's where DOS runs programs. In the old days, this was an issue because not every computer came with the full complement of 640K. Some came with 256K; others with 512K. Today, most systems come with the full 640K.

The microprocessor can run programs anywhere in memory, regardless of these silly terms. However, because DOS controls your computer, it restricts programs to conventional memory. This creates a terrible conundrum because today's computers can play with much more memory than 640K.

Upper memory

The next chunk of memory in your computer, right after conventional memory, is called *upper memory.* It may also be referred to as *reserved memory* or *high DOS memory.* When IBM designed the original PC, this memory was marked "hands off." It's primarily used for ROM chips and special instructions that tell the computer's various parts what to do.

Upper memory totals 384K in size. Combined with the 640K of conventional memory, that brings the total to 1,024K of memory, or 1 megabyte. That's how much memory was available in the first IBM PC. Because all PCs made since then are compatible with the first PC, they too are limited to this setup: 640K of conventional memory plus 384K of upper memory.

Extended memory

If you have an 80286 or 386 family PC, any memory you have beyond the first megabyte is referred to as *extended memory.* For example, if you have an 80386 system with 4 megabytes of RAM, then you have 3 megabytes of extended memory. An AT-class system with 2 megabytes of RAM total has 1 megabyte of extended memory.

Extended memory isn't good for much when your computer runs DOS. There are some things you can do with it, but for the most part, it remains a white elephant; DOS programs cannot access the extra memory. (This is a limitation of DOS — not anything that's your own fault.)

Hold off on that sudden sorrow, however. Extended memory is a blessing when you run Windows. Windows loves extended memory — the more the better. Also, some special programs, referred to as *extended DOS applications,* can use extended memory. They include common programs such as 1-2-3 Release 3, the Paradox database, AutoCAD, and other popular and powerful programs.

Expanded memory

The short-term solution for DOS's memory woes is *expanded memory.* This is extra memory in a PC that DOS programs can use. Expanded memory is available to all levels of PCs, from the 8088/8086 through the fastest 386 family microprocessor.

Expanded memory can be used by a variety of DOS programs. The memory is supplied with some fancy hardware and software techniques — stuff too complicated to describe here or even to think about aloud. Suffice it to say that expanded memory is a good thing.

Don't confuse extended and expanded memory! They're very similar terms but describe two entirely different things (don't look at us — we didn't make this up). Just remember that expanded memory is what you need for DOS programs. If you don't have expanded memory, you can add it to your PC. Consult your guru for more information.

Memory management

All the bizarre murkiness of memory and memory terms comes together under the leaky umbrella of *memory management.* DOS users get more chuckles about this part of computing from competing types of computers than anything else. Memory management is an issue because DOS doesn't do it. Instead, you — the poor user — are left to suffer through it. This is akin to having to manually throw cogs and gears to shift a car while the rest of the world drives automatics.

Performing the kind of wizardry necessary to do memory management on a PC is beyond the level of this book. However, to give you a small grasp of what's going on, here are the basics:

- Memory management is possible only with the proper combination of hardware and software. For 8088/8086 and 80286 PCs, you need expanded memory (which you must buy as extra hardware), plus a memory management program (software).

- The best memory management is possible only on a 386 family PC.

- The gist of memory management is to give you control of all your memory. The basic objective is to make the most of the 640K of conventional memory. You do this by moving special programs from conventional memory into upper memory.

✔ DOS does some memory management, which is like saying your barber could pull your teeth provided that he had the proper implements. Better memory management is provided by third-party memory management software programs.

The BIOS

In addition to a microprocessor and memory, your computer needs some instructions to tell it what to do. Those instructions are written on a special ROM chip called the *BIOS,* which stands for *basic input/output system.*

The BIOS's job is communication. It allows the microprocessor to control — or "talk with" — other parts of your computer, such as the screen, the printer, the keyboard, and so on. Those instructions were written by the people who built your computer and are permanently etched on the BIOS chip (or chips) soldered onto the motherboard.

✔ The BIOS is what starts your computer. In fact, you probably see the BIOS copyright message every time your computer starts.

✔ DOS is the true program that controls your PC. It tells the microprocessor what to do, controls the disk drives, manages your files, organizes information, and communicates with the BIOS to get things done.

✔ In addition to the main BIOS, your computer may have other BIOSs. For example, the VGA BIOS controls your system's graphics display, the hard drive BIOS controls the hard disk, and so on. Your network adapter may have its own BIOS. Normally, when you see the term *BIOS* by itself, it refers to the PC's main BIOS.

Expansion Slots and Cards

On the back of the motherboard, near the rear of the computer, you'll find several long, thin slots. These are *expansion slots,* into which you can plug special *expansion cards.* The idea is that you can expand your system by adding options not included with the basic PC.

✔ Your PC can have from 3 to 12 expansion slots. The average is 8.

✔ Although it's possible for anyone to plug in a card and expand a computer system, this is a job best left to those willing to risk both life and machine. (No, it's not life-threatening — at least if the PC is unplugged first — but it is complicated.)

✓ They never tell you this one: Most expansion cards come squirming with cables. This makes the seemingly sleek motherboard look more like an electronic pasta dish. Some cables are threaded inside the PC; others are left hanging limply out the back. It's the cables that make the upgrading and installation process so difficult.

✓ The variety of expansion cards for a PC is endless. In the early days, expansion cards provided what are now considered the basics: more memory, a printer port, a joystick port, the system clock, and so on. Today, expansion cards can give you a music synthesizer, a fax machine, a CD-ROM drive, a scanner, external video input, and a whole gaggle of extra goodies.

✓ Expansion cards are sometimes referred to as *daughterboards*. Cute, huh? But explain this: The expansion slot is also referred to as *the bus*. Computers. . . .

✓ Some motherboards have the newest thing: *local-bus* expansion slots. Most computer manufacturers drop a local-bus video *card* into one of those slots so that pictures move around the screen a little faster. Don't have a local-bus card for that spot? Then any regular card will work there. It just doesn't work as quickly as one designed for that magic, local-bus spot.

Some blazingly fast Pentium computers come with a blazingly fast *PCI* slot. Just like the local-bus slots, PCI slots let special PCI *cards* work faster. A regular card works fine in an unused PCI slot, but don't even think about sticking a local-bus card into a PCI slot. Heavens!

I wouldn't read this expansion slot stuff if I were you

There are different systems for expansion slots and cards in a PC. The most common is the *ISA*, which stands for *Industry Standard Architecture*. If you have an IBM PS/2 system, it's likely that you're using the *MCA*, or *Micro Channel Architecture*, expansion slot/card system. (Some PS/2s use the older ISA.)

Why these different slot systems? Because the ISA isn't as technically advanced as some users require. IBM set out to improve that with its PS/2 series of computers, but not everyone followed suit. So today, the older ISA standard is still more popular, and a greater variety of expansion cards is available for it.

A third standard, used only in very high-end engineering and network server systems, is the *EISA*. The E must stand for *expensive*.

Power Supply—The Thing That Goes Poof!

The final mystery item "in the box" is the power supply, which, much to your relief, doesn't go poof! hardly at all. The power supply does three things: It brings in power from the wall socket, it supplies power to the motherboard and disk drives, and it contains the on/off switch.

✔ The power supply makes most of the noise when your PC runs. It contains a fan that regulates the temperature inside the console, keeping everything nice and cool. (Electronic components get hot when electricity races through them. This has the ugly consequence of making them misbehave, which is why cooling is needed.)

✔ Power supplies are rated in *watts*. The more stuff your computer has — the more disk drives, memory, expansion cards, and so on — the greater the amount of watts the power supply should provide. The typical PC has a power supply rated at 150 or 200 watts. More powerful systems may require a power supply of 220 or 250 watts.

✔ Boom! If lightning strikes or something deleterious comes marching down the power line, your power supply will blow. Don't panic. It's designed to pop and smolder. This in no way damages the rest of your computer. You just need to buy a new power supply and have someone replace it. Everything else in your system should survive the disaster (which is how the power supply is designed, fortunately).

Summary

This chapter took you on a whirlwind tour of the inside of your computer:

▶ You learned about motherboards and daughterboards — what they are and what they do.

▶ You examined the computer's "brain" — also known as a microprocessor. You reviewed various microprocessors and discovered how they differ from each other.

▶ You looked at different types of computer memory.

▶ You learned how the BIOS tells your computer what to do.

▶ You learned that you can add features to your computer through expansion slots and cards.

▶ You learned how the design of the power supply protects your computer in the event that lightning strikes.

In the next chapter, we teach you about your computer's keyboard.

Chapter 7
Your Keyboard
(Is Not a Coffee Filter)

• •

In This Chapter

▶ Examining the functions of the keys on the keyboard

▶ Learning how to type foreign words

▶ Understanding why four keys have a left-pointing arrow

▶ Learning where the Help and Any keys are

▶ Examining how to ease the muscle soreness that can occur when you're typing at a rapid rate

▶ Learning what a template is

▶ Getting the coffee out of your keyboard

▶ Examining why they screwed up the keyboard on your laptop

▶ Learning whether Dvorak's keyboard is better

• •

*E*xcept for when shopping for headphones, *Star Trek*'s Mr. Spock had it easy. Whenever he had a question, he just called it out to the computer. The computer said "Working," made some weird teletype noises from two centuries earlier, and called out the right answer. Spock never had to call out "Backspace" if he burped while telling the computer what to do. The computer simply understood what he wanted and did it.

Unfortunately, our computers aren't as smart. They hail from the typewriter era and cling to the same keyboard that has been used for more than 100 years.

This chapter examines the keyboard, the primary tool you use to boss the computer around. You learn why a computer keyboard is packed with so many more keys than a typewriter keyboard. You learn what all those extra keys are supposed to do. And you learn why some of those extra keys perform no function at all. They just stay with the keyboard year after year, like tassels on golf shoes.

Why Doesn't It Look Like a Typewriter?

A typewriter can only do one thing: print letters and numbers onto a piece of paper. You press a key, and the character appears on the page. It's beautifully simple. Even the concept of a Shift key doesn't wear out many brain cells. The only complications come when you try to change the ribbon or retrieve the french fry you dropped in the mechanism.

Computers, in contrast, must handle many more chores. Computers enable you to balance checkbooks, copy files, calculate mortgage rates, and catalog recipes for easy kitchen access. (OK, does anybody *really* catalog recipes?) Therefore, the computer keyboard needs a few extra keys. After all, an airplane's dashboard has more buttons than a car's dashboard.

The typewriter's faithful 45 keys can still be found on a computer's keyboard; they're usually the respectfully white-colored ones near the center. The weird computer-oriented keys around the edge are usually a drab gray, and they appear in different places on different keyboards. Figure 7-1 shows a typical PC-style keyboard, which contains 84 keys. Figure 7-2 shows an Enhanced Keyboard, which contains 101 keys.

Although different manufacturers style their keyboards differently, all keyboards have four main parts:

Typewriter keys: These keys are the normal-looking white keys in the center of the keyboard. They include letters, numbers, and punctuation symbols.

Function keys: These keys are positioned either horizontally across the top of the keyboard or in two vertical rows down the left edge. They're labeled F1, F2, F3, and so on. Some keyboards have F11 and F12 keys. Others don't. If you don't have F11 and F12 keys, don't feel left out; hardly any software uses them, anyway.

Figure 7-1:
A typical
PC-style
keyboard.

Figure 7-2:
An
Enhanced
Keyboard.

Cursor-control keys: These four keys are often called *arrow keys* because each one has an arrow on the key cap. These keys move the screen's cursor in the direction of their arrows. Near the arrow cursor-control keys are keys labeled PgUp, PgDn, Home, and End. The PgDn key, for example, enables you to flip to the next on-screen page. PgDn actually stands for Page Down. The Home key usually takes you either to the top of your document or to the beginning of the line. It varies depending on your software. Some word processors deliberately enable you to decide what the Home key does so you can feel powerful and in charge.

Numeric keypad: Popular among bank tellers with zippy fingers, the numeric keypad contains the calculator-like keys. (The numeric keypad is on the right side of the keyboard.) In addition to containing numbers, some of the numeric keypad keys also contain arrows; these keys normally act like cursor-control keys. If you press the Num Lock key, however, the keys containing the arrows create the numbers listed on them, instead.

- ✔ Computer keyboards are available in two main styles. Most people use the newer, 101-key (count 'em) keyboard, known as the *Enhanced Keyboard.* Other people use the older, 84-key keyboard. On the Enhanced Keyboard, the function keys are across the top; on the 84-key keyboard, the function keys are along the left-hand side (where it's harder to put sticky notes next to them).

- ✔ The keys labeled F1, F2, and so on, are called *function keys.* Newer keyboards also contain the F11 and F12 keys, but lacking them isn't a major drawback.

- ✔ The keys that have arrows on the key caps, either in the upside-down T layout or on the numeric keypad, are called *cursor-control keys* or sometimes *arrow keys.* The keys labeled Home, End, PgUp, and PgDn are also cursor-control keys.

✔ The PgUp and PgDn keys stand for Page Up and Page Down. The labels on the key caps may be fully spelled out or abbreviated.

✔ The Print Screen key may also be labeled PrtScr or Print Scrn. Either way, this weird key is discussed later in this chapter.

✔ If you're a lousy typist, don't worry. Plenty of computer users hunt and peck. In fact, many people buy computers because they're lousy typists. They can press the Backspace key instead of messing with gooey globs of Whiteout (and trying to get that little brush back inside that tiny hole).

✔ You don't need to be speedy when typing commands. The computer won't hang up and move to the next caller while you're deciding what to do next. It just sits there and waits patiently, silently yearning for macho computer chores like calculating wind-chill factors in Alaska.

On a typewriter, the lowercase letter l and the number 1 are often the same. Not so with a computer. If you're typing 1,001, for example, don't type l,00l by mistake — especially when working with a spreadsheet. (The same holds true for the uppercase letter O and the number 0. They're different.)

The Toggle Keys

Several keys act as a *toggle,* or an on/off switch of sorts. Press the key once to turn on its feature and press it again to turn off the feature — like a light switch. The toggle keys examined in this section work pretty much like their typewriter counterparts (except for a few weird exceptions, which are noted).

Shift: No surprises here. The Shift key works just like it does on the typewriter. Hold it down to make capital letters. By pressing the Shift key, you also can create the %@#^@ characters that come in handy for comic strips. (These types of characters are listed on the keys containing numbers along the top row.) When you release the Shift key, everything returns to normal, just like with a typewriter.

For math whizzes only (like any would be reading this book)

Look around the numeric keypad. You see the /, *, − , and + keys. These keys are the ones a computer uses for division, multiplication, subtraction, and addition. Noting this fact is very important. Don't use the letter X when you want to multiply stuff in a spreadsheet. The computer uses the asterisk (*) instead. The forward slash (/) is used for division because there isn't a ÷ character on the keyboard. The other numerical operators — the plus sign (+) and the minus sign (−) — are used as you would expect them to be used. (Odd, but true.)

Caps Lock: This key works like a typewriter's Shift Lock key; it's as if the computer holds down the Shift key so you can create all-capital letters. Press Caps Lock again and the letters return to their normal lowercase state. But look at the sidebar "The Caps Lock key doesn't work exactly like the typewriter's Shift Lock key" for some additional information.

Num Lock: This key isn't on the typewriter, but we discuss it here anyway. Pressing this key makes the numeric keypad on the right side of the keyboard produce numbers. Press this key again and you can use the numeric keypad for cursor control (for moving the cursor around on the screen).

✔ On some keyboards, the Caps Lock and Num Lock keys have lights. When the light is on, the key's feature is turned on.

✔ The strange Scroll Lock key is covered later in this chapter.

The Caps Lock key doesn't work exactly like the typewriter's Shift Lock key

Although the Caps Lock key enables you to type all-capital letters, just like the typewriter's Shift Lock key, the similarities end there. Be aware of these key differences:

1. The Caps Lock key only affects letters; it doesn't affect the number keys along the top row. If you try to type a G-rated swear word by using the Caps Lock key, you type 837645, for example, which doesn't have the same panache.

2. The Caps Lock key doesn't affect any punctuation marks.

3. If the Caps Lock key is on and you hold down the Shift key, you counteract the Caps Lock key's effect: Letters return to lowercase. The numbers along the top of the keyboard,

however, turn into %$@#^@ characters, for example. (Welcome to the Twilight Zone.)

4. If you type "This Text Looks Like A Ransom Note" and it ends up looking like "tHIS tEXT lOOKS lIKE a rANSOM nOTE," the Caps Lock key is inadvertently turned on. Press it once to return everything to normal.

5. Sometimes, the computer confuses itself and leaves the Caps Lock key on all the time. There's no way to solve this frustrating problem. Curse, save your work, exit your program, and reset the computer. Curse again for good measure.

6. Oh, yeah, and the Shift key reverses the Num Lock key in the same weird way it affects the Caps Lock key.

The Weird Keys

Technoweenies, struck dumb by the surreal concept of the typewriter's Shift key, decided to create two similar keys for the computer keyboard. They called one a *Control key* (known as *Ctrl*) and the other an *Alternate key* (referred to as *Alt*).

Like the Shift key, the Ctrl and Alt keys are never used by themselves. Instead, they give new meaning to a second key. For example, holding down the Ctrl key and pressing Y (referred to as "pressing Ctrl-Y") deletes a line of text in the WordStar word processing program. In some programs, if you hold down the Alt key and press S (press Alt-S, in other words), you save something. Likewise, in some programs, you press Alt-P to print (and so on for each clever letter of the alphabet).

Ctrl: The Control key, abbreviated as Ctrl on the keyboard, is usually on the left side of the keyboard near the Shift key. The Enhanced Keyboard has two Ctrl keys — one underneath each Shift key for easy access. (There's no difference between the two Ctrl keys, though.)

Alt: The Alternate key, abbreviated as Alt on the keyboard, is also next to the Shift key on the left side of the keyboard. The Enhanced Keyboard has two Alt keys — one on each side of the spacebar. Like with the Ctrl key, it doesn't matter which Alt key you press.

 ✔ Some manuals use the term ^Y rather than Ctrl-Y. They both mean the same thing: Hold down the Ctrl key, press the letter Y, and release the Ctrl key.

 ✔ OK, we lied. With some programs, you do press the Alt key by itself. This practice isn't normal, but it's often used to pop up a menu or something. For example, in Windows, you press the Alt key to activate the menu bar.

The Keys You Don't Know Are Weird but Really Are

When moving from a typewriter to a computer keyboard, you need to be aware that the meaning of several keys subtly changes. These keys may look the same as on a typewriter and may even look like they're performing the same duty on-screen. But bad things can happen if you're not aware of the differences.

Tab: On a typewriter, you press the tab button, and the carriage moves forward five spaces to create a neatly indented paragraph. When you press the Tab key on a computer keyboard, however, the tab is not treated as five spaces. The computer treats the tab as a *single* character. As a refreshing change from general obfuscation, computer nerds call this special single character the *Tab character.*

✔ This single Tab character often represents five spaces on-screen in word processing programs. But, in some programs, it represents eight spaces. Still other programs enable you to adjust the tab to be any number of spaces you want.

✔ Sometimes a tab doesn't stand for any characters at all. In fact, when filling out on-screen forms, you must usually press the Tab key to move to the next box. If you try pressing the spacebar five times instead, the program hollers, causing coworkers to turn their heads in amazement.

✔ To confuse matters, the Tab key sometimes isn't labeled Tab. Instead, it has two arrows on it — one pointing left and the other right. That's because when you press Shift-Tab in some word processing programs, your indent moves backward, toward the left side of the screen. Weird stuff.

✔ The computer treats a tab as a single, separate character. When you backspace over a tab in a word processing program, the tab disappears completely in one chunk — not space by space.

✔ Use the Tab key to indent paragraphs; don't press the spacebar five times. You'll thank yourself later when your word processing program doesn't mangle paragraphs. (Or at least it gives your word processor one less way to mangle paragraphs.)

Enter/Return: Pressing the Enter key (called Return on some keyboards) tells the computer that you've finished typing a statement: a paragraph in a letter, for example, or a command at the DOS prompt or a calculation on a calculator.

✔ On an electric typewriter, you must press the Return key at the end of each line, or else you start typing off the edge of the paper. Computers, in contrast, sense when the words are about to run off the edge of the screen; they automatically drop down a line and continue the sentence so you don't have to worry about it. (This feature is known as *word wrap* by the in-crowd.)

✔ You only need to press Enter when you're done typing a paragraph and want to start a new one.

✔ Keyboard designers couldn't figure out whether computer keyboards should have a Return key, like a typewriter, or an Enter key, like a calculator. The nerdy calculator crowd naturally won, so most keyboards have an Enter key. (Today, only Macintosh computers — plus a few other oddballs — use the Return key.)

✔ Some keyboards have two Enter keys — one in the normal typewriter location and the other next to a separate numeric keypad on the far right side of the keyboard. You can use either Enter key at any time, but your pinky must be 9.7 inches long to use the numeric keypad's Enter key when you're word processing.

The Pause (or Hold) Key

The keyboard may have a special toggle key labeled Pause or Hold. Pressing that key instantly freezes the computer, halting all operations. Press that key again to continue the operation.

Pause (or Hold): This key comes in handy when things are spinning out of control. Primarily, you'll use it in DOS when information is moving so fast up the screen that you can't see anything. When that happens, press the Pause key, take a look around, and then press the Pause key again to get the ball rolling.

- ✔ If the keyboard lacks a Pause key, pressing Ctrl-Num Lock does the same thing.
- ✔ Another traditional pause key is the Ctrl-S key combination. Pressing Ctrl-S suspends all computer activity. Pressing Ctrl-S again resumes everything. (Actually, the traditional resume key is Ctrl-Q.)
- ✔ The Pause key is shared by the Break key on the Enhanced Keyboard.

The Keys That Are Too Weird to Bother With

Simply pretend that the Scroll Lock and SysRq keys aren't there. Don't mess with them and skip past the following section on them. Don't bother reading the information about the Print Screen key either. Just pretend all three keys don't exist.

The secret behind the Scroll Lock and SysRq keys

DOS doesn't use the Scroll Lock or SysRq key, so you don't need to bother with them either. In the early days of computing, the Scroll Lock key would "lock" a spreadsheet onto the screen. When people then pressed the cursor-control keys, they would move the entire spreadsheet around — not just the cursor from cell to cell. It gave them a welcome feeling of accomplishment. Very few programs still use the Scroll Lock key today.

IBM added the SysRq key to the keyboard many years ago to be used in a future version of DOS. We're still waiting. So, although the SysRq key has kind of a cool name, it never really amounted to anything. Feel free to press it whenever you don't want to do anything.

Why doesn't the Print Screen key work right?

In theory, the Print Screen key (labeled PrtScr or something similar on most keyboards) sounds incredible. At the press of a single key, the entire screen is sent to the printer. What a convenient time-saver!

But it's too good to be true. First, it only prints text on the screen — no graphics. And even then, the printed material looks only as good as it does on-screen. You just can't win.

Next, if you press Print Screen when the printer is not hooked up or turned on, everything stops. The computer freezes. If you can't hook up the printer for some reason, you have to reboot. You won't be able to save your work first, either. What a mess.

Last, there's no standard for the Print Screen key. When you press it on some keyboards, you get an asterisk (*); you must simultaneously hold down the Shift key and Print Screen key to make the screen print. On other keyboards, if you hold down the Ctrl key while pressing Print Screen, the computer starts printing everything that appears on the screen, from that point on. (Press Ctrl-Print Screen again to make it stop.)

In today's world of glossy graphics, the Print Screen key is like an 8-track tape holder. Only consider using it if you have the simplest of text on-screen (and you know the printer is on-line and ready to go).

  ✔ There's a glimmer of hope for the Print Screen key, however. When you press it in Windows, a picture of the current screen is sent to the Windows Clipboard. From there, you can insert it into a Windows graphics program. (Sometimes, you must hold down the Shift key while you press Print Screen.)

  ✔ If you use the Print Screen key and see a bunch of junk, your printer probably isn't capable of printing IBM graphics. If it has an IBM graphics mode, you can try to switch it on and press Print Screen again. Otherwise, read the following item.

  ✔ If you like the concept of sending screen shots to the printer, head to the software store and ask the salespeople to get you a graphics package when they're through playing their computer games.

The "Knock It Off!" Keys

The technogeeks who designed the computer knew it would head for the clouds every once in a while. That's why they made a special key to tell the computer to immediately stop misbehaving and start listening to the master. When that key didn't always work, they added another key to do the same thing. And another.

Today, computer users have a whole series of keys they can press desperately to put their computers back on track.

Esc: The Escape key, labeled Esc on most PCs, is supposed to enable you to escape from your current situation and seek higher ground. For example, if you make a mistake while typing a DOS command, press the Esc key and the offending line disappears. Some programs stop when you press Esc; others bring a menu to the screen. Still others ignore you. But Esc can be a good pinch hitter to try first when something goes wrong.

Break: By itself, the Break key does nothing. But when you hold down the Ctrl key and press the Break key, you can often break the computer's current fascination with itself and get back to something constructive. For example, if a program is running in some sort of awful loop, try the Ctrl-Break combination: Hold down the Ctrl key and press the Break key (disguised as the Scroll Lock or Pause key on some keyboards).

Ctrl-C: This key combination does almost the same thing as the Break key. Ctrl-C is DOS's hand brake. It halts almost any operation and gets you back to the calming — albeit confusing — DOS prompt.

✔ If none of these keys has a positive, calming effect, see the following section on making your computer go poof!

✔ Why is the key called Break? Why not call it the Brake key? Wouldn't that make sense? Who wants a computer to "break" anyway? Golly.

If I Hold Down the Ctrl-Alt-Del Keys, Everything Goes Poof!

Sometimes, the computer ignores you, even when you peck out a keystroke sequence that's supposed to do something special. The computer may just beep incessantly or repeat some command in an endless loop, like a flickering 8 mm home movie.

To completely reset the computer *as a last resort measure,* hold down the Ctrl, Alt, and Del keys at the same time. (Don't worry; even most technoweenies use two hands for this one.) The computer reboots, starting from scratch.

- Ctrl-Alt-Del is called Control-Alt-Delete. It's also called the Vulcan Nerve Pinch and the Three-Finger Reset button.

- On the negative side, the Ctrl-Alt-Del sequence wipes out all data that hasn't been saved to disk. After the third time or so that you lose all your work, you'll gently form a habit of saving your work in progress every few minutes.

- On the positive side, the Ctrl-Alt-Del sequence almost always makes the computer come back to life.

- If, after contorting your fingers into the positions required by the Ctrl-Alt-Del sequence, the computer doesn't go poof, use your index finger to push the Reset button on the front of the case. The same negative connotations about losing all work in progress apply here as well.

The Good, the Bad, and the Backslash (and Other Funky Keys)

When creating the computer keyboard, IBM — the maker of the touch typist's favorite Selectric keyboard — didn't stop after loading it up with function keys, toggle keys, cursor-control keys, and a numeric keypad. IBM had to sneak in two funky characters. They're called the backslash and the pipe, named after the weapons used in the video arcade game Street Computin' Ninja.

The backslash (\) and the pipe (|)

IBM saw how typewriters always come with a forward slash key (/) so people could type "I'll split the proceeds/earnings with you 50/50." The technogeeks leaned the forward slash backward to create a backslash key (\). Its location is kept a secret on the keyboard (although rumor has it last sighted near the big Enter key).

The pipe (|) is on the same key as the backslash. (When you hold down Shift and press the backslash key, you get the pipe.) It may or may not have a tiny space in the middle. Either way, it's a pipe.

✔ You need to use the backslash key quite a bit when using DOS commands, to move around on the hard drive (see Chapter 13). Don't mistake the backslash (\) for the common forward slash (/).

✔ The pipe is used in utilitarian DOS commands; other people use it just to create vertical lines when making a fancy letterhead.

The grave accent (`) and the tilde (~)

On the top-left side of the keyboard, another key masquerades as a typewriter key: the grave accent (`). (Some people call it the backward apostrophe.)

The tilde (~) is on the same key as the grave accent. (When you hold down Shift and press the grave accent key, you get the tilde.)

You won't use these keys nearly as much as you'll use the backslash and the pipe. In fact, you'll probably never use them at all. But by now, you should be used to seeing keys that don't do anything useful.

✔ Typesetters like the grave accent so they can type "John said 'Wow' when the cat knocked his monitor to the floor."

✔ When you're typing Spanish words, the tilde (~) is pretty useless. Typing "Man~ana, man" isn't quite the same as typing "Mañana, man." Refer to the following section to learn how to make real foreign characters.

How Do I Type Foreign Words like Crème de la Crème?

Sooner or later, you'll find yourself trying to type a foreign word, which stops you cold. Where's the é in *ménage,* for example? You can type such a character on your own keyboard; you don't have to buy the French version.

When creating DOS to be used worldwide, the computer nerds figured that people would need these foreign characters. But they thought that putting foreign characters on the keyboard would be too confusing and would take up too much room. Instead, they came up with the Alt keyboard trick.

It goes like this: If you look in the back of the most boring computer manuals, you'll probably see a chart of characters and symbols. Each funky character is assigned its own number. The number for é is 130.

TIP

Impress the folks in your French class with these hip new keys

To create one of the following characters, hold down the Alt key and type the number listed before that character. (Make sure that the Num Lock feature is turned on.) Release the Alt key and the foreign character appears in your document. *Voilà!* Here's your list:

129	ü	137	ë
130	é	138	è
131	â	139	ï
132	ä	140	î
133	à	147	ô
135	ç	148	ö
136	ê	164	ñ

You'll find charts with the secret codes for creating other foreign characters in the back of many boring computer manuals. Check the index for the *Extended ASCII Characters.*

To create the é character, you use the numeric keypad (the square field of numbers on the right side of the keyboard). Press the NumLock key to use the numerical keypad to type numbers. Then, while holding down the Alt key, type the number **130** on the numeric keypad. When you release the Alt key, the funky character appears.

✔ You must use the numeric keypad; you can't use the numbers along the top row of the keyboard. You must hold down the Alt key while you type the numbers. The characters appear only after you release Alt.

✔ The Alt keyboard trick works in most word processors and other DOS programs. It works at the DOS command line, too.

Why Do Four Keys Have a Left-Pointing Arrow?

Many keys have arrows on the key caps so you can identify them more easily. This setup creates a few problems. Three keys have a left-pointing arrow, and one key has two arrows — each pointing in opposite directions! What's going on?

Some Tab keys aren't labeled Tab; instead, they have two arrows on them (see "The Keys You Don't Know Are Weird but Really Are"). Pressing the Tab key creates a special character that indents your text to the right. In some programs, you can indent to the left by pressing Shift-Tab. Also, in some programs, you must press Tab to move from option to option in a menu or when filling out forms.

On some keyboards, the Enter key is labeled Return instead (see "The Keys You Don't Know Are Weird but Really Are"). Press Enter at the end of a paragraph in a word processor or at the end of a command line you've typed at the DOS prompt.

Press the left-arrow cursor-control key to move the cursor one character to the left. If the Num Lock feature is turned on, however, this arrow key creates the number 4 on the numeric keypad.

How can you tell the Backspace key apart from the left-arrow cursor-control key? Because of its position on the keyboard. It's usually located on the keyboard's top row, near the right-hand side. Some keyboards even have the word *Backspace* on the key cap to avoid confusion.

✔ Both the Backspace key and the left-arrow cursor-control key move the cursor one character to the left. The Backspace key simultaneously deletes that character; the left-arrow key doesn't. Use the Backspace key to correct your mistakes; use the left-arrow key to move around on-screen.

✔ There may be other confusing arrows on the keyboard as well. One innocent user counted 11 over the phone to a well-known computer guru. Where were the 11 arrow keys? On the older PC keyboard, there were arrows on both Shift keys (now those keys also have the label Shift), plus the two arrows on the Tab key, the arrow on the Enter key, the arrow on the Backspace key, and the four arrows on the cursor-control keys. Where's the eleventh? Above the 6 key on the numeric keypad.

✔ Incidentally, the ^ character is often called the caret, or hat, character. It's also used for abbreviating the word Control when you're describing key combinations like Ctrl-C. That's ^C to many of the computer elite.

Where's the Help Key?

When computer dweebs transferred the typewriter keyboard to the computer, they added plenty of goodies. But, in all the excitement of adding the pipe, backslash, Esc, and SysRq, they forgot the most important key of all: Help.

To correct this oversight, they instructed all the programmers to make the F1 key (the top-left function key) a help key in their programs. That way, when stumped users press the F1 key, the program brings a list of helpful suggestions to the screen.

- ✔ Unfortunately, WordPerfect programmers lost that memo, and the company assigned help to the F3 key. Despite that programmers' oversight, WordPerfect has become one of the biggest sellers of all time. (The company that makes it has also received the most phone calls to its toll-free help lines.)

- ✔ When looking for help in a program, try pressing the F1 key. You may get lucky.

And Just Where Is the Any Key?

This is an old, old computer joke. Many programs prompt Press any key to continue. So where is the Any key? No key is labeled Any anywhere on the keyboard. So what exactly do the programs mean?

Literally, they mean for you to press any old key. In fact, the programmers think that they're being friendly by saying "press any key you want." However, the Shift key doesn't work. Neither does Ctrl, Alt, or the 5 in the middle of the numeric keypad.

What the programmers really should say is "press the spacebar to continue" or "press the Enter key to continue."

Ouch! My Wrists Hurt!

Several years ago, the *New England Journal of Medicine* published an article documenting "Space Invaders Wrist," a soreness caused by rapid hand movements at the controls of the Space Invaders arcade game.

Because typists move their fingers at a similarly rapid rate, they're subject to the same muscle soreness. In fact, Labor Department statistics show that a typist's fingers move farther in an hour than the fingers of every nose-picking commuter driving on the freeways right now.

Because of the strain, many typists suffer from Carpal Tunnel Syndrome, a soreness caused when muscles rub against each other in the small wrist passage. Some victims wear expensive reinforced gloves that, if they don't actually help alleviate the pain, at least draw sympathetic stares from coworkers.

- ✔ A chair's seat and backrest should support a comfortable posture — one that can be adjusted to your own preference. When your hands are resting on the keyboard, the upper arm and forearm should form a right angle, with the hands extending in a reasonably straight line from the forearm. Many keyboards come with adjustable legs underneath for positioning the keys to a comfortable angle.

✔ If you can't adjust your desk or keyboard to the right height, buy a chair that can be adjusted up or down.

✔ Try using a palm pad. These foam or rubber devices rest in front of the keyboard and support the palms while you're typing.

What's a Template?

When trying to remember which key does what, many people put sticky notes on their keyboards. Entrepreneurs, recognizing a new market, created keyboard templates. A *template* is a piece of cardboard or plastic that fits around the keyboard. The keys stick up from holes cut strategically through the middle.

The template contains a description of each key's function, conveniently placed next to each key.

✔ Because key commands change with each program, you need a different template for each program you use.

✔ Keyboards come in many different styles. Make sure that you specify your exact model of keyboard when ordering or purchasing a template.

✔ Depending on templates can be dangerous, especially when the cleaning crew accidentally throws yours away, leaving you with no clues on how to operate your computer. Make a backup version by using the copy machine and a pair of scissors and keep it in a safe place.

How Do I Get the Coffee out of the Keyboard?

Sooner or later, you'll spill something gross into the keyboard. The grossest liquids are thick or sugary: soft drinks, fruit juice, cheap sherry, or St. Bernard drool. These things can seriously damage the keyboard. Here's what to do:

1. **Pick up the glass or push the St. Bernard out of the way.**

2. **Save your work (if the keyboard is still functional), turn off the computer, and unplug the keyboard.**

3. Turn the keyboard upside down and give it a few good shakes (away from your coworkers' keyboards, if possible).

4. Use a sponge to sop up as much stuff as possible and then just let the keyboard dry out. It usually takes about 24 hours.

✔ Surprisingly enough, the keyboard will probably still work, especially if there wasn't much sugar in the beverage. Unfortunately, you've probably cut its life expectancy in half. The dried gunk beneath the keys will attract dust and grime, making the keyboard get dirty much more quickly than normal.

✔ If you find the keys stickkkkkking when you try to type, compare the cost of a new keyboard with the cost of having the old one professionally cleaned.

✔ Some companies sell plastic keyboard covers. These covers are custom fitted to the keyboard and work quite well. Smokers, especially, should consider purchasing one. (A simple sheet of plastic wrap works almost equally as well, but research shows that it lasts no longer than three days.)

✔ While Andy Rathbone was laptopping by the pool at his sister's house, her friendly St. Bernard innocently sniffed his keyboard. Andy was able to flick off the major drool gobs, but the incident left him a much more cautious man.

Why Did They Screw Up the Keyboard on My Laptop?

In the process of shrinking a full-sized keyboard into a svelte, "sharper image" type of computer, almost all manufacturers chose a different optimum size for their keyboards. To add to the confusion, the keys on some laptop keyboards barely move down when you press them. (It's known as their *travel* distance.)

✔ When buying a laptop, make sure that the keyboard layout matches the desktop computer's keyboard, or you'll have to learn to type all over again.

✔ Most of the keys work the same as they do on a full-sized keyboard; they're just smaller.

✔ Everything else can wait until the laptop chapter, Chapter 12.

Is Dvorak's Keyboard Better?

The first typewriters were piano-sized beasts with a few mechanical problems. If anybody tried to type faster than about ten words a minute, the keys jammed.

To slow people down, the designers made the typewriter's keyboard as awkward as possible. They placed the most common keys along the outside edges of the keyboard, forcing a typist's fingers to move as far as possible. All the extra finger work slowed people down; nobody could jam the keys, and the repair people were happy.

This key arrangement is called *QWERTY* because the Q, W, E, R, T, and Y keys all sit along the top row, from left to right.

By the 1930s, the engineers had the typewriter mechanics down pat. They didn't have to slow anybody down anymore. So a guy named August Dvorak designed a new keyboard layout. This new layout placed the most commonly used keys directly underneath the right hand so that it could do most of the work. The other common keys appeared directly under the left hand's fingers. No more finger stretches. With Dvorak's layout, people could type much faster and with less finger strain.

But, although the general public has given up its 8-tracks for cassettes, few people want to give up their old keyboard for a new, more efficient layout. If you're up for it, you can buy special software to convert your keyboard to the Dvorak layout. You'll have to relearn your typing skills, as well as move around all the key caps. Or you can buy a new keyboard from a mail-order outfit.

  ✔ If you decide to learn the Dvorak keyboard, be sure to learn the QWERTY method, too, or you'll be lost when trying to use keyboards at libraries and offices (or any of the 99 percent of all keyboards you'll encounter).

  ✔ The Dvorak keyboard doesn't spell DVORAK like the QWERTY keyboard spells QWERTY. And August Dvorak is a cousin of the famous musical composer Antonin Dvorak. Also, nobody knows this, but Alfred Nobel invented plywood as well as dynamite.

  ✔ Unless you perform high-speed typing for a living, there's really no need to learn the Dvorak keyboard. It's just mentioned in most how-to computer books so people can say "that's neat" and quickly turn the page.

- -

Summary

This chapter introduced you to the computer keyboard:

▶ You learned the functions of the various keys on the keyboard (including all those keys with left-pointing arrows).

▶ You learned how to type foreign words.

▶ You learned what the Help and Any keys are.

▶ You examined how to ease the muscle soreness that can occur when you're typing at a rapid rate.

▶ You examined the benefits of keyboard templates.

▶ You learned how to get the coffee out of your keyboard.

▶ You examined the differences between the QWERTY keyboard and the Dvorak keyboard.

In the following chapter, you learn about disks and disk drives.

- -

Chapter 8
Using Disks and Disk Drives

● ●

In This Chapter

▶ Learning all about floppy disks and disk drives

▶ Preparing floppy disks for use in your computer (or "Why won't my disks work right out of the box?")

▶ Examining the difference between a hard disk and a hard drive

▶ Finding lost disks and dealing with "Write Protect Error" messages

▶ Taking care of your disk drives

● ●

*F*loppy disks, like Oreos, come in several shapes and flavors. Right on!

Why do computers need disks at all? Well, computers use disks for storage. They can store small amounts of information on little floppy disks and large amounts of information on a hard disk, that thing inside your computer called *C:*. A computer can handle only as much information as it can fit into its memory at one time. When you turn off the computer, its memory disappears, and so does the information. Where did it go? Hopefully, you copied it onto a disk somewhere.

This chapter explains why two floppy disks can look identical, yet only one of them works on your computer. You learn why you can't use most floppies straight out of the box. (You have to learn about "that formatting stuff.") You learn how to *write-protect* your disk in the right way. And you hear about those new CD-ROM discs that everybody spells with a "c." (No relation to hard drive.)

The Floppy Disk

When you open the shiny, colorful software box, you find drab little plastic disks inside. The actual program — the instructions for your computer — is stored on those disks, much like sound is stored on an LP record.

Unless you have a father in the music business, it's very difficult to make a record. But it's quick and easy to put information onto a disk. It's such a convenient method of storage, in fact, that it's the main way that software companies move information from their computers to your computer.

- ✔ Because you can touch floppy disks and even drop them behind your desk, disks are considered *hardware*. The *software* is the program, or the information stored on the disks. The disk itself is not software.

- ✔ Before your computer can read a disk's information, you must insert the disk into a *disk drive*. Disk drives are those funny slots on the front of your computer.

- ✔ Your computer can't use the data right from the disk. Instead, it copies the data to its memory. From there, the computer can manipulate the data, send it to the printer, or occasionally lose it. Because the computer is only working with a copy of the data, the original data is still safe on the disk.

- ✔ After the computer finishes processing the data in memory, it writes it back to the disk, overwriting the original information. If the computer mangles the information while you're working with it, don't save that information back to the disk. Instead, abandon that data and load the original data from the disk again.

Almost all floppy disks come in two sizes: 5¼-inch and 3½-inch. The former usually are black, and the latter come in colors to match most any decor. Each size of floppy disk can be either high capacity or low capacity, leaving the consumer with four main varieties to choose from. Figure 8-1 shows a 5¼-inch disk, and Figure 8-2 shows a 3½-inch disk.

Who really cares how a disk works?

A musical record contains a single, spiraling groove. Tiny peaks and valleys line the edges of the groove. When the record player's needle rides over these tiny peaks and valleys, it starts to vibrate. Your amplifier picks up these subtle vibrations and amplifies them, and the result is the music bursting from your stereo. Any small scratches or other defects in the record turn into loud pops.

Computers can't tolerate any pops, so they use a system that's much less mechanical. Floppy disks are coated with a layer of magnetic material. To store information, the disk drive writes the data magnetically — similar to the way information is recorded on a videotape or audio cassette. But, unlike video or sound, the information that a computer stores on a disk is electronic. Specifically, it is bits and bytes of information.

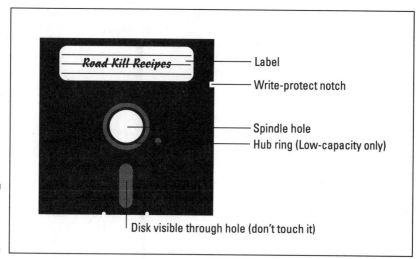

Figure 8-1:
A 5¼-inch
disk.

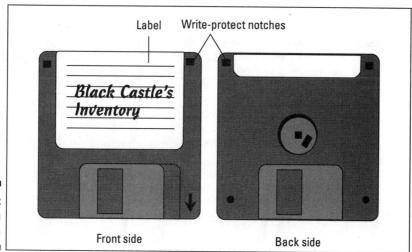

Figure 8-2:
A 3½-inch
disk.

5¼-inch low-capacity disks

Other names include *low-density, 360K,* and *DS/DD (double-sided/double-density).*

Everybody used this type of disk a few years ago. It can store 360 kilobytes of information. Five years ago, that was plenty of storage room. Today, you'd need about 40 of these disks to store a single copy of Microsoft's Word for Windows word processing program. The disks are terribly outdated, but because so many people once used them, they're still around. (It's like record albums; they're on their way out, but you can still buy them in a few stores.)

The actual disk is housed inside a plastic case that's supposed to protect the disk from damage. But the casing has several open windows. A large hole in the center, called the *spindle hole,* shows the center of the disk, or the *hub.* A large, oval-shaped hole exposes the black disk glistening inside. Don't touch the disk, or you'll leave gross finger stuff on it, confusing the computer. Keep your fingers on the plastic cover instead.

✔ These 360K floppy disks are considered the lowest common denominator. If your disk drive has a slot that's wide enough for one of these disks to fit inside (without folding it), you can use these low-capacity disks. For more on this subject, see "The Disk Drive" later in this chapter.

✔ Don't confuse these disks with their high-capacity counterparts, described next.

5¼-inch high-capacity disks

Other names are *high-density, 1.2MB, DS/HD (double-sided/high-density),* and *96 TPI.*

These disks hold 1.2 megabytes, which is four times as much data as the 360K disks. Yet the two types of disks look almost identical. How can you tell the difference? Look at the hole in the center of the disk. Low-capacity disks have a *reinforcing hub ring,* a small piece of plastic that runs along the inside edge of the disk. High-capacity disks don't have this reinforcing ring.

That's it. That's the only way to tell, and even it isn't always reliable.

Somehow, the computer industry prospers, even though the same lack of labeling would kill the cereal industry the first time consumers found Teenage Mutant Ninja Sugar Bombs inside the box instead of All Bran Total.

✔ Only high-capacity drives can read high-capacity disks. Older-style drives, those built for the 360K disks, can't read them. You'll see the message `General failure` if you try.

✔ If you're lucky, the words "1.2MB" or another of the high-density disk names will be printed on the disk label. That's another way to tell them apart from their lower-capacity cousins.

3½-inch low-capacity disks

Other names are *low-density, 720K,* and *DS/DD (double-sided/double-density).*

The Macintosh, in keeping with its "foolproof and fun" look on life, popularized these hardy babies. These disks don't have gaping holes in them, effectively heading off the temptation to touch the sacred disk inside. They're made of much thicker plastic, so they're much harder to damage.

✔ That shiny metal plate moves aside to let the disk drive access the disk inside. You can slide the plate aside yourself if you want to look, but don't touch the actual disk itself. The metal plate will snap back into position when you're through snooping.

✔ It's tempting to use these disks as beverage coasters. *Don't.* Moisture can seep underneath the sliding metal thing and freak out the disk inside.

✔ Any drive with a 3 ½-inch slot can use these 720K disks. They do not work in 5 ¼-inch disk drives, however, even though they'll fit. (Sort of.)

✔ These disks have a hole in one top corner. That's a *write-protect hole.* There's a little tab in the hole that can slide back and forth, opening or closing the hole. If the hole is closed, the disk works fine. If the hole's open, your computer can read information from the disk, but you won't be able to write anything to the disk. See "What Does 'Write Protect Error' Mean?" in this chapter for more on this.

3½-inch high-capacity disks

Other names are *high-density, 1.4MB,* and *DS/HD (double-sided/high-density).*

These guys hold 1.4 megabytes of data, and they're easy to distinguish from their low-capacity, 720 kilobyte counterparts. Look at the top corners, farthest away from the shiny metal sliding thing. In each corner, you'll see two tiny, square indentations. One hole has a square sliding tab next to it; the other is merely a hole. The sliding tab is a *write-protect notch,* which enables you to protect the disk from accidental erasure. (Refer to "What Does 'Write Protect Error' Mean?" in this chapter.)

✔ Try to resist the temptation to put these disks in your shirt pocket and carry them around. First, you'll look like a nerd. Second, your shirt pocket collects almost as much dust and lint as the area beneath your refrigerator. This gross pocket stuff can slip inside the rugged plastic casing, possibly scratching the disk inside.

✔ These disks often have the letters "HD" printed on them to indicate "high density." (If you hold the disk with the metal part toward you, the letters become "CH," as in "pure cane sugar." Regardless, the disks were still probably manufactured in Taiwan.)

3½-inch extended-capacity disks

Other names are *2.8MB* and *DS/ED (double-sided/extended-density).*

These disks are still too new to be widely used, but you may run into them anyway. You can tell them apart from their cousins by the letters "ED" stamped on a corner.

Disk do's and donuts

Disks store information in the form of magnetic impulses. That means that if you bring them close to a magnet, you copy new, random magnetic impulses over your important data. Don't use the water man's refrigerator magnet to stick a floppy to the refrigerator.

✔ Keep your disks away from disguised magnets, as well. Telephone handsets have magnets; so do speakers on radios and TV sets, executive-style paper clip holders (and some paper clips themselves), desk fans, photocopiers, and electric-guitar amplifiers.

✔ Don't set books or heavy items on top of disks. The pressure can push dust granules into the disk.

✔ Avoid extreme temperatures. Don't leave a disk sitting on the dash of your car or even on a window sill. And, even if the novel thought occurs to you, don't store your disks in the freezer.

✔ At least make an effort to put each disk back in its protective jacket after use. This is much more important for 5¼-inch disks than the smaller ones.

✔ Don't touch the disk surface itself; only touch the protective cover. Don't spray WD-40 inside, even if the disk makes a noise as it spins. (Your disk drive is probably making the noise, anyway. Keep the WD-40 out of there, too.)

✔ When mailing a 5¼-inch disk, pick up a floppy-disk mailer from the drug store. Don't fold the disk in half and mail it in a standard-size envelope.

✔ Never use a ballpoint pen to write on a disk's label. The hard pen point can damage the disk inside. Use a felt-tipped pen or, better yet, write on the label before you put it on the disk.

✔ Your computer must have special, expensive drives to read these disks. Because these disks aren't as popular as the other types, most software doesn't come on them.

✔ If you *do* have these special expensive drives, you can still read the other two varieties of 3½-inch disks.

In movies made in the '50s, computers looked like monster tape-decks, with two huge reels of tape jerking back and forth. But those things weren't the computers; the computers filled the entire room next door. Those huge, tape-deck-looking things were yesteryear's equivalent of a floppy disk: They stored all the programs and data. When the computer geeks wanted a piece of information from the front of the tape, they rewound the tape. When they wanted something near the back, they'd fast-forward. In both cases, it was slow going.

So some wise guy got the idea of grabbing some magnetic recording tape *before* it was sliced into strips. He cut it into a disk shape and then slipped the disk into a plastic jacket to keep off any stray french-fry grease. When this special disk was inserted into a newly invented disk drive, computers could read the information off the spinning disk, just as they'd read it from the tapes, but much faster. But what to call these flexible things? Flexible disks? Quivering disks? Somehow, the word *floppy* caught on, leading to *floppy disks*.

The Disk Drive

The disk drive is the thing in your computer that eats disks. Actually, although you stick the disk in the drive, little chewing is involved. Instead, the disk drive is the mechanism by which the computer reads information from the disk. You must put the disk into a disk drive before your computer can use it.

Disk drives contain a motor that spins the disk around at least 300 times each second. A thing called a *head* inside the drive hovers over the spinning disk, reading or writing information from or to the disk. The disk drive translates the stuff on the disk into information the computer can use (put into memory).

- Disk drives are described in two ways: by the size of the disks they eat and by the maximum amount of storage available on the disk.

- The two disk drive sizes are 5¼-inch and 3½-inch. An appropriately sized slot exists on the front of your computer for each disk size.

- You cannot put a 5¼-inch disk into a 3½-inch drive and vice versa. It just won't work.

- Table 8-1 shows the five different types of drives, based on the storage capacity of the disks they eat. No, you don't need to memorize the table. Just put a sticky note on it so you can refer to it later.

- High-capacity drives can eat both high- and low-capacity disks. Don't let this issue confuse you! If you purchased your computer in the past five years, odds are straight-on that you have a high-capacity disk drive (or drives). If so, you don't need to worry about a thing.

Table 8-1	Types of Disk Drives
Storage Capacity	*Disk Size*
Low (360K)	5¼-inch
Low (720K)	3½-inch
High (1.2MB)	5¼-inch
High (1.4MB)	3½-inch
Extended (2.8MB)	3½-inch

Locating drives A and B

Unlike parents who buy books when trying to name baby, computers save time and money by referring to drives as single letters. Every computer has a *drive A,* which is your first (and the computer's favorite) floppy drive.

If you have a second floppy drive, your computer refers to it as *drive B.*

- ✔ Usually, the drive closest to the top of the computer is drive A. Computers that put drive A on the bottom are rare, but they may exist. If you have one, and you confuse drive A with drive B, get one of those punch-tape things and label your drives "A" and "B."

- ✔ DOS refers to your floppy drives by their letters as well. However, DOS tacks on a colon after the letter, just to be different. So, in DOS, drive A is called *A:* (that's *A* followed by a colon). Drive B is likewise called *B:* (a *B* with a colon).

- ✔ Your computer may also have another disk drive. This one, stored inside the computer, is a *hard drive,* and it's usually called *drive C.* It's a special kind of disk that stores much more information than a floppy disk.

Putting a disk into a disk drive

You can slide a floppy disk into a floppy drive in several ways, but only one method is correct: Grab the disk along the labeled edge, making sure that the label faces up. (Usually your thumb will be resting on the label; that makes it easy to remember.)

On 5¼-inch drives, you'll see a small knob next to the slot. This is the *drive door latch,* and it can be in one of two positions: open or closed. The open position is horizontal so that the latch is parallel with the slot. The latch must be open before you can slide a floppy disk (label side up and toward you) into the drive. Give the disk that last little push with your thumb until the drive swallows it completely. Then push the latch down until it's in a vertical position and locks in place.

On 3½-inch drives, there isn't any latch. Just push the floppy disk (label side up and toward you) firmly into the drive. Give it that last little push with your thumb. When you push it in all the way, the drive clicks and swallows the disk. Gulp!

Getting a disk out of a disk drive

On the 5 ¼-inch drives, flip open the latch. It flips up (or down) to a horizontal position. The magic of this is that it also partially spits out the disk, usually pushing the thing right against your fingers. Grab the disk and pull it the rest of the way out.

On the 3 ½-inchers, push the little plastic button just beneath the slot. When you do, the drive ejects your disk. No need to stand back; it's more of a dainty push than a Frisbee fling. Grab the edge of the disk and pull it the rest of the way out.

Follow these safeguards to keep your drive healthy:

- ✔ Don't leave a disk in the drive when you're finished computing for the day. This leaves the drive's little sensing device (its head) resting on the disk's sensitive surface, which is a no-no.

- ✔ *Never* remove a disk while the drive's little light is turned on. The light means the drive is trying to read or write some data. Pulling the disk out when the light's on is like pulling a plate of spaghetti away from somebody who's already placed a fork into it. It's a messy situation you can easily avoid.

Why You Need to Format Floppy Disks before You Use Them

For many years, all brands and styles of computers used those ugly, black 5 ¼-inch-square floppy disks. But the computers all stored information on those disks in slightly different ways.

Unlike a phonograph record, which comes with a single groove on it, computers store information on multiple "tracks." And different types of computers use different schemes for putting those tracks on a disk. So, instead of selling dozens of different kinds of disks, floppy-disk manufacturers threw up their hands (an ugly sight) and said computer owners had to add their own tracks to the blank disks.

When computers add these special tracks, they're said to be *formatting* the disk. Today, IBM-compatible computers are just about the only computers left that still use 5 ¼-inch disks. But the disks usually are still unformatted. (You can buy some disks that are already formatted, but they cost a lot more.)

✔ You must format all disks before you can use them. The formatting process prepares a disk for use by putting those little tracks on it.

✔ When you buy a box of disks, sit down at your computer and format the whole batch of 'em at once. It's a drag, but it's better than trying to make a quick copy of a file a few weeks down the road and finding out that you don't have any formatted disks on hand.

✔ When you're formatting your disks, just press Enter when you're asked to type in a volume label. The label is entirely optional.

✔ The disk's *serial number* is simply a unique number (with a few letters mixed in) assigned to each disk. It's nothing you can change, and you don't need to memorize it.

Formatting a disk

It's not difficult to format a disk — just time-consuming. To format the disk in drive A, type the following command:

```
C:\> FORMAT A:
```

That's the word **FORMAT**, followed by a space, and then the letter **A** (for drive A), immediately followed by a colon. The computer responds by asking you to insert a disk in drive A and press the Enter key. Put the disk in the drive if you haven't done so already. For a 5 ¼-inch disk drive, close the drive's door latch after you insert the disk. Then press the Enter key.

The formatting process takes a minute or two, so pick at the spots on your desk for a while. When the computer finishes formatting a disk, it asks you to enter a *volume label.* You can press Enter for "no volume label." If you prefer, you can type something descriptive about the disk, but you're limited to 12 characters, so what the heck, just press Enter. (More information on the volume label is covered later in this chapter, in the section "How to Find Lost Disks.")

Next, the computer asks whether you want to Format another? Press N. You can now use the disk.

To format a disk in drive B, repeat the same formatting command but substitute the letter **B** for **A**:

```
C:\> FORMAT B:
```

> ✔ If you want to format more than one disk, press Y when the computer asks `Format another?` Remove the first disk from the drive and replace it with another disk. You can format several disks in a row this way.
>
> ✔ After you format a disk, label it. Use one of the sticky labels that came in the box of disks. Write on the label *before* you peel and stick it onto the disk. (You don't want to write on the disk itself; that can damage the disk.)

You must format all disks before you can use them!

Never, ever, ever format drive C. If you do, all the data on your hard drive disappears, leaving you with nothing but empty tracks and a "gosh, I really blew it this time" gaze.

Formatting low-capacity disks in high-capacity drives

Computers with the more expensive, higher-capacity drives can format both high- and low-density disks. If you don't have a high-density drive, don't bother with this section.

The only time the situation arises is when you want to make a copy of a disk for a friend who has low-capacity drives (and subsequently can't read your high-capacity disks). Otherwise, you should never format a low-capacity disk. Always buy high-capacity disks and format them by using the commands mentioned in the preceding section.

If you're formatting a low-density, 5¼-inch disk in a high-capacity drive A, type the following command at any prompt:

```
C:\> FORMAT A: /F:360
```

That's the word **FORMAT** followed by a space, the letter **A**, a colon, another space, a forward slash (the slash that shares your question mark key), the letter **F**, another colon, and then the number **360**. Press Enter and follow the instructions that appear on the screen.

When the drive's through formatting, your computer politely asks whether you want to format another disk. If you press Y for yes, you'll be formatting more low-density disks — not the high-density disks you normally use.

To format a low-density, 3 ½-inch disk in a high-capacity drive A, type the following command:

```
C:\> FORMAT A: /F:720
```

That's the same as before, but substituting 720 for 360. Again, if you format any additional disks by pressing Y at the computer prompt, those disks also are formatted at a low capacity.

Don't ever try to format a high-capacity disk to a lower capacity. That ruins the disk. You need to find a disk of the correct capacity for each of the format commands you use. The friends for whom you're going to all this trouble should be able to provide you with disks that are the same capacity as their drives.

It's usually foolish to use low-capacity disks in a high-capacity drive. It's like buying raisin-bran cereal and then picking out all the raisins. You spent extra money for a disk drive that has extra storage capacity, and you should use it.

What's a Hard Disk, or Hard Drive?

Floppy disks can be cumbersome for day-to-day computing. Your computer takes a long time to read and write information from them, and they can't hold very much information in the first place.

So the Dorito-breathed geeks who invented floppy disks came up with the ultimate floppy disk: a large, spinning plate that lives inside your computer. The computer reads and writes to this large, spinning plate as if it were a floppy in a disk drive. But unlike floppies, hard drives stay sealed up inside your computer, away from dust, magnets, and carbonated-beverage spray. (In fact, the people who build these hard drives have to wear special suits and work in sterile, spaceship-like rooms to keep any contaminants out. One sneeze, and it's all over for that batch of disk drives.)

Because the large, spinning plate, or platter, is so big and thick, it can hold more information than hundreds of floppy disks. It's also much speedier.

✔ Like their floppy drive counterparts, hard drives have lights on the outside that turn on when the computer is accessing data. If your computer is taking a particularly long time to load a program, look at the hard drive light. It should be blinking in a somewhat random series of flashes. If it's not on at all, or it's on all the time, that may mean that something bad is happening (see Chapter 26 for troubleshooting tips).

- Hard disks are labeled with letters just like floppy disks. The first hard drive in your PC is drive C — whether or not you have a drive B. Additional hard drives are given letters D, E, F, and so on, all the way up to Z. (No joke.)

- Nobody will laugh if you call a hard drive a "hard disk." Only technoweenies call it a "fixed disk," however.

- Hard disks normally function invisibly. You don't have to look for them underneath your desk or try to pick labels off them. But if you have a hard drive, remember that it's there and can fail at any time. Copy your important data (and some of your unimportant data, too) onto floppy disks and keep the copies in a safe location. You won't be considered paranoid if you make two copies — keeping one set of disks near your computer and the other at the house of a friend or relative.

Here are the real differences between *hard disk* and *hard drive:* The hard disk is the physical disk spinning inside your computer. The mechanism that houses the disk is the hard drive. You can speak of everything collectively as the "hard drive." But, just as a floppy drive has floppy disks, a hard drive has hard disks. They're just not removable, that's all. (Or are they? See the next section.)

Removable Hard Drives

Some people became so enthused about the portability of floppy disks, they wanted a portable hard disk, too. It costs more, of course, but some hard drives are removable. You can pull them out and carry them around like a lunch box.

- A removable hard drive can be convenient when you work at two different computers. When you're done at the office, you yank out the hard drive and slide it into your computer at home. All your data is there waiting for you, ready for play.

- Some people like removable hard drives for security reasons. They can lock up the hard drive in a safe each night. Of course, if they forget, anybody else can walk off with the hard drive, making it even less secure.

- The most popular type of removable hard disk is the *Bernoulli disk,* named after the famed 16th-century Swiss mathematician, Daniel Bernoulli (no relation to Daniel Gookin). The Bernoulli disk is really a big floppy disk, but thanks to aerodynamic principles discovered by D. Bernoulli, it acts like a hard drive — and a removable one at that. Incidentally, Bernoulli also pioneered the principles by which all airplanes fly.

How to Find Lost Disks

To find out what's stored on a disk, use DOS's DIR command. Place the unknown floppy in drive A and type the following command:

```
C:\> DIR A: /P
```

That's the word **DIR**, a space, the letter **A**, and a colon. Follow all that with another space, the forward slash (/), and a **P**.

The DIR command lists the names of all the files on that disk, one screenful at a time. To see the next screen, press Enter. This shows you everything on the disk, and you can quickly tell whether it's the lost disk you're looking for.

A quicker way to keep track of your disks is to label them. You'll find sticky labels inside every box of disks. (If you run out, blank address labels often work in a pinch.) Here's the procedure:

1. **Use the DIR command to see what you stored on the disk. Then, using a pen, write a descriptive phrase on the label: "Spreadsheet Files," "Letters to Mother," or "Backup Disk," for example.**

2. **Avoid the temptation to label a disk "Stuff," "Miscellaneous," or "Computer Data." (Be descriptive!)**

3. **Peel off the label and apply it to the disk. Be sure that you're not covering up any holes or notches in the disk's casing.**

4. **Rejoice in that "I'm prepared!" feeling when you can find your disks easily.**

A disk's label is different from its volume label. When you format a disk, DOS asks you to supply a volume label. That's an electronic name the computer gives the disk — not the same as the sticky label you put on the disk's outer hull. (In fact, how could the computer tell what you've written there anyway?)

Because you get hit with the volume-label question each time you format a disk, here is a handy DOS command you can use to scope out any disk's volume label, provided that the disk is in drive A:

```
C:\> VOL A:
```

That's the word **VOL**, a space, the letter **A**, and a colon. The computer tells you the disk's label or says that the disk has no label. Remember, this is regardless of whether the disk has a sticky label. So why bother with a volume label? Beats us!

To better organize your data, consider buying different colored disks. Use one color for word processing files, another color for spreadsheets, and another color for backups.

- Don't use a ballpoint pen to write on a label after it has been applied to a disk. The pressure of the pen point can damage the disk inside.

- Don't use sticky notes as labels. They can flick off while the disk's on your desk or, even worse, while it's inside your disk drive.

- If you did enter a volume label when you formatted the disk, you'll see it displayed when you use the VOL command. Again, the volume label isn't required by anything.

What Does "Write Protect Error" *Mean?*

Sometimes, a computer flat out refuses to copy anything to a floppy disk. If you see the words Write Protect Error, it doesn't mean the disk is bad. It means it's protecting you from yourself.

By *write-protecting* your important disks, you prevent the computer from writing anything to them, so you don't accidentally copy over your vitally important files. Your computer can read information and even run programs from a write-protected disk, but it won't be able to write any data to it.

- To write-protect a 5¼-inch disk, grab one of those little stickers that came in the disk box. Find the square notch on the side of the floppy disk and fold the tab over the disk's edge, covering the notch on both sides. When the notch is covered, the disk is protected.

- To write-protect a 3½-inch disk, look at the little square hole or holes in the corners. In one hole, you see a small plastic tab (you may have to turn the disk over; the tab only shows from one side). The tab slides back and forth, effectively opening or closing the hole. When it covers the hole, the disk is normal. You can read and write to it. Push the tab with your fingernail or a pencil tip so that it opens the hole. When you can see through the hole, the disk is write-protected.

- To make a disk normal, reverse the procedure. Either remove the plastic sticker or slide the tab to cover the hole.

- *Cover* the notch to write-protect a 5¼-inch disk. *Uncover* the hole to write-protect a 3½-inch disk. The computer nerds didn't bother looking for a system that was easy to remember.

- It's a good idea to write-protect any program disks you have. Most come that way, straight out of the box.

- In a pinch, you can use masking tape to write-protect a floppy.

Write-protecting a disk sounds like a cool idea. However, for 5 ¼-inch disks, with their write-protect tabs, it can be a messy proposition. If you constantly add and remove the sticky tabs, you create a greasy film on the disk, making it stick to everything. This is actually worse than losing your data, so don't write-protect a 5 ¼-inch disk you plan on repeatedly unwrite-protecting in the future. (The 3 ½-inch disks don't suffer from this problem.)

Should I Clean My Disk Drives?

So-called head-cleaning disks usually cost no more than five or ten dollars, and well-meaning friends and relatives often give them as gifts to proud new computer owners. The concept is simple: You squirt the cleaning disk with some liquid, shove it into your drive, and let it spin around for a while. The disk, made of an abrasive kitchen-scrubber material, is supposed to remove the iron oxide (rust) buildup from your disk drive's heads.

Some people say that you should clean your disk drives every week with a head-cleaning disk. Others say these abrasive disks can damage your drives. Who's correct?

- ✔ If your disk drive doesn't work, give it a shot. It may work, and if it doesn't, you had nothing to lose anyway.

- ✔ Don't use head-cleaning disks on a regular basis, however. Your disk drive is a sensitive piece of equipment, not meant for serious scrubbing. Don't use head-cleaning disks more than once a year. (If your disk drive isn't broken, why try to fix it?)

- ✔ Andy Rathbone hasn't used a head-cleaning disk for the past three years, and his disk drives work just fine. Dan Gookin bought a head-cleaning kit ten years ago and used it once.

- ✔ Nothing beats taking your disk drive (and therefore your entire computer) to a technician for proper cleaning. This isn't something that needs to be done on a regular basis at all; only if you experience consistent disk problems should you consider the trip.

● ●

Summary

In this chapter, we sorted out the differences between drives, disks, floppy disks, CD-ROM drives, and other disk- and drive-related lingo:

▶ You examined the different kinds of floppy disks and disk drives.

▶ You learned how to prepare floppy disks for use and how to get them in and out of your computer.

▶ You learned about hard drives and hard disks.

▶ You reviewed the process known as write-protecting your floppy disks — a handy way to keep you from erasing valuable data.

In the next chapter, you learn all about your computer monitor.

● ●

Chapter 9

Learning about the Monitor (That TV Thing)

In This Chapter

▶ How monitors and display adapters work to display images on-screen

▶ A look at different types of monitors and display adapters

▶ A guide to graphics adapters

▶ The answer to the question "Which display is best?"

▶ The difference between a computer monitor and your TV set — and why the two aren't interchangeable

▶ How to keep your monitor safe, clean, and happy

*Y*ou've heard it called the monitor, the screen, and the display, but whatever the terms, they all refer to that TV-like thing sitting on top of or nearby your console. No computer is complete without a monitor. Otherwise, how would your PC talk to you, display pretty pictures, or flash disgusting error messages? In fact, the monitor is such an essential part of a PC that many users forget it's an option that can be changed or upgraded.

This chapter discusses various aspects of the computer monitor. Although this seems like a cinchy thing to deal with, the truth is that awkward and annoying terms attach themselves to a computer monitor like a thick layer of dust. These include the weird acronyms CGA, VGA, and EGA, as well as bizarre concepts such as monochrome, graphics, and pixels. They're all *screen-dumped* here for your examination. And, as usual, the aisles are clear, exit signs illuminated, and escape hatches clearly marked.

The Bonehead's Guide to PC Monitors

In a way, the PC's monitor is like its mouth. It displays information as a type of visual feedback, enabling you to know what's going on or to see the result of some operation. But, while you stare at the computer's monitor, you should know that there really are two things that make up the entire video system: the *monitor* and the *display adapter*.

The monitor is the physical, television-like thing you see on top of or near the console. It looks just like a TV but without the tuner or volume knobs. It has a brightness and contrast knob, plus other adjustments similar to those on many TV sets. But that's where the similarity ends. Your computer monitor is *not* a TV set, and you cannot use it as a TV set without very (very, *very*) expensive computer hardware. (We're being emphatic because there's always some basement scientist who sets out to try.)

The display adapter is the part of your video system you probably don't know about. It's actually an expansion card plugged into the motherboard inside your console. (Take another look at Chapter 6 for a review of motherboards and expansion cards.) The display adapter enables information to leave your computer and appear on the monitor. The adapter card contains the special circuitry that drives the monitor, telling it what to display, where to display it, and what colors to use — like an electronic interior designer.

Of the two, the monitor and display adapter, the latter is the more important. The display adapter determines how many colors you see and how fancy the graphics are that appear on your monitor. Also, only certain monitors work with certain display adapters. (This is that confusing aspect we warned about in the introduction.) Fortunately, after everything is properly matched, you never need to worry about monitors or display adapters again.

- ✔ You need both a monitor and display adapter. There are a variety of monitors and display adapters you can use. The rest of this chapter elaborates on different options, including the advantages and drawbacks of each. Note that there are special monitors for each display adapter; you cannot (and should not) mix and match them carelessly.

- ✔ In some PCs, especially laptops, the display adapter is built into the motherboard.

- ✔ The term *monitor* refers to the physical device — the monitor that sits on top of or to the side of your console. The terms *screen* and *display* are both used to describe what appears on the monitor's screen — information the computer is showing you.

- ✔ The display adapter may also be called the *display adapter card, video card, video hardware,* or *video system*. Other terms describe the graphics standard used; the terms *Monographics, Hercules, CGA, EGA, VGA,* and so on, tell you how fancy the graphics can be on the screen. Refer to the section "PC Graph-a-bets Soup (a.k.a. Graphics Adapters)" in this chapter.

- ✔ Laptop computers have special monitor/display adapter arrangements. Refer to Chapter 12 for more about this.

Monochrome vs. color

There are two main styles of monitors on the PC planet: *monochrome,* which displays information in only two colors — like a black-and-white TV set — and *color,* which displays information in several colors. Color monitors are more expensive and more popular than monochrome, primarily because they show great graphics displays in the computer store.

Up front, note that a monochrome monitor is *not* the same as a black-and-white TV set. In some cases, it's actually more desirable than color. Monochrome monitors are cheaper and display text more crisply and cleanly than color monitors. You may not suffer from eye fatigue as rapidly when using monochrome. And many applications don't need color at all. Word processing and database creation are two popular applications that don't require color displays. For tasks such as these, a monochrome monitor is preferable.

On the other hand, color displays are more popular because, well, they're prettier to look at. Also, many applications now use color creatively. These programs just plain look gross on a black-and-white monitor. And advanced, graphical applications, such as Microsoft Windows (not to mention computer games), really need color to show their stuff. So unless you use your computer for monotonous programs, color is recommended.

- Monochrome displays show text in white, green, or amber against a black background. They can also show underlined text, bright or boldfaced text, flashing text, and inverse (black-on-white) text.

- In addition to bright, flashing, or inverse text, color displays show text in any of 16 colors against eight different background colors. Note that color displays cannot (with a few exceptions) show text underlined. (Usually, programs resort to showing underlined text in some special color — typically blue.)

- Monochrome displays generally don't offer anything in the way of graphics. Special types of monochrome displays, called *Hercules* or *Monographics,* can show some graphics but not with the variety and richness offered by color displays.

- It's possible to upgrade from a monochrome to a color display. However, you must replace both your monitor and adapter card with color versions. And here's another secret: It's possible to run two monitors on the same PC — one color and one monochrome. Few people do this and few programs take advantage of it, but it can be done.

- Some color adapters can be used with monochrome displays. Particularly, a special breed of monitor called the *paper white VGA monitor* can display shades of gray rather than colors. The effect is nice, but this type of system — although cheap — isn't for everyone.

Graphics vs. text

You see one of two different things on a computer monitor: graphics or text. *Text* refers to characters, letters, numbers, and symbols you see on the screen. These are displayed in neat rows and columns — what you expect to see on a computer display. *Graphics* are pictures, images, circles, lines, and squares, and can also include text.

The reason for making a distinction between graphics and text is that some monochrome monitors can display only text. If you attempt to run a graphics program on such a system, your screen goes blank. This happens most often when you try to run a color graphics game on a monochrome system. The solution? Upgrade to a color system.

- ✔ Color systems can display both graphics and text but only in two different *modes.* In *text mode,* you see text (in color). In the *graphics mode,* you see colorful graphics as well as text.

- ✔ Text is displayed on a PC in *rows* and *columns.* Rows march across the screen from right to left, like lines on a page. (In fact, the terms *rows* and *lines* are used interchangeably.) Columns are like vertical columns of text, up and down. An *A* in the upper-left corner of your screen is said to be in the first row and first column.

- ✔ The typical PC's text display has 25 rows and 80 columns — room for about half a page of single-spaced text. This is true for both monochrome and color systems.

- ✔ Rows and columns are used most often to position information on the screen. For example, you can put an asterisk (*) at row 13, column 40, and it will be just about smack dab in the middle of the screen.

The PC also can display text at 25 rows by 40 columns — in other words, *fat text.* Various other combinations of rows and columns are possible, but usually only the advanced or extremely bored user messes with them. If you're curious, you can change to a 40-column screen in DOS by typing the following command:

```
C:\> MODE 40
```

Note that this only works with color displays; monochrome systems can't show fat text. To change the screen back, type this:

```
C:\> MODE 80
```

PC Graph-a-bets Soup (a.k.a. Graphics Adapters)

Welcome to one of the most confusing aspects of using a PC monitor: the hell we call *graph-a-bets soup*. That refers to the unconventional way the computer industry describes different graphics adapters. (Graphics adapters are the secret, internal part of your video system; see "The Bonehead's Guide to PC Monitors" at the start of this chapter.)

What's the difference?

Each graphics adapter is given a specific name or acronym. This is the name of the graphics standard created by IBM. It tells those-in-the-know how fancy the adapter is, which means whether or not it can display graphics in high resolution with bazillions of colors.

Graphics terms and such not worth reading about

When describing a graphics display on a PC, you usually use the following terms:

Pixels: This refers to an individual dot on the screen. All graphics you see on a PC are composed of hundreds (or thousands) of graphics dots, or *pixels*. Each pixel is a different color, which creates the image.

Resolution: This refers to the number of pixels on a graphics screen — specifically, the number of pixels across (horizontal) and down (vertical). The more pixels — and greater the resolution —the finer the graphics image will be. High resolution, with maybe 640 pixels horizontal and 480 vertical, creates an almost photographic image. Low resolution, with perhaps 80 by 100 pixels, produces a blocky, "stair step" image.

Colors: This describes the number of colors available for a given graphics resolution. At lower resolutions, you have more colors; higher resolutions, which use more memory, give you fewer colors. For example, at the high, 640 by 480 resolution, you may see only 16 different colors. Low, 320 by 200 resolution may give you several hundred colors.

Mode: The combination of pixels, resolution, and colors is described by a graphics mode. These modes have confusing number values, primarily for use by programmers. However, it's safe — as a beginner — for you to refer to a *high-resolution mode* or *low-resolution mode*.

All of this is basically information for programmers. However, you will hear the terms pixel, resolution, colors, and mode used often when people describe graphics. Just smile, nod your head knowingly, and no one will be the wiser.

Table 9-1 lists graphics adapter acronyms and offers some observations about each type.

Table 9-1	A Guide to Graphics Adapters		
Adapter	*Meaning*	*Type*	*Why Bother*
Monochrome	Like the original IBM monochrome display	Monochrome (duh)	It's cheap.
Hercules	Like monochrome but can also display graphics	Monographics	Some programs support its black-and-white graphics.
CGA	Color Graphics Adapter	Color	It was the first color adapter — few colors, low resolution, and ugly.
EGA	Enhanced Graphics Adapter	Color	It's better than CGA but more expensive.
VGA	Video Graphics Array	Color	It's currently the color graphics standard.
Super VGA	Better than Video Graphics Array	Color	It's better than VGA but more expensive.
PGA, XGA, and so on	Professional Graphics Adapter, Extended Graphics Adapter	Color	It's used mostly by professionals in high-end situations and is very expensive.

✔ When the PC first came out, it had only monochrome and CGA video. Monochrome was cheap and recommended by IBM. The CGA adapter was the only way to get color text and graphics. IBM downplayed the CGA because it assumed that only users who wanted to play games would buy it. IBM underestimated the importance of graphics in business software, and CGA took off. It eventually was replaced by EGA and then VGA.

✔ The Hercules adapter was the first major third-party hardware addition to the PC. It offered all the capabilities of IBM's monochrome adapter, plus limited two-color graphics. As a historical note, Hercules and 1-2-3 helped propel each other to fame and fortune; 1-2-3 produced interesting graphs and charts on Hercules-equipped PCs.

✔ A monographics card is a clone of the Hercules card. It's a combination of "monochrome" and "graphics."

✔ The EGA graphics standard was introduced as an improved type of CGA adapter. It offered more colors and a higher resolution but was very expensive. EGA soon was shadowed by the currently popular VGA standard.

✔ VGA and Super VGA are the current PC video graphics champs. They offer high resolution and lots of colors at an affordable price.

Which display is best?

Simple question, simple answer: Super VGA.

✔ Many manufacturers make Super VGA display adapters. They offer a wide range of features and prices. We can't recommend individual brands, but it's a good strategy to avoid the cheaper, no-name brands.

✔ You need a monitor that can handle the output of a Super VGA adapter — if that's the way you want to go. Although some places claim that Super VGA works with any monitor (and that may be true), the best results are possible only on monitors built to handle Super VGA.

✔ If you're really in this for a pretty picture, try getting a Super VGA system with one megabyte (1MB) of video memory. It will cost you, but the display will look *real good*.

✔ Yes, adapters more expensive and fancier than Super VGA do exist. The PGA and XGA standards go way beyond what Super VGA offers. But, unless you're using advanced software that requires these adapters, you're wasting your money.

What's an accelerated video card?

For years, IBM-compatible computers merely tossed words and numbers on-screen. Occasionally, some word processors and spreadsheets would spice things up by adding a flashy, blue background, but that didn't slow things down much.

But when Microsoft Windows hit the scene and tossed all its fancy graphics into little "windows" on-screen, Windows users found themselves twiddling their thumbs: The old-style video cards were too slow to keep up.

So some savvy manufacturers tossed a special "graphics-stomping" chip onto a special breed of video cards. These special *accelerated video cards* can flick little windows onto the screen as fast as Windows dishes them out.

If you're using Windows much, an accelerated video card lets you use Windows much faster. The card doesn't make Windows print any faster or calculate spreadsheets faster, but you can switch from window to window almost instantaneously.

If you're not using Windows or any other graphics-happy programs, the card's power isn't nearly as noticeable. Don't run out and buy an accelerated video card if you're still using WordPerfect 5.0.

Some computers speed things up with a slick *local-bus video* card. This quick little card plugs into a special slot on special motherboards to make things move on-screen especially fast.

The local-bus video wasn't confusing enough, so some designers swiped the term and applied it to motherboards that don't have a video card: The video card stuff is built into the motherboard. That makes it work much faster and makes it much harder for the shop to replace if it goes bad.

Technical Monitor Stuff to Numb Your Brain

Thinking about all the technical issues surrounding a PC monitor will make you shudder. Do it now: Shudder. Egads! Here are some nonlayman terms that describe various parts of a PC monitor. The gist of this section is to tell you which option is best. Keep in mind the basic computer axiom: The better it is, the more expensive it is.

One final warning: You really don't need to read this section. We'd skip it, if we were you.

Analog: This is a type of monitor, as opposed to a *digital* monitor. VGA adapters must be connected to analog monitors. All older graphics adapters work with digital monitors. Generally speaking, analog monitors are better because they can produce more colors than a digital monitor.

Bandwidth: This is the speed at which information is sent from the computer (actually the graphics adapter) to the monitor. The bandwidth is a value, measured in megahertz (MHz), and the monitor must be capable of accepting the bandwidth of the graphics adapter. The higher the bandwidth value, say 70 MHz or so, the better.

Composite: This is a type of monitor that's similar to a TV set. In olden days, PC owners often bought a composite monitor as a cheap alternative to the more expensive *RGB* monitor. These monitors were used primarily with CGA video systems, and they displayed their images in (fuzzy) green on black.

Digital: A digital monitor must be used by older graphics adapters, such as monochrome, Hercules, CGA, and EGA. These monitors received digital signals from the PC and were limited in the breadth of colors they could display. The most common type of digital monitor was the *RGB* monitor (more on that in a bit).

Dot pitch: This refers to the distance between each dot, or *pixel,* on the screen (as measured from the center of each pixel). The closer the dots, the better the image is. A dot pitch of 0.28 mm (millimeters) is really good, with smaller values being even better.

Interlacing: This is a method of tricking the monitor into displaying a picture that is better than it should be able to display. Interlacing takes twice as long to paint the image on-screen by painting only half of it at once.

Multiscanning: This is the capability of a single monitor to switch between multiple *analog* and *digital* modes. This is the type of monitor you want if your graphics adapter supports several graphics modes and your software often switches between them. (Some manufacturers refer to this as *multisync.*)

Picture tube size: This is the diagonal measurement of your monitor's picture tube, from corner to corner. Bigger monitors mean more display areas and are more expensive. The 12- to 14-inch monitors are common, but you can buy special monitors up to 19 inches and beyond, given the size of your ego or vision problems.

RGB: This is an acronym for red, green, and blue. This described the basic digital monitor users preferred with the old CGA. An RGB monitor was a digital monitor.

Scan rate: This is the rate at which a monitor's *electron gun* paints the image on the screen. It's measured in kilohertz (KHz), and the higher the value, the better.

TTL: This is a totally unnecessary term that crops up a lot and confuses the heck out of everyone. Basically, the old monochrome monitors were referred to as TTL monitors by the IBM documentation. *TTL monitor equals monochrome monitor.* No sweat. But what TTL stood for was a mystery for years. Here's the long-held secret answer: transistor-to-transistor logic. Now, aren't you glad you read that?

Why You Don't Want to Use a TV Set

IBM was so nervous about its first PC not being accepted that, well, it thought of everything. One thing was to make sure that it would display an image on a TV set, which is what many Apple II owners were doing at the time. To make that possible, the old CGA display adapter had what scientists call a *doohickey.* You plugged a cable into the doohickey and then into your TV, and, *voilà,* the TV acted like your monitor. Cool.

The problem with using a TV set is that it is designed to display low-resolution TV images — typically, low-brow dramas and inane game shows. These look OK on the screen, but computer text never will. Sit down a foot or so away from your TV, and you can see how blurry the picture is up close. Bluntly, your TV set makes a lousy PC monitor.

✔ No display adapter since the old CGA has had output for a TV set.

✔ Recording an image from your TV is possible but only with advanced — and expensive — video hardware. You can locate this stuff in the back of computer and video magazines, if it interests you.

✔ As an aside, the reason DOS has a 40-column mode is so that the screen looks readable on a TV set (see "Graphics vs. text" earlier in this chapter).

How to Adjust, Clean, and Otherwise Pamper Your Monitor

The typical computer monitor has many knobs. The two you find in front are the brightness and contrast knobs. Other knobs include a horizontal and vertical adjust, image sizing, color, hue, and on and on. Most often, the only ones you need are brightness and contrast.

The best way to adjust your monitor is to display text and turn the brightness way up. With the brightness up, adjust the contrast. Then turn the brightness down until you can't see the scan lines (that hazy square that appears when the brightness is all the way up). Ta-da, your monitor is perfectly set.

Some monitors come with a swivel base. This enables you to adjust the monitor angle and pitch to something comfortable. If your monitor lacks this luxury, you can purchase a special tilt-and-swivel stand that gives you the same freedom. Leave some slack in the monitor's cords; otherwise, you could pull the cords out of the back of the computer by swiveling the monitor too far in one direction.

Troubleshooting or "I can't see anything!"

Sometimes, the monitor appears totally blank. Other hints may tell you the computer is on — it's making noise, its lights are on, and so on — but the monitor appears to be broken. If so, follow these steps:

1. **Make sure that the monitor is plugged in.**

2. **Make sure that the monitor is turned on. Some monitors have on/off switches separate from the computer's main on/off switch.**

3. **Touch a key. Sometimes special programs called *screen blankers* turn off the display. Touching a key — either a Shift key or the spacebar — restores the image.**

4. **Check the brightness knob. Someone may have turned it down, in which case adjusting the brightness (or contrast) knob brings back the image.**

✔ Another problem may be the software you're running. Some software is dumb. It won't let you know if you don't have the proper graphics adapter. Instead, you see a blank screen. If you try the steps we just mentioned and they don't seem to work, reset your computer. Press the Reset button or hold down the Ctrl, Alt, and Del keys all at once.

✔ If the monitor goes blank often and a press of the key restores it, a screen blanker is to blame. Refer to the next section.

Preventing phosphor burn-in

Leaving your monitor on all the time leads to something called *phosphor burn-in.* It's insidious. After time, the same image becomes "etched" on your screen. You see 1-2-3 or WordPerfect even with the monitor turned off! This happens because displaying the same image over a long period of time burns up the phosphors lining the inside of your display. Needless to say, this looks tacky.

To avoid phosphor burn-in, turn off your monitor when you're not using the PC. Even if you'll only be away for a few minutes, it's a good idea to turn down the brightness. This saves your monitor, keeping the image as brilliant as it was when your monitor was new.

✔ Although everyone argues about the benefits of leaving a computer turned on 24 hours a day, the consensus is that if you're not looking at the monitor after a period of time, you should turn it off or turn down the brightness.

✔ A way to avoid phosphor burn-in is to buy *screen dimmer* or *screen blanker* software. These special programs blank or erase the screen after a given amount of time, usually when you haven't touched the keyboard after several minutes. Pressing any key on the keyboard — even a Shift key — restores the image.

Windows contains its own screen saver. You can find it in the Control Panel, the Desktop item. Other screen blanking software is available as well, including the popular After Dark application. When the screen blanks in After Dark, you may see flying toasters on your screen!

Cleaning your monitor

Nothing attracts more dust than a computer monitor. These things grow dust like a five o'clock shadow. And, in addition to the dust, you always find finger prints and sneeze globs on your screen. Monitors are messy.

To clean your monitor, spray some window cleaner on a soft towel or tissue. Then gently rub the screen. You also can use vinegar if you want your computer to have that fresh salad smell.

Never spray window cleaner directly on the screen. It may dribble down into the monitor itself and wreak electronic terror.

✔ For cleaning the monitor's housing (the nonscreen part), you can use some Formula 409 or Fantastik. Again, spray it on a cloth and wipe the monitor. This also works for cleaning the PC itself if you're in one of those moods.

✔ A fond term for that layer of dust that coats your monitor is *pixel dust*. Ah, computers can be painfully cute at times.

Summary

This chapter took you through the ins and outs of computer monitors:

▶ You learned about the two major components that make it possible for your computer to display images: the monitor and the display adapter.

▶ You reviewed different types of monitors, display adapters, and graphics adapters, and you learned which types are best for which computing tasks.

▶ You learned how to adjust the display on your monitor, how to keep your monitor clean, and how to prevent phosphor burn-in.

In Chapter 10, you learn about another vital part of your computing system: your printer.

Chapter 10
The Printer
(the Paper, the Document Maker)

● ●

● ●

"**S**end this off to the printer," they say.
Then they wink their eye in a mischievous way.
Press Shift-F7 here, and F or 1.
Zip, zippity, zip, and your printing is done.
It's clean and it's quick, but not a memorable trick.
Yet why does it look like the printer is sick?
There are weird funny characters, an @ and a 4.
This doesn't look like it did in the store!
You want hassle-free printing and envelopes to address.
But now you're not printing. Everything is a mess.

So many people worry about making a computer easier to use. But there's this rogue element: the printer, an equally ornery element of all computers, as tough to master as DOS and as fussy as any computer hardware. Your printer is like an unwanted relative: easily ignored most of the time but occasionally stopping by for an annoying visit. Under DOS we're burdened with printers that must be set up with each and every program we own. It's a once-in-awhile hassle. But nothing a few pages of text — or a large caliber weapon — can't solve.

Types of Printers

Forget brand names and all the technical mumblings for a moment. There are two major types of printers: *impact* and *laser* (kind of like two characters you'd see on *American Gladiators*). The difference between the two types of printers is the quality of the image and the price.

Laser printers are more expensive and produce higher-quality text and graphics. Odds are fairly good that if you're in business, you want a laser printer.

Impact printers produce lower-quality images but are relatively inexpensive. They are ideal when quality and speed don't count, such as for the home or in the government or any other large bureaucracy.

- ✔ Impact printers are also called *dot matrix* printers. The name refers to the grid of dots used to create the image. On the really cheap printers this shows up annoyingly well.

- ✔ An older type of impact printer was the *daisy wheel*. This printer is essentially an electronic typewriter, and it produces similar output — but no graphics. The laser printer has replaced the daisy wheel as the printer of choice in business today.

Only a die-hard computer geek would read this

Computer printers are like teenagers' cars: Speed and image are what counts the most. Speed refers to how long it takes the printer to produce its image. Impact printers print one character at a time, so their speed is measured in cps (characters per second). A speed of 80 cps is about middlin', with smaller values indicating slower printers and high values describing printers that would rip a hole in the wall if their little rubber feet weren't securely gripping the table top.

Laser printers print a sheet of paper at a time, so their speed is measured in ppm (pages per minute). A swift laser printer can crank out 8 ppm.

Image is referred to as *letter-quality* among impact printers. They try to approach the quality of a typewritten page but usually fall short. This earns them the moniker *near letter-quality*. Laser printers print much better than letter-quality. Their quality is measured by the number of dots they can laser beam into a linear inch. A laser printer with 300 dpi (dots per inch) is about average, and 600 dpi is possible with the proper hardware and sufficient funds. When you get up to 1,200 dpi, you're approaching the quality of a professional typesetting machine.

The object behind image is to create something that doesn't look as if it was made on a computer. Which makes you wonder why you've spent all that money when a typewriter's output ain't so bad. . . .

✔ Specialty printers abound. One of the most popular is the *ink-jet printer* that actually spits ink onto the page. Contrary to that image in your head right now, the ink-jet printer produces clean, almost laser-printer-quality output. It's slower than a laser printer but much more economical. Also, some ink-jet printers can produce color images.

✔ Doinky little printers are available for laptop computers. They're called *thermal printers* because (like many fax machines) they print with heat on waxy paper. These printers are impractical for anything but portable computing.

The printer produces *hard copy.* That's anything you do on your computer screen that eventually winds up on paper.

What Is a Compatible Printer?

Most of your software — including DOS — prefers certain brand-name printers. They are what we call "the biggies" — IBM, Epson, and Hewlett-Packard. Everything else will work, just as you can put any brand of tire on any car. It's just that the hassle rate rises when you stray from the major names.

The reason these are the biggies is that most of the software out there prefers to work with these printers. With other printers, whether or not software will like them is an iffy situation. Most of the time, as long as you don't buy weird and non-Japanese-sounding printer equipment, you'll be OK. But, if you have one of the three biggies, you're doing OK.

✔ You don't have to buy the same brand of printer as your computer. There are hundreds of different brands of printers. The one best suited to your computer is the one most compatible with your software — not your hardware.

✔ All printers, whether or not they are the biggies, plug into and operate with all PC software. The compatibility issue here describes how much you'll get out of the printer. Fancy printing, including graphics, is a touchy issue. If your software knows about and is willing to cooperate with your brand of printer, that's great. And, if you have one of the three biggies, that's even better.

✔ Even if you don't have a big-name-brand printer, it may still be compatible with an IBM, an Epson, or a Hewlett-Packard printer. Check the manual, where the manufacturer usually boasts about such a feature right up front. It's referred to as *emulation,* which means one printer will behave like, or *emulate,* the features of another. (Emulation has nothing to do with a printer's setting itself on fire.)

✔ Hewlett-Packard is often abbreviated *HP*. IBM is already an abbreviation. And Epson isn't an abbreviation at all, nor is it a type of salt. (Skip this following stuff if you're a busy executive.) The company that makes Epson printers used to make paper tape printers for calculators. The company called its printer the Electrical Printer-1 or EP-1. The second printer was the EP-2. And its first computer printer was the "son" of the EP printer line, hence EPson or Epson. Amaze your friends at the next user group meeting with that piece of trivia. Maybe you'll win the Twinkie.

✔ WordPerfect is the most printer-friendly program. It currently supports more than 800 different brand-name and model printers. Odds are that your printer will work with WordPerfect, which is good for both them and you. Contrast this with the dumb mailing label program one of the authors uses: It works only with IBM and HP printers. Now you know why WordPerfect sells more copies.

✔ Another type of printer compatibility is PostScript. If that concerns you, refer to the section, "What Is PostScript?" later in this chapter.

Setting Up the Printer (Hardware)

This is the easy part: to set up your printer, you plug it into your PC. Specifically, you find a connection called the printer port on the rear of the PC's console. It may be labeled as such or "LPT1." Plug one end of the printer cable into the printer port on the console and then plug the other end into the printer. If you get good at this, you can charge your friends fifty bucks to perform the same feat for them.

Your printer needs to be loaded with paper. For impact printers, this requires either feeding in a continuous sheet of *fanfold paper* or lining up one sheet at a time as you would with a typewriter. Laser printers load up a cartridge of paper at a time, similar to a photocopier.

Impact printers require a ribbon. Loading it will get your hands all smudgy no matter how careful you are. We suggest buying rubber gloves or those cheap plastic gloves that make you look like Batman. Laser printers require drop-in *toner cartridges*. These are easy to install and come with their own handy instructions. Just don't breathe in the toner or you'll die of cancer.

✔ The printer port is also called the *parallel port*. There may be more than one of them, in which case they're referred to as LPT1, LPT2, and so on. If you have more than one, plug your printer into LPT1, the first printer port. A single computer is capable of handling two printers, but you must have a terribly big ego to be that possessive.

✔ Always make sure that you have enough printer paper.

✔ You can buy standard photocopier paper for your laser printer. Special paper is available for a nicer output, but steer clear of the finer, fancier papers and especially of erasable bond. Those papers have talcum powder coatings that come off in your laser printer and gum up the works.

✔ Some ink-jet printers require special paper for the colors to really come through. This paper is horribly expensive, so buy it in bulk.

✔ Fanfold paper is a continuous piece of paper that snakes into an impact printer. This paper must be manually separated after you print on it: tear off each sheet, as well as the "holes" on the sides of the paper. You can't put fanfold paper into a laser printer, but you can sit around all day and argue about what the little holes are called.

✔ Your printer may have a row of tiny switches, called *DIP switches* (named after the French Dip sandwich). Some printers have a front panel with buttons and an LCD display instead of the switches. The object is to configure and control your printer. For example, if your Wannabishi printer can emulate the more popular Hewlett-Packard LaserJet, that's where you'd tell it to do so.

✔ Three important switches on the front of your printer (or on its control panel, wherever that may be) are the On-Line or Select switch, plus the Form Feed and Line Feed switches. The functions of these switches are covered later in this chapter, in the sections "Doing the Line Feed" and "Doing the Form Feed (Ejecting a Page)."

Setting Up the Printer (Software)

Hooking the printer up to the computer is the easy part. The hard part is getting your software to "talk" with the printer. It's the software that tells the printer what to print and how to print it. For that to happen, you must tell the software about the printer.

Telling your software about your printer is usually done during installation. You supply your program with the brand name and model of the printer you're using. This information is saved with the program, and you'll never have to mess with it again. From that point forward, your printer will print the information you expect it to, not counting any hassles required getting it to look "just so."

✔ If you don't see your printer's name listed, then you have two choices. The first is to contact your printer manufacturer to see whether he or she can help. But that requires many years of learning Japanese, and by that time the printer is obsolete anyway. The second option is to use your printer in the dumb mode. In that mode, your printer will print text just fine. But fancy fonts and graphics — forget it. To use the dumb mode, select Generic Printer or Dumb Mode from the list of available printers.

✔ All of the biggies, IBM, Epson, and HP printers, will work with just about anything. Other brand-name printers will be known to a few major applications as well. It's when you get specific that problems arise.

✔ Windows requires you to install your printer only once — when you start. After that, all Windows software runs just fine; you'll never need to mess with printer software setup again. (Windows currently supports more than 250 different makes and models of printer.)

Easy-to-skip cryptic information on printer drivers

The device that controls the printer is called the *printer driver.* That's special software written to communicate between your printer and the program that's being used. Some large-headed computer programmers can write custom printer drivers, and some applications come with programs that enable you to build printer drivers. Under no circumstances should you, a mere mortal, attempt to do this. If it's important enough, pay someone else.

If you do decide to create a printer driver, you'll need your printer's manual, which is conveniently not sold with the printer any more. The manual contains all the printer's control codes and commands. These tell the printer to print in boldface or italics, change fonts, draw graphics, jam the paper, and so on. Creating the printer driver is a matter of filling in the blanks. Personally, I'd rather run through a quilting convention with my hair set on fire than write a printer driver.

Using a Serial Printer

Not all printers plug into the printer port. The exception is the *serial printer,* which, surprisingly enough, plugs into your computer's serial port. If you don't have a serial printer and are smart enough never to buy one, then you can happily skip this section.

Serial printers work just like parallel printers. This still doesn't make them oddballs. DOS, and probably the Lord Himself, intended all PC printers to be of the parallel type. Serial printers can be used but only after some tedium and hassle.

✔ Some serial printers are a dual-mode type. They can be run as a serial printer or as a parallel printer. Unless there's some grave need to run the printer as a serial printer, hook it up as a parallel model.

✔ To use your serial printer with any major application, you must install it as a serial printer. Most programs can handle this, taking care of the fuss by themselves. You'll need to know some technical detail, discussed at the end of this section.

✔ To use your serial printer with DOS, you need to type in two DOS commands. First, configure your serial printer to these settings: 9600 (baud or bps), 8, N, 1. You do this on your printer by throwing tiny switches — or by referring to your guru and asking him or her what the settings are. And, while you're at it, try to get your guru to configure DOS as well. If that fails, type the DOS command that follows:

```
C:\> MODE COM1:9600,N,8,1
```

In other words, type **MODE** (for the MODE command), a space, **COM 1,** a colon, **9600,** a comma, **N,** another comma, **8,** yet another comma, and then **1.**

After your computer swallows that command, type this in:

```
C:\> MODE LPT1 = COM1
```

There. Your printer is set up to be used with DOS and the handful of programs that don't ask for your printer type when they're installed.

✔ If your printer is connected to the second serial port, type **COM2** rather than **COM1.**

✔ Serial printers require special serial cables. These are radically different from the standard serial cable you may use to connect to a modem. When buying a serial printer cable, make sure that it's labeled as such.

✔ Aside from these brain-swelling hassles, using a serial printer under DOS is a charm. *Not.*

Turning the Printer On

Flip the switch.

✔ Always make sure that your printer is on before you start printing. Some programs will inform you of this and urge you to turn the printer on to continue printing. Others will sit and wait. And wait. (Get the picture?)

✔ Your printer doesn't need to be on all the time. Only turn it on whilst you print. When you're done printing, you can turn the printer off. (This is economical for laser printers, which use up to 1,000 watts of electricity when they're on.)

✔ Make sure that your printer is *on-line* or *selected.* Even though your printer is on, it needs to be switched on-line before it prints. A button on the control panel handles this chore; when the light is on, the printer is ready to go.

Easily ignored information on serial settings

Serial ports need special care and attention, which makes them too bothersome for most people. You must make sure that the computer and the printer are on proper speaking terms, which requires the setting of four items — both under DOS and on the printer:

The speed: This refers to how fast the printer and computer talk with each other. Most serial printers talk at 9600 bits per second (bps) or baud.

The word size: Never mind. Set this to 8.

The parity: Ditto, set this to N for No parity.

The stop bits: You need only one stop bit; no sense pushing your luck.

Why the complexities? For the same reason the sky is blue and you can't see into your own ear. Seriously, serial printers can talk at different speeds, which is why everything must be set up this way.

Printing (and Other Routine Hassles)

Printing is handled differently by each DOS program. The end result is always the same: something on paper — hard copy — that somewhat resembles what you wanted in the first place. How you get there depends on which software you're using.

Before printing with software, you can test your printer to make sure that it's working properly. Some printers have a handy test button for this purpose. If you don't want to hunt for it on the printer (or dredge through the manual), then you can do the following steps at the DOS prompt (for information on typing at the DOS prompt, refer to Chapter 13):

1. **Turn your printer on.**

2. **Make sure that your printer is on-line (check for the light).**

3. **Type the following DOS command:**

```
C:\> MEM > PRN
```

In other words, type **MEM** (for the MEM command), a space, the greater-than symbol (above the period on your keyboard), another space, and then **PRN**. Press Enter. If you have an impact printer, you'll see (and hear) something right away. If you have a laser printer, sit and smile.

4. Now type this in:

```
C:\> ECHO THIS PRINTER WORKS! > PRN
```

In other words, type **ECHO THIS PRINTER WORKS!** Follow it with a space, the greater-than sign, another space, and **PRN**. Press Enter.

5. Finally, type this in:

```
C:\> ECHO ^L > PRN
```

Type **ECHO** and a space; then press and hold the Ctrl (Control) key and press **L**. This produces the ^ and L characters on your screen. Then type a space, the greater-than symbol, another space, and then **PRN**. Press Enter. Now your laser printer will print.

Check the output to make sure that it looks OK. Don't expect anything fancy.

> ✔ If you want a real test, load up a software program and print with it. Printing methods for some of the more popular applications are covered in the following subsections. If a program isn't listed, then it probably has some funky method of printing that we ourselves don't know about.

Printing with 1-2-3

Printing can be fearsome in 1-2-3, so bribe someone to write a macro for you. Otherwise, do the following (which 1-2-3 users will understand, but no one else will): Press the forward slash and select the Print command. Then select Printer and press Home, which is on your keyboard. Then type a period, press End, and press Home. Finally, select Align, Go, and then Page.

After the printer spits it out, press Q to quit. This will get the spreadsheet out on your printer. Fancier ways of printing are reserved for those loony enough to learn 1-2-3 all the way through.

Printing with Quattro Pro

Printing in Quattro is insane, like all spreadsheet printing. A lot more is possible than just printing out raw numbers (and it's easier than 1-2-3). But we're not going to bother with the fancy stuff in this book. For now, follow the bouncing cursor. Press the forward slash key, select Print, and then select Block. Press Home, type a period, press End, and then press Home again. Press Enter and then select Spreadsheet-print.

Sometimes printing stops and the page doesn't spit out of the printer. When that happens, press the forward slash key and then select Print, Adjust-printer, and Formfeed, in that order.

Printing with Microsoft Word

This is for the text-based version of Word — the one Microsoft abandoned in favor of Word for Windows. (And do you still think Microsoft is going to keep text-based Word around? Will the Dalai Lama return to Tibet?) Here we go:

Click on the File menu with the mouse and then select the Print menu item. Answer OK when the window pops up.

Some older versions of Word used Ctrl-F8 to print.

Printing with WordPerfect

WordPerfect's soul is printing what you've written. Sometimes it just seems like the soul has gone out for tea with the Antichrist. Nevertheless, until you buy *WordPerfect For Dummies,* print by pressing Shift-F7 and then pressing F.

There. That prints your entire document. To print just a page, press Shift-F7 and then press P.

Enough said.

Printing in Windows

Windows removes most of the pain from using DOS. Printing under Windows, although slower than a frozen pig rolling uphill, is done with the same commands in all programs. With your mouse deftly poised in the proper hand, click on the File menu, click the Print item, and click OK.

This works for all Windows programs that can send something to the printer. Want more information? Yes, we're going to plug *Windows For Dummies* here as well.

Printing on a network

Network printing is simple: Let someone else handle it. As far as you're concerned, the printer just may not be in the same room with you. Everything else, including how you use your programs and all that, works the same.

🖛 Network printing doesn't offer that sense of immediacy that having your own printer brings. Instead of seeing it "right there," you'll have to wait for something called *despooling* to take place. In fact, bring *despooling* home as your new buzzword. When the boss asks you why you're not working, exclaim, "That darn printer is despooling!"

🖛 With some networks you'll have your choice of printer. You can print on a printer nearby or print on Bob's printer across the office. Selecting a printer depends on two things: how close it is and what kind of output you want (because some printers produce better hard copy than others). And, if Bob's been bugging you, it's entirely possible to have his printer spit out "Bob is a dork" eight zillion times.

What Is PostScript?

A *PostScript printer* isn't a name-brand printer. It's more of a type of printer. PostScript printers — no matter who makes them — will work with all applications that support the PostScript printing language. This makes them a universal type of printer.

🖛 PostScript is actually a printing language — like a programming language — that tells the printer exactly what to do, what to print, and how it looks. The printing language can be very precise, which is why many printers support it and most applications will send their output to a PostScript printer.

✔ If your printer supports PostScript, then all you need to do is check your application. If it supports a PostScript printer, then you just set everything up to work with the PostScript printer and you're in business. Kiss those worrisome pains good-bye!

✔ All Apple (Macintosh) laser printers use PostScript. (At least the expensive, good ones do.) If that excites you, rush out right now and buy some Apple stock.

✔ PostScript printers are expensive.

What Are IBM Graphics?

This has absolutely nothing to do with any type of printer. Instead, IBM graphics are those weird characters you may see on your screen. Anything that you can't find on your keyboard is doubtlessly an IBM graphics character. These include foreign characters, ugly symbols, and weird "line drawing" characters. At issue is whether your printer can print those characters. Some can't, and instead of the graphics characters, they print italicized *M*'s, colons, and other unsightly junk.

✔ Some printers, compatible with IBM and Epson printers, will print the IBM graphics characters but only in a secret mode. After you activate that mode, your printer will emulate the IBM printer, producing the graphics.

✔ Life isn't over if your printer can't do IBM graphics. Only a limited number of programs will attempt to print those characters anyway. *All* printers, on the other hand, can print graphics, which is much more important.

The IBM graphics characters are the same *extended ASCII characters* you may hear the Dorito-eaters talk about. These characters are all displayed in Table 10-1. If you see any of these characters on your screen and not on your printer, then you can't print the IBM graphics characters. Do not pass Go; do not collect your quarterly dividend check.

Doing the Line Feed

A *line feed* is the process of advancing a sheet of paper up one line in your printer. It's from the old manual typewriter's line feed bar, which you aggressively whacked to reach the next line down on the page.

Table 10-1   Extended ASCII Codes and Characters

Character Number → 98 corresponds to: Text character set = b, Symbol character set = β, Wingdings character set = 𝒬

Number	Text	Symbol	Wingdings
32			
33	!	!	✎
34	"	∀	✂
35	#	#	✈
36	$	∃	👓
37	%	%	🖐
38	&	&	📖
39	'	∋	✋
40	(	(	☎
41	)	)	○
42	*	∗	✉
43	+	+	☒
44	,	,	✉
45	-	−	✉
46	.	.	✉
47	/	/	✉
48	0	0	□
49	1	1	🗁
50	2	2	🗀
51	3	3	▦
52	4	4	🗎
53	5	5	▤
54	6	6	🗏
55	7	7	🗐
56	8	8	↺
57	9	9	🖳
58	:	:	□
59	;	;	▬
60	<	<	🖮
61	=	=	🖰
62	>	>	⊕
63	?	?	⌨
64	@	≅	🖱
65	A	Α	✂
66	B	Β	✂
67	C	Χ	✂
68	D	Δ	✎
69	E	Ε	☎
70	F	Φ	✒
71	G	Γ	✏
72	H	Η	☎
73	I	Ι	✇
74	J	ϑ	☺
75	K	Κ	☹
76	L	Λ	⊗
77	M	Μ	🖘
78	N	Ν	🖙
79	O	Ο	℞
80	P	Π	🖚
81	Q	Θ	✈
82	R	Ρ	✇
83	S	Σ	✦
84	T	Τ	✺
85	U	Υ	✡
86	V	ς	✢
87	W	Ω	✣
88	X	Ξ	✳
89	Y	Ψ	✇
90	Z	Ζ	☾
91	[	[	●
92	\	∴	❄
93	]	]	✦
94	^	⊥	♈
95	_	_	♉
96	`	(overscore)	♊
97	a	α	♋
98	b	β	♌
99	c	χ	♍
100	d	δ	♎
101	e	ε	♏
102	f	ϕ	♐
103	g	γ	♑
104	h	η	♒
105	i	ι	♓
106	j	φ	☞
107	k	κ	&
108	l	λ	●
109	m	μ	○
110	n	ν	■
111	o	o	□
112	p	π	□
113	q	θ	□
114	r	ρ	□
115	s	σ	◆
116	t	τ	◆
117	u	υ	◆
118	v	ϖ	◆
119	w	ω	◆
120	x	ξ	⌧
121	y	ψ	✍
122	z	ζ	✼
123	{	{	⊕
124					●
125	}	}	✦
126	~	∼	"
127			⌂
0128			⓪
0129			①
0130	,		②
0131	ƒ		③
0132	„		④
0133	…		⑤
0134	†		⑥
0135	‡		⑦
0136	ˆ		⑧
0137	‰		⑨
0138	Š		⑩
0139	‹		⓿
0140	Œ		❶
0141			❷
0142			❸
0143			❹
0144			❺
0145	'		❻
0146	'		❼
0147	"		❽
0148	"		❾
0149	•		❿
0150	—		▪
0151	–		▪
0152	˜		▪
0153	™		▪
0154	š		▪
0155	›		▪
0156	œ		▪
0157			▪
0158			▪
0159	Ÿ		▪
0160			
0161	¡	Υ	○
0162	¢	′	○
0163	£	≤	○
0164	¤	⁄	○
0165	¥	∞	●
0166	¦	ƒ	○
0167	§	♣	▪
0168	¨	♦	□
0169	©	♥	▲
0170	ª	♠	+
0171	«	↔	★
0172	¬	←	✱
0173	-	↑	✦
0174	®	→	●
0175	¯	↓	●
0176	°	°	⊕
0177	±	±	+
0178	²	″	✦
0179	³	≥	¤
0180	´	×	◆
0181	µ	∝	○
0182	¶	∂	★
0183	·	•	○
0184	¸	÷	○
0185	¹	≠	○
0186	º	≡	○
0187	»	≈	○
0188	¼	…	○
0189	½	│	○
0190	¾	—	○
0191	¿	↵	○
0192	À	ℵ	○
0193	Á	ℑ	○
0194	Â	ℜ	○
0195	Ã	℘	♪
0196	Ä	⊗	♫
0197	Å	⊕	✦
0198	Æ	∅	✧
0199	Ç	∩	✎
0200	È	∪	♪
0201	É	⊃	♦
0202	Ê	⊇	♫
0203	Ë	⊄	✗
0204	Ì	⊂	▨
0205	Í	⊆	ß
0206	Î	∈	☒
0207	Ï	∉	☒
0208	Ð	∠	♪
0209	Ñ	∇	☺
0210	Ò	®	✧
0211	Ó	©	✦
0212	Ô	™	☒
0213	Õ	∏	☒
0214	Ö	√	☒
0215	×	⋅	◄
0216	Ø	¬	►
0217	Ù	∧	▲
0218	Ú	∨	▼
0219	Û	⇔	◄
0220	Ü	⇐	⊃
0221	Ý	⇑	○
0222	Þ	⇒	⇒
0223	ß	⇓	←
0224	à	◊	→
0225	á	〈	↑
0226	â	®	↓
0227	ã	©	↘
0228	ä	™	↗
0229	å	∑	↙
0230	æ	(	↲
0231	ç	⎛	←
0232	è	⎜	↑
0233	é	⎡	↑
0234	ê	⎢	↓
0235	ë	⎣	↘
0236	ì	⎧	↙
0237	í	⎨	↖
0238	î	⎩	↗
0239	ï	⎪	↔
0240	ð	◊	↔
0241	ñ	〉	⇑
0242	ò	∫	⇓
0243	ó	⌠	⇔
0244	ô	⎮	⇕
0245	õ	⌡	⤴
0246	ö	⎞	⤵
0247	÷	⎟	↵
0248	ø	⎤	⤶
0249	ù	⎥	□
0250	ú	⎦	□
0251	û	⎫	✗
0252	ü	⎬	✓
0253	ý	⎭	☒
0254	þ	⎪	✓
0255	ÿ	▯	■

A line feed is done in two steps on most printers:

1. **Take the printer off-line: Press the On-Line or Select button so that the little light goes out. This tells the printer to ignore the computer without turning the printer off.**

2. **Press the Line Feed button on the printer.**

With an impact printer, you'll see the paper jump up a line, one line for every press of the Line Feed button. Laser printers don't show any visible effect; however, "inside" the paper is moved up a line (shhh!).

✔ When you're done, remember to press the On-Line button again so that the computer can print once more.

✔ What good is the line feed? No good on a laser printer. On an impact printer, where you can see what you're printing, line feeds are good for adjusting the paper inside the printer, as well as poking the paper up a bit so that you can see what you've been typing.

Doing the Form Feed (Ejecting a Page)

A *form feed* is the process of spitting a page — or the rest of a page — out of the printer. This is done for an obvious reason: to see what you've printed.

To make the printer eject a page (a form feed), take the following two steps:

1. **Press the printer's On-Line or Select button. The little light will go out, which puts the printer into its "command mode."**

2. **Press the Form Feed button on the printer. This may also be labeled "Eject."**

With an impact printer, one whole sheet of paper will pop out. On a laser printer, the printer will warp up to speed, drag in a piece of paper, print on it, and then slide it back out.

✔ Remember to press the On-Line button after you're done. The computer won't talk to the printer until it's on-line again.

✔ Doing the form-feed is the only way to see what you've printed in a laser printer. Laser printers do not print until you either print an entire page or give the printer the form feed command.

✔ Form-feeding paper also gives you a blank sheet of paper if you need one.

Diabolical and nerdy ways to pull a form feed

Form feeds are important for laser printers; you can't see the hard copy without one. When paper stubbornly sits in your printer without printing, press the Form Feed button. Better still, type the following at the DOS prompt:

```
C:\> ECHO ^L > PRN
```

Type **ECHO** and a space; then press and hold the Ctrl (Control) key and press L. That produces the ^ and L characters on your screen (so don't type ^ and L). That's followed by a space, the greater-than symbol, another space, and then **PRN**. Press Enter to send the contraption to the printer. Your page will eject shortly.

What you're doing is sending the character Control-L to the printer. That's the universal "page eject" command for all printers. This can be done without the hassle of taking the printer off-line, standing up, walking around, and other stuff that — for a computer user — too closely resembles exercise.

* *

Summary

This chapter told you how to make your printer work for you and how to avoid some common printer hassles:

▶ You learned about different types of printers and how to tell which ones are compatible with your hardware and software.

▶ You found out that although it's easy to hook a printer up to your computer, getting the software to "talk" with the printer is more difficult.

▶ You learned some tricks for making a serial printer work and what settings to use for a serial printer.

▶ You found out how to print in DOS and how much easier it is to print in Windows. You also learned how to print when you are running 1-2-3, Quattro Pro, Microsoft Word, and WordPerfect in DOS.

▶ You learned how and why to use line feed and form feed and why form feeds are important for laser printers.

In the following chapter you find out about all the gizmos that can make your computer more fun, more useful, or both.

* *

Chapter 11

Peripherals
(Just Hanging Around)

*M*ost parts of an IBM-compatible computer are pretty boring: a monitor, a big box, and a keyboard. The fun stuff comes with computer peripherals: gizmos you can add to your computer to make it more useful or more fun. And certainly more expensive.

Some peripherals plug into your computer with a cable; others fit right inside your computer itself. In fact, about a third of your computer's console box consists of empty space, or "slots," for people to slide in their own goodies (which come on "cards"). Slots and cards. It sounds a lot like Vegas.

If you play your cards right, your PC can become a fax machine, jukebox, video arcade system, or all three (even at the same time). This chapter takes a look at some of the more popular peripherals that attach to a PC: a mouse, a fax/modem card, joysticks, scanners, and other fun toys. (Oh, your printer could be considered a peripheral, too, but that's covered in Chapter 10.)

Messing with the Mouse

Almost every brand of computer comes with its own mouse, but IBM waited several years before it finally gave in to the trend. A mouse was simply too much fun to be associated with a serious business machine. Today, however, nearly everybody has a little plastic rodent running around on the desk.

Actually, a mouse looks like a bar of soap with a large, rolling ball embedded in its underside. On the top, you'll find at least two push-buttons. A tail, or cord, runs from the mouse into the back of your PC. Figure 11-1 shows a typical mouse.

When you move your mouse, it sends a signal through its tail to the computer, telling the computer which direction the mouse is moving. This controls the movement of a small arrow on the screen: When you move the mouse to the left, the arrow on the screen moves to the left, too. In fact, the only time the arrow doesn't move in the same direction as the mouse is when you lift the thing up in the air. The arrow just stays put, wondering what you're doing.

A mouse is not only fun, but it's useful, too. For instance, you can move the mouse until its arrow rests over a word you've misspelled in a letter. Then, when you click a button, the word processor's cursor will jump to that word. This can be much quicker than tapping on the cursor keys to move the cursor, line by line, character by character.

The mouse buttons can do more than move the cursor around. For instance, some programs will place a picture of something on the screen. The something displays a message, saying, "Push me to check the spelling in your document." Move the mouse until the arrow points to that something and then click the mouse's button. The program acts as if you've pushed a "button" on the screen, and it will start chastising you for your louzy speling.

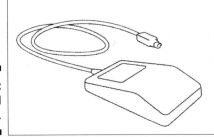

Figure 11-1:
A typical
mouse.

Using a mouse can be not only quicker than typing program names at a DOS prompt, but also a lot more fun. After using a mouse for the first time, you'll want to move it in wild circles on your desk so that you can watch the spirals on the screen. This urge takes a long time to wear off (if it ever does).

- A computer mouse doesn't come with a PC for a reason: Only a few programs use them. DOS doesn't. But Windows does. WordPerfect and other programs enable you to use a mouse, but they're not as dependent on the furless rodents as Windows.

- If you have more than one mouse, you have mice, not mouses.

- A mouse comes with its own software, but that won't do anything by itself. It merely places information about the mouse's geographic location in a special place in your computer's memory. Then any software you run will look at that location to figure out where the mouse happens to be at that particular time. This software, called a *driver,* needs to be in either your AUTOEXEC.BAT or CONFIG.SYS file. For more information about these two bothersome files, see your guru.

- You need to designate a special "mouse area" on your desk and keep it clear of desk debris so that you'll have room to move the mouse around. Clean off an area a little smaller than the size of your monitor's display because that's roughly how far you'll be rolling the mouse around.

- A mouse works best when moved across a *mouse pad,* which is a small piece of plastic or rubber that sits on your desk. The mouse pad provides more traction than your slippery desktop, so the mouse's movements are more accurate. (Also, it reminds you to keep that area of your desk clean.)

Which is best: a bus mouse or a serial mouse?

A bus mouse and a serial mouse look identical, and they both work in the same way: An electronic signal from the mouse flows into your computer through its tail. The difference is the way the tail plugs into the back of your computer.

The tail from a serial mouse plugs into your computer's serial port. Your computer probably came with at least one serial port already installed, typically called COM1.

The tail from a bus mouse plugs into a special card that plugs into a slot in your computer's expansion bus. You install the special card by taking the case off your computer and fiddling around, a process best left to professional fiddlers.

Which mouse is better? Well, because they both work the same way, it doesn't really matter. If you have a serial port already installed and ready to use, buy a serial mouse. That way you can plug in the cord yourself and get right to work.

If you don't have a spare serial port, buy a bus mouse and a jumbo bag of Doritos to bribe a computer guru to install it for you.

> ✔ The best mouse pads have a rough surface, which the mouse can really grip. Poorly designed mouse pads are slick and should be avoided. Also, it's a status symbol to have something cool on your mouse pad: your PC's logo, a photo of your favorite movie star, or a fractal pattern. Uncool mouse pads have the names of computer stores on them or pictures of cats.

Using a Mouse

When holding a live mouse, you'll keep it in your palm, but with the palm up. A mechanical mouse is held against the desktop with your palm down; its tail extends away from your hand, heading toward the back of your computer.

Most people hold the mouse cradled in their palm with their thumb against the left edge and their ring finger against the right edge. The index finger and middle finger can then hover over the buttons along the top. (If this were medieval times, the mouse would be a fist weapon, not a finger weapon.)

> ✔ Computer nerds grab potato chips with the middle finger and thumb of their right hand. That way their index finger won't get greasy stuff on the mouse button.

> ✔ Left-handed mice are the same as right-handed mice. It's only a matter for your software program to create the difference.

> ✔ The buttons need to be tapped only lightly, which is why you can rest your fingers on them at an angle.

> ✔ When the mouse cord becomes tangled, raise the mouse in your hand and whip it about violently.

Examining the mouse button

This is a little push-button switch on top of the mouse. It makes a clicking noise when you push it. All mice have at least two buttons; some mice have three buttons for good measure. (Some macho mice have 20 or more buttons, but those are for the seriously computer mental.)

Regardless of how many buttons your mouse has, you'll use the button on the left about 90 percent of the time. The left button falls naturally under your index finger when you hold it with your right hand, so it's easily available. (Can you believe it? A computer concept that actually makes sense!)

✔ When a software manual tells you to "push the mouse button," it's referring to the left mouse button. This is also known as "clicking the mouse
   button."

✔ When the manual tells you to "drag" with the mouse, you push and hold
   down the button, roll the mouse around (the dragging part) and then
   release the button.

✔ A "double-click" consists of two quick clicks of the mouse button in a row.
   It must be made on the same spot; you cannot roll the mouse around and
   do a double-click.

Examining the mouse pointer

The little arrow that appears on the screen is called the _mouse pointer_ or _mouse
cursor_. Its job is to move on the screen in the same manner as the mouse moves
on your desktop.

When your mouse pointer disappears, roll your mouse in wild circles across
your desktop; this usually brings it out from its hiding place, whether it was
lurking off-screen someplace or lost in a sea of text.

✔ If your mouse pointer doesn't appear when you first start a program, see
   Chapter 20.

✔ The pointer never appears when you're at the DOS prompt, so don't think
   your mouse is broken (at least, not yet).

Clicking the mouse

Now don't go calling the SPCA. We're talking about computer mice here —
electronic devices you're supposed to handle and "click" on.

When you push the button on your mouse, it makes a clicking noise. So most
programs tell you to "click" your mouse button when they really mean for you
to press the mouse button.

✔ When clicking the button, push it down once and release it. Don't hold it
   down continuously. (Actually, it makes two clicks — one when pushed,
   and another when released. Is your hearing that good?)

✔ If your program says to "click on the Eject option," move the mouse until
   the pointer on the screen rests on (or hovers over) the box or button that
   says Eject. Then click the button on your mouse. This tells the program to
   activate that Eject option.

Double-clicking the mouse

Pushing a mouse button once and releasing it is called *clicking*. If you click the button twice in rapid succession, you're *double-clicking*. Software programs treat clicking and double-clicking as two separate entities.

> ✔ Click, click. Or, if your ears can hear two clicks, then it's click (click), click (click). Here a click. There a click. Everywhere a click-click. Old MacDonald had a PC, IEEE I/O. (Nerd humor.)

If you double-click your mouse and nothing happens, you may not be clicking fast enough. Try clicking it as fast as you can. If this speed is uncomfortable for you, most software lets you adjust the double-click rate so that you don't have to click so fast.

Dragging the mouse

You scream in horror as the manual says, "Drag your mouse around the desktop." Yet you're a persistent user. So you go into li'l Billy's room, pluck Mickey out of his tank, walk over to the kitchen table, and . . .

To *drag* means to hold the mouse's button down while moving the mouse around. You do this to move objects around on-screen. In some programs, you can position the mouse pointer over an item, hold down the button, and move the mouse to place that item in a different location. This makes sense when you do it but not when you read about it.

> ✔ To drag, press and hold the mouse button, move the mouse, and then release the mouse button. This works like a tiny claw under the mouse cursor on the screen; you pick up, move, and then drop various items.

Selecting with the mouse

To select an item means to "highlight" it or mark it as the target for action. For instance, you click the mouse on a file and its name becomes selected. This is usually shown as highlighted text — white on black or inverse graphics.

Selecting is the same as clicking. When the manual says to "select that doohickey over there," you move the mouse pointer and click on the doohickey. Simple.

Mouse hygiene: cleaning your mouse ball

Your desk constantly collects a layer of dust and hair, especially if you have a cat around. If your mouse isn't behaving the way it used to, you may need to clean its ball. It's easy; there's no need for the repair shop or a guy in a van.

Turn the mouse upside down, and you'll see a little round plate holding the ball in place. Push or twist the plate in the direction of the arrow that says "open." The plate should come off, and the ball will fall out.

Pull out any hair or debris from the mouse-ball hole and brush any stray viscera off the ball itself. Put the ball back inside, reattach the plate, and you'll be on your way.

Try to keep the mouse pad clean as well: brush it off occasionally to clear away the potato chips, drool, and other debris that accumulate there.

Knowing the differences between a mouse and a mousse!

A *mouse* is either a furry little rodent — like Mickey — or a handy peripheral for your PC. A *mousse*, on the other hand, is either this stupid French dessert that pretends to be pudding or something people put on their hair to make it look messed up. Know which is which before you buy.

Rolling the Trackball: The Upside-Down Mouse

The concept of a mouse is great; it makes it easy to control what's on your screen. In practice, however, it's sometimes a bother. The mouse's cord can get hung up on obstructions, and sometimes there's simply not enough room on your desktop for the mouse to roll around. (If that's true, it's time to call the clutter police.)

So some smart designer turned a mouse upside down. Instead of rolling the mouse around, you use your thumb or index finger to roll the ball itself. The whole contraption stays stationary, so it doesn't use up nearly as much room. A trackball has buttons, just like a mouse. In fact, your software won't know whether you're using a mouse or a trackball.

- Trackballs work great on laptops, so you don't have to use the leg of the guy next to you when you're laptopping on the plane.

- You can't just turn your mouse upside down to make it a trackball. You'll have to buy one.

- Some people clip a laptop's trackball onto the keyboard of their desktop machine; it doesn't use any desktop space at all. Plus, they can just clip it onto their laptop when they want to hit the road; that way they have to buy only one trackball.

- Trackballs are more expensive than mice. They seem to work best in graphic arts environments (because artists probably can't type anyway). Some people really hate them.

Introducing the Cool, New Cordless Mice

The latest rage in mice-ware is a *cordless mouse*. Instead of sending the signal down the tail to the computer, the mouse sends it through the air, using either radio waves or infrared technology. The mouse of the 21st century has arrived!

In either case, the cordless mouse sends the signal to a small "receiving unit." The receiving unit relays the signals down a cord that plugs into the back of your computer. (I can hear it now: "Mickey Niner to base, Mickey Niner to base! Bogey at three o'clock! Prepare to release mouse button." Kachinka!)

A radio-controlled cordless mouse usually costs more than an infrared cordless mouse, and both types cost more than their tailed counterparts.

- The receiving unit for a radio-controlled cordless mouse can be anywhere within a six-foot radius of the mouse. The receiving unit for an infrared mouse can be up to six feet away too, but it must be within a direct line of sight. (The radio signal can transmit through objects; the infrared light can't.)

- Both types of cordless mice need batteries. Be sure to keep a spare set around so that you can still work when they fail at a crucial moment.

- If your infrared cordless mouse starts acting strangely, you've probably set something in front of its receiving unit. It's easy to do because that "line of sight" area will be the only clean spot on your desk.

- This is for J. Fred Niedermeyer of New Brunswick, Rhode Island: No, Fred, you can't use your TV remote control when the infrared mouse fails. And it's not the mouse that keeps changing the channel to *Gilligan's Island*. I'd call the cable company if I were you.

Communicating with a Modem

Modems have been around for years, but they've only now received big-time ad campaigns. You may have seen glossy magazine ads or TV commercials for Prodigy, for instance. (Does "Ya gotta get this thing" sound familiar?) To use Prodigy, or services like it, you need to connect a modem to your computer.

A modem serves as a "translator" between two computers. It's a little box that takes a PC's digital language and converts it into sounds that can be sent over the phone line. A modem on the other end of the phone line translates the incoming sounds back into digital language so that the receiving computer can understand it.

✔ By itself, a modem can't do much. You need special communications software to tell the modem when to start talking. Luckily, some cheap communications software usually comes packaged in the box with the modem.

✔ Most modems have two phone jacks built into them. A standard phone cord connects between the phone jack in your wall and the modem jack marked "Line." Plug your telephone into the modem's second phone jack, just as if you were plugging it into the wall. (That way you can still use your telephone when your computer's not talking to its friends.)

✔ Computer nerds say that the box is modulating and demodulating the computer's signal, so they call it a modem (pronounced "ya gotta get some mo' dem things").

✔ You can't use your phone while your modem is using it to transmit information. In fact, if somebody picks up another extension on that line, it will garble the signal, possibly losing your connection.

✔ Modems and communications software can be very complicated and cryptic until they're set up just right. You need to worry about things like modem speed (measured in bits per second, or bps), parity, stop bits, and all sorts of other gobbledygook. Bribe a computer guru to hook yours up for you and set it up right. After it has been tweaked in just the right way, a modem is easy to use.

✔ Just like mice, modems come in serial and bus versions. But this time they're called *internal* and *external* versions. If you're worried about the differences, read the following box. Otherwise, tighten your shoelaces and move on.

Which is the best modem, internal or external?

Modems come in two breeds: One fits inside your computer (known as *internal*), and the other is a box that sits outside your computer (*external*). They both work in exactly the same way; the external modem just has a little plastic box housing the mechanism.

An internal modem is cheaper. It comes on a card that plugs into a slot inside your computer. Refer to "Playing Cards on the Expansion Bus" later in this chapter. The back of the card is visible at the back of your computer; that's where its phone jacks are.

An external modem costs more because you have to pay for its little plastic box. You'll also have to buy a serial cable to connect it to your serial port, just as with a serial mouse. (That can be a problem: If you have only one serial port, you can't have a mouse and a modem plugged in at the same time.)

Although external modems cost a little more and take up shelf space near your computer, they have several advantages:

First, they have a little row of lights along the front that correspond to the action. A light goes on when the modem's connected to another computer, for example. Other lights convey similar informational tidbits.

Second, external modems have a better speaker. You can listen when the modem dials, and you can hear if you have a busy signal. (This comes in handy when setting the modem on autodial to win radio station giveaways). Also, because the external modem sits on a shelf, it's easier to reach its volume control knob. With an internal speaker, you must ferret around for a small switch hidden beneath the mass of cables behind your computer.

Third, external modems are more transportable. They're easier to take to the repair shop, for instance. You can also use them with other computers or take them to a friend's house. (This is a serious step toward computer nerd-dom, however.)

Using a modem

Most people use their modems for two things: calling on-line services and calling local bulletin boards.

On-line services: An on-line service is a huge computer that's hooked up to a whole bunch of modems. When you tell your computer to call the on-line service, your modem dials the number and connects with the other computer's modem; then the other computer starts filling your screen with information. From your end, an on-line service looks like any other software program. But, although most programs make you feed *them* information, the on-line service sends *you* information.

His modem modulates and demodulates faster than my modem!

Just as some computers are faster than others, some modems are faster than others. But all modems are relatively compatible: The fastest modems can still talk to the slower ones.

Modem speed is measured in bits per second, or how many bits they can toss across the phone line in one second. (Some people use the word *baud* to describe modem speed. That's inaccurate, and they should be saying *bps*. Correct them enthusiastically if you want to sound like a nerd.)

For more information on modem speeds, see Table 11-1.

On-line services offer hundreds of reference materials, like news, weather, stock reports, encyclopedias, and forums. Forums are places where people gather to send messages to one another about their interests. They are somewhat like a bathroom wall. One person will type in a message; another person will read it and respond, another responds to the response, and pretty soon it turns into a worldwide conversation.

You're paying for the fellowship, however; charges appear on your credit card. On-line services charge their subscribers anything from $5 per month to $20 per hour.

BBS: Short for bulletin board service, a BBS can be considered a tiny on-line service. It's usually a PC some hobbyist has connected to a modem in his or her living room. Most BBSs offer forums, just like the commercial on-line services, but they don't charge anything for access.

Table 11-1	Modem Speeds
Speed	**Helpful Information**
300 bps	This is one of the first modem speeds; it has become a "standard." Almost all modems can communicate at this snail's pace.
1200 bps	Although this speed is four times as fast as 300 bps modem speed, it is still regarded as too slow by today's standards. (That tells you how slow 300 bps modems are.) The Prodigy on-line service works very slowly at this speed.
2400 bps	This is the current standard; this speed is currently most popular.
4800 bps	This speed never really caught on; some slow fax machines use it.
9600 bps	These guys can really jam; they're four times as speedy as the previous standard. Several on-line services, including Prodigy, America Online, and CompuServe, let people call at this speed.

(continued)

Table 11-1 *(continued)*

Speed	Helpful Information
14.4 kbps (14400 bps)	The fastest modem standard today, it's not yet as well supported as the 9600 bps modems. Buying a 14.4 bps modem is like buying a 165 mile per hour Porsche — and having to drive it at 55 miles per hour until you find the right freeways.
19.6 kbps (19600 bps)	A few modems can speak this quickly, but only to each other. It's a proprietary standard, which means that you can only call other 19.6 kbps modems made by the same manufacturer. That's like not being able to take your Porsche out of Germany.
28.800 kbps (28800 bps)	By the time this book is printed, this new standard, sometimes known as V.Fast should be an approved standard. This is an international standard, so you will soon see lots of modems that have this feature.

Using fax/modems

The latest rage, these modems can send and receive information from fax machines, as well as from other computers. You tell the software what file you want to send, along with the fax machine's phone number. The software converts the file into a graphic image and passes it to the fax/modem, which calls up the fax machine and sends the picture over to the fax machine.

You can receive faxes, too. Your fax/modem will answer the phone when a fax machine calls. It will receive the transmission and store the picture on your hard drive for later viewing. If you want to keep the fax, send it to your printer. If not, delete it.

✔ Faxes are graphic images: They're pictures of pieces of paper. When you receive a fax of a letter, you won't be able to put that letter into your word processing program unless you have special OCR, or Optical Character Recognition, software. That's pretty expensive and complicated stuff.

✔ Unless you have a scanner, you'll be very limited in what you can send with your fax/modem. You won't be able to sign your letters, for instance. (Scanners are covered in the next section.)

✔ If you're serious about faxes, hook your fax/modem up to its own phone line so it can receive faxes all the time. It's a drag to pick up your phone at 3 a.m. only to hear the whine of a fax machine on the other end.

✔ If you don't have a scanner, sign a piece of paper and have somebody fax it to your fax card. Then, when you're viewing that fax on your screen, use a graphics program to "grab" your signature. Save it to a file for future faxes where you need a signature.

Scanning with a Scanner

A scanner works like a photocopier. But instead of producing a duplicate of a sheet of paper, the scanner converts the image to numbers and stores it on a disk. This has two very useful purposes. The first is to scan graphic images for inclusion in documents and for desktop publishing. The second is that software can "read" documents, converting the image into text for input in the computer. This is truly amazing stuff.

Scanners come in two basic styles: *handheld* and *desktop*.

A *handheld scanner* looks like a miniature vacuum cleaner. You slide the scanner across a picture, and the picture appears on your screen. After it's on the screen, it can be dropped into party fliers, faxes, newsletters, books, or any other printed material.

Larger scanners, known as *flat-bed* or *desktop scanners,* work more like copiers. You place the paper on top of the scanner, close the lid, and push a button, and the image appears on your screen, ready to be saved to disk.

- ✔ Handheld scanners work best for importing small images: logos, signatures, or small pictures.

- ✔ If you don't move your hand smoothly while sliding the scanner over the image, the resulting picture will look weird.

- ✔ Desktop scanners can import images more clearly and much more expensively.

- ✔ All scanners come with special cards; you won't find any serial port scanners. Bribe a guru to do the dirty installation work.

Reading in text with a scanner isn't as easy as it sounds. Scanners understand only the image they scan. To convert that image into text, you need special software called *Optical Character Reading (OCR)* software. Even then, the software can read only certain types of characters. Although OCR software is getting better — it's even tossed in with most fax software to read text from incoming faxes — be sure to run your spell checker afterward.

Playing Cards on the Expansion Bus

The designers of the IBM PC didn't want their machine to end up in the thrift shops after a few years. To ensure a long lifetime, they made the PC expandable by creating a method of upgrading each PC, customizing it with special features.

The way to upgrade a PC is to plug those extra options into special slots in the back of the console. The slots are called the *expansion bus*. (This is not the same type of bus you see on the street with one of those accordion-like things in the middle.)

An expansion bus has anywhere from 3 to 12 slots into which you can plug special expansion cards. If you look behind your computer, you'll see a bunch of cables protruding from its back. These cables all plug into cards that have been slipped into the expansion bus.

For instance, both a bus mouse and an internal modem come with cards, ready to be snuggled into any available slots. Sound cards come on a card; so do game cards with their joystick port.

✔ Installing a card is relatively simple, so have a relative who knows something about computers do it for you.

✔ The variety of cards available is seemingly endless. Some of the standard items come on cards: the video adapter, printer and serial ports, joysticks, modems, and so on. But there are some incredible, creative expansion cards that you can get for your computer. Visit your local computer hardware store or browse the many techno-nerdy magazines to see what's out there.

The great majority of computers use an *ISA* bus. Because almost every card for sale at the computer store is an ISA card, there's usually no problem. If you have an IBM PS/2, however, you probably have an *MCA* bus: Those computers require special MCA cards, and the plain old ISA cards don't work.

If you bought one of those expensive computers with an EISA bus, you can buy expensive EISA cards or those cheap ISA cards everybody else uses. EISA computers can use both. (EISA computers cannot use MCA cards, though. Go figure.)

Making Your PC Sing

IBM and compatible computers have always treated sound as something to be avoided. The computer beeps rudely when you've pressed the wrong button or when your spreadsheet figures don't add up. The PC's tiny speaker can barely be heard; there's not even a way to adjust the volume. Luckily, a few companies began creating *sound cards,* mostly so game players could hear music and antediluvian space grunts.

Today, sound cards have become one of the most trendy add-ons in the IBM computer world. People say they're buying them for business presentations and educational uses, but that really means they want to hear the sound of a club swinging in Accolade's new Jack Nicklaus golf game.

✔ For you to hear the sound of a golf club swinging, your sound card must be capable of playing *digital audio.* Digital audio is a sound that's been examined by a computer, translated into a string of numbers, and stored to disk. For example, your compact discs contain digital audio.

✔ Most sound cards can synthesize music, as well. When a sound card plays music, it's usually using its own built-in synthesizer, just as if it were an electric organ. Instead of playing back actual digital sounds, the sound card just generates musical tones on the fly.

✔ Sound cards don't come as a complete package. To hear them, you'll need speakers or some cables to connect the sound card's output into your home stereo. If you want to record sounds, you'll need to buy a microphone. Plus you'll need cables to hook up a small radio to the auxiliary port if you want to hear music in the background.

✔ Two standards dominate the sound card market: AdLib leads the synthesized sound/music market, and Sound Blaster leads the digital sound market. Make sure that your sound card is compatible with AdLib and Sound Blaster, or most software won't recognize it.

✔ Even if your CD-ROM drive can play digital sound, you'll probably need a sound card too. When your CD-ROM drive is playing back digital sound, it's very busy — much too busy to access any other data on the disk. So companies usually store the sounds on the CD-ROM drive but route them through a sound card so that the CD-ROM won't be tied up.

✔ If you put speakers on your desk, remember that they contain magnets. If any stray floppy disks come too close, they may lose their data.

✔ Digital sound takes up huge amounts of room on a disk. That's why most digitized sounds are limited to short bursts like golf swings and grunts.

Playing Games with Joysticks

Joysticks get no respect in the computer world. IBM released some joystick specifications in volume two of its reference manual for the PC XT, and that antique joystick had only one button. Manufacturers have had to group together to find some sort of standard.

✔ IBM was very sneaky when it designed its first joystick expansion card. It referred to the card as an *analog to digital* card and mumbled something about scientific experimentation. Yeah. Meanwhile, all those guys in white lab coats were busy killing aliens.

- A joystick from an Atari or Commodore computer won't work on an IBM computer. They use a different format for transmitting data. (They use different plugs, too.)

- A joystick from an Apple computer *will* work on an IBM computer, however. It's rated slightly differently, though, so it won't work quite as well.

- In order to use a joystick, you need a *joystick port,* usually called a *game port.* These ports come on expansion cards and plug into expansion slots.

- Luckily, most sound cards come with a built-in game port, so you don't have to buy a separate game card.

- A joystick port is about half the size of a parallel port and a little bigger than those tiny serial ports and the VGA port. This is handy: You will never try to plug a joystick into anything other than a joystick port.

- Some expansion cards geared toward the game player have two ports on the end — one for each joystick. Others have only one port. You can plug two joysticks into a single game port by using a *Y adapter,* available at most computer stores. Don't try installing a second game card to get a second port; that will only confuse the computer.

- If your game allows it, be sure to calibrate your joystick before playing. All joysticks are slightly different, and the game must be customized to each joystick's individual quirks.

Do I *really* care about the mechanics of a joystick?

Each joystick contains two gizmos called *potentiometers.* By turning the knob on the potentiometer, you vary the flow of electricity running through it. (It's just like those fancy adjustable light switches people put in their dining rooms.)

When the joystick moves from right to left, it turns the knob of one potentiometer; when it goes up and down, it turns the knob of the other. When it moves in angles, it moves both potentiometers. The game card reads the electricity levels being sent down the cord by each potentiometer, so it can tell which way the joystick's being moved.

Amiga and Atari joysticks are digital: They contain little on/off switches instead of potentiometers. That's why those joysticks can move on-screen characters in only eight different directions. Because IBM joysticks measure subtle variations in electricity flow, they can move in infinite directions.

The problem came when computers began to run much faster. Game designers didn't take this into account, and the extra speed threw off the joystick's calibration. The newer games use better programming techniques to avoid this problem. If it bothers you, consider buying a fancy *adjustable calibration* game card. It has a little knob you can turn until the joystick works the best with each particular game.

Can I Play Led Zepplin on a CD-ROM Drive?

As stereos become more computerized, computers become more like stereos. In fact, computers now can read information stored on compact discs, or CDs — the same discs you've bought at the record store for years. A compact disc stores music in the form of numbers, making it a perfect match for the computer.

Unfortunately, you can't hook up your stereo's CD player to your computer. No, the computer industry says you must buy another CD player, called a *CD-ROM drive*. This works almost identically to the one on your stereo but costs a lot more.

- ✔ Some CD-ROM drives fit in your computer like a regular floppy disk drive. You push a button, and a caddy emerges. You set your disc on the caddy and push it back in. Your computer can then read the information stored on the disc.

- ✔ A compact disc can hold a *lot* of information, or about 600 megabytes. That's the equivalent of 1,800 360K floppy disks. Because they can store so much information, compact discs usually contain entire encyclopedias, as well as sounds and pictures (two notorious space hogs).

- ✔ You can only read information from a compact disc; you can't write information to it.

- ✔ Although you can't use your stereo's CD player with your computer, you can use some CD-ROM drives with your stereo. You need a few extra cables. Before you buy, check with the salesperson; not all CD-ROM drives let you listen to Led Zepplin while you compute.

Each compact disc manufacturer thought that it had discovered the best way to store information on a compact disc, so today's compact discs are stuffed with information in several incompatible ways. The solution? CD-ROM drive manufacturers try to make their drives support *all* the standards out there. Table 11-2 gives you a rundown of the weird words you might see. The more weird words your drive can support, the better.

Table 11-2	CD-ROM Acronyms
Acronym	*Meaning*
MPC	Defines compact disc drives that can handle designated "Multimedia" discs, complete with pictures and sound. The MPC label is pretty easy to earn, however; most drives say MPC or MPC-2 — the latest version — somewhere on the box, thank goodness.
CD-I	Short for CD-Interactive and an important standard for both data and hardware. Make sure that your drive supports CD-I.

(continued)

Table 11-2 *(continued)*	
Acronym	*Meaning*
ISO-9660/	Almost all CDs adhere to this standard.
High Sierra	Basically, it means that they store their information in ways that DOS computers can recognize.
Kodak Photo CD	Why stick with 8-by-10 glossies? Some photo developers can store your pictures on a compact disc. A Kodak Photo CD-compatible drive can read these discs and display their pictures on your computer's monitor. The more expensive drives are *multisession* — they let you add additional photos to the same disc. The *single-session* drives cannot read the multisession discs, so the photo developer gives you a new discful of pictures every time you take a batch in for developing.

Safeguarding Your Equipment with Surge Protectors

Ever been chewing your meatloaf one evening and seen the lights flicker slightly? Electricity rarely flows to outlets at a constant level, and it can fluctuate for several reasons: The washing machine could start the spin cycle, a car could knock down a power pole, or lightning could strike a nearby satellite dish.

Although a flicker in the lights during dinner is a minor annoyance, it's downright scary to a computer. Computers depend on a constant flow of electricity, and their sensitive internal organs can be damaged by quick changes in the current.

✔ Surge protectors, also known as *line conditioners* or *surge suppressors,* keep fluctuations in electricity from reaching your computer. You plug the computer into the surge protector and plug the surge protector into the wall.

✔ Some surge protectors have enough outlets for you to plug in all of your computer goodies. But multioutlet *power strips* aren't necessarily surge protectors. You can tell the real surge protectors by their expensive price tag.

✔ Surge protectors wear out. They're good for only a few blasts. Because you don't know when these blasts occur, you should replace them on a yearly basis.

✔ If the power goes out completely, a surge protector won't help you at all. You'll still lose all the data you haven't yet saved to disk. To keep on computing, you'll need an *uninterruptible power supply,* or *UPS,* described in the next section.

Protecting Your Data with Uninterruptible Power Supplies

Your computer's memory disappears when the power shuts off. If somebody trips over your computer's cord and pulls it out of the wall, you'll lose any work you haven't saved to your hard disk or a floppy disk.

Even less predictable than clumsy friends, power outages can happen during air-conditioning overloads on hot days or because of traffic accidents.

An uninterruptible power supply contains special batteries that will keep electricity flowing to your computer if the power should ever die. It will kick in so quickly that your computer will never know anything happened.

✔ Most uninterruptible power supplies last only 5 to 20 minutes. They're designed to give you enough power to save your work and shut down your computer. If you have a gas range, make some popcorn and wait for the lights to turn back on.

✔ Uninterruptible power supplies cost several hundreds of dollars. But think of it as only a fraction of the national debt.

Backing Up Your Data with a Tape Drive

When watching public access documentaries about the history of computers, you'll invariably see big spinning wheels on the early computers. Back then, computers stored all their information on magnetic recording tape — a slow and cumbersome process.

Floppy disks eventually replaced tape, but you'll still find tape used for one purpose: backup copies of data. A tape backup unit plugs into the back of your computer (like everything else) and copies the information on your hard drive to tape.

✔ Tape backup drives are an optional extra on all PCs. They may or may not require their own expansion card.

✔ Some tape drives are external, and some are internal. The external ones are more expensive but have the advantage of being capable of being put on a cart and wheeled around to different computers.

✔ Tape backups generally aren't faster than floppy disk backups, but they are less time-consuming. As long as the tape is large enough, you won't have to switch them as often as you do floppy disks. Also, tape backups can be automated to take place after-hours.

✔ Most of the time, you'll find a tape backup on a network file server. This way, all the company's files can be backed up on one system, as opposed to several tape backup units for each PC.

✔ Although some tape backup units look like VCRs, don't believe the guys who say you can use a regular old VCR. An occasional flicker is no big deal during a Roseanne Arnold movie, but it's no fun at all when you discover a new glitch in your income tax records on April 14.

Summary

This chapter introduced you to many of the peripherals that you can attach to your computer to make it more versatile:

▶ Mice speed up your computing and make it easier to do your work.

▶ Trackballs are useful in small spaces where you don't have room for a mouse.

▶ Modems connect your computer with other computers so that you can communicate with other users and gain access to information from on-line services and bulletin board services.

▶ Scanners copy images and text into your computer so that you can incorporate them into your files.

▶ Adding joysticks and some games enables you and the neighborhood kids to get to know each other better (if you're willing to share).

▶ You can use a tape drive to back up your data.

▶ You learned about the differences between your stereo's CD player and a CD-ROM drive.

▶ Surge protectors keep your computer safe from fluctuations in electricity, and uninterruptible power supplies keep your data from being lost right away if the power goes out completely.

▶ You can enable your computer to accept many of these peripherals by inserting expansion cards into special slots in your machine, or, better still, you can get someone who knows something about computers to insert them for you.

Now that you've learned about many of the peripherals that you can add to your computer to make your system occupy more space, move on to Chapter 12 for a discussion of computers that are small and portable.

Chapter 12
The Laptop
(or Were Laps Always This Big?)

● ●

In This Chapter
▶ Laptop, notebook, portable, or palmtop?
▶ What's wrong with this keyboard?
▶ Screen stuff
▶ NiCads and other bad memories
▶ What plugs in where?
▶ Traveling with a laptop
▶ The myth of working outdoors
▶ Special laptop software
▶ Laptop care and feeding

● ●

Some people love the thought of a laptop computer. Who needs a big computer in a small, stuffy office? Let's crank out that corporate report poolside! For others, a laptop's a nightmare. Their boss has taken away their trusted desktop computer, thrust a strange new computer at them, and said, "We're expecting a 20-percent productivity increase by next month."

Laptops work pretty much the same as desktop computers but in strange, new, cramped ways. The keyboard is smaller. The screen's harder to read. There's no room for a coffee mug on the seat of a Buick Skylark.

This chapter helps to ease the transition from desk to lap. It explains how laptops differ from desktops, why the mouse pointer keeps getting lost on the laptop's screen, and why laptopping on the beach really isn't a good idea. And please, if you're going to put your laptop in your overnight bag, make sure that your Head and Shoulders is in a plastic bag. That ugly blue color clashes with the normal decor, especially around the keyboard.

Is It a Laptop, Notebook, Portable, or Palmtop?

COMPAQ made the first IBM-compatible computer that you could pick up and carry around like a piece of luggage. The company called it a *portable* because its 22 pounds would crush all but the most steel-reinforced laps.

The term *laptop* replaced *portable* when the machines slimmed down to less than 10 pounds. As they dropped below 7 pounds, the word *notebook* took over. The computers most people are buying today are called *notebook computers,* not *laptops.* These new, smaller computers are roughly the same size as a college notebook (8 inches by 11 inches) and about the thickness of an elementary chemistry text (2 inches).

Increased computer dieting has brought notebook computers down to an even smaller level: *palmtops.* These little puppies weigh under a pound and allow anybody with toothpicks for fingers to touch-type.

- ✔ Palmtops are used mostly as high-powered calculators or personal information managers. Palmtop owners can calculate profit/loss statements during lunch, check their schedule for the next free Tuesday night, and then look up Pat's number to make a date to play squash. They peck out grocery lists, not novels.

- ✔ Notebook computers can replace all but the most high-end desktop machines. The best notebook computers have color screens, huge hard disks, and decent-sized keyboards. The only problem is that they cost about three times as much as a desktop computer.

- ✔ Laptop-sized 12-pound computers, like their portable uncles, are being dumped in droves as people move toward the smaller, lighter-weight, trendier notebook computers.

- ✔ Because this book doesn't cater to trendy buzzwords like *notebook,* we'll use the word *laptop* to refer to all portable computers that open and shut like a clam shell.

- ✔ The latest buzzword, *subnotebook,* describes a notebook computer that has been squashed even thinner. To save weight and space, some subnotebooks even leave out the disk drive. Instead, the disk drive comes as a separate, plug-in box, which can be left at the office accidentally when you need it on the road.

AAAARRRRGGGGHHH! What's Wrong with This Keyboard?

In their effort to shrink large desktop computers to the size of a notebook, computer designers did some nasty things to the keyboard. Luckily, not even computer nerds have the guts to mess with the typewriter's "QWERTY" keys; those will be in the same location. But most of the other keys have smaller key caps, appear in different locations, and don't move down as far when pushed (that's a key's *travel distance*). If your desktop computer's keyboard has a different travel distance, typing on a laptop will be like getting used to the clutch and brake pedals on a rental car.

- The term *full travel* refers to keys that travel the same distance as they do on a standard desktop keyboard.

- Almost every laptop brand but Toshiba puts Caps Lock next to Shift on the left side of the keyboard and puts Ctrl beneath it. This arrangement may be different from your desktop keyboard, causing much aggravation. And keep an eye out for Backslash. It can show up just about anywhere on the keyboard.

- Today, everybody but haughty French intellectuals agree that laptop cursor-control keys should be arranged in an *Inverted T.* That means they're placed in an upside-down T shape: the up arrow rests on top, with the down arrow immediately below it. The left and right arrows lie to the left and the right of the down arrow. It's logical, and it makes it easy to tell which key is which. Watch out for the older, L-shaped arrangement. Or worse, the dreaded I-shaped grouping.

- Laptop keyboards often substitute combination keys for keys normally found on a desktop keyboard. For instance, PgUp won't be separate on a laptop. You'll have to hold down a special function key while pressing the up arrow to move the screen up a page.

- Some laptop keyboards won't have dedicated function keys. Instead, you hold down a single function key and press one of the number keys — the number 1, for example, to mimic F1.

- The keyboards on IBM's latest laptops have a bright red pencil eraser that protrudes upward from the keyboard near the G and H keys. Although an eraser would be handy, IBM has turned it into a mouse: By moving the eraser head back and forth with your finger, you move the mouse pointer back and forth across the screen. No bulky mouse cord to get in a laptopper's way.

Screen Stuff: Passive Matrix, Active Matrix, and Supertwist

Remember everything you learned about monitors in Chapter 9? Forget it, because laptops use a completely different technology. Laptops would weigh an extra 15 pounds if they used the same cathode ray tube technology as monitors. Instead, they use LCD screens or gas plasma screens.

The following are some descriptions of the various laptop monitors you'll encounter, along with opinions and such on each.

Liquid crystal displays (LCDs)

Most laptops use liquid crystal displays, or LCDs. It's basically the same display you'll find on most digital wristwatches but a little flashier. Most people today have backlit or sidelit LCD screens, making them easier to see. Rich people use the new color LCD screens.

How does the LCD screen work? If you want to know, read this.

Liquid crystal reflects light even though it's a liquid. The substance can be manipulated easily by electricity, heat, or simply your finger. Gently push a finger against an LCD screen and watch as the screen changes under pressure.

In laptops, the liquid crystals are squirted between two sheets of polarized glass or plastic. Just like sunglasses, the polarized sheets keep out all light except for the waves that are parallel to their particular plane.

The two planes in the liquid crystal display are normally at right angles; that means they filter out all the light. But because the liquid crystals are twisted, they can bend the light enough to let it pass through.

When tiny electrodes embedded in the display pass current through the liquid crystals, however, they untwist, blocking the light. This makes a small black dot on the screen. By varying the flow of electricity to various parts of the screen, the liquid crystal does a hula dance of twists, effectively lighting and darkening portions of the screen.

- Confused people in both categories deal with the terms *active matrix, passive matrix,* and *supertwist.* Luckily, they're all described later in this section.

- Liquid crystal displays reflect light, so they work best in well-lit rooms or even outdoors in heavy sunlight. You won't be able to see the screen at all in the dark, however. These screens don't create any light of their own; their batteries last for a long time.

- Sidelit or backlit LCD screens shine their own lights on the screen, so any excess room lighting has the opposite effect, making them harder to see. Because the screen must generate its own light, battery life is limited to a matter of hours.

- LCD screens have notoriously slow *refresh rates,* meaning the images don't snap on and off the screen quickly. When you're scrolling the text up or down, the lines of text blur into each other. Your mouse arrow disappears as it moves across the screen. This is called *comet tailing.*

- The color LCD screens on today's laptops look better than the displays on their desktop counterparts. And they'd better: They cost more than what some people pay for an entire computer system.

Several features of Windows 3.1 help laptop owners. First, the Control Panel can add *trails* to your mouse: When you move the mouse, the pointer leaves ghost images behind it, so it's easier to find on an LCD screen. Second, the Control Panel contains color combinations designed especially to make LCD screens more visible.

Active matrix/passive matrix

Most laptops use *passive matrix* displays; this means the pixels share electrodes. In English, that means their screens can be rather slow and murky when compared with their more expensive cousins. But they're still very readable and suitable for most applications.

With *active matrix* displays, each pixel gets its very own transistor. Active matrix displays require *a lot* of transistors, making them much more difficult to construct, heavier, and a larger drain on the batteries.

All that means is that active matrix screens are easier to read and cost a lot more.

Supertwist (and triple-supertwist)

Liquid crystal molecules must twist in order to reflect the light properly. Due to the Richard Simmons Molecular Workouts, the latest breed of liquid crystal molecules can twist more easily than earlier types. Chemists call this new breed of molecule *nematic.* Advertisement blurbs call them *supertwist* or even *triple-supertwist.* Sometimes they get carried away and call them *triple-supertwist nematic,* or *TSTN.*

Like active matrix screens, TSTN ensures that the screen is both easier to read and a lot more expensive.

Gas plasma screens

Because LCD screens have such a slow refresh rate, anything that moves across the screen becomes a blur. People who need quicker refresh rates opt for gas plasma technology instead of LCD screens.

- ✔ Gas plasma screens are those ugly, orange screens that are always described as "garish."
- ✔ The screens are intended for specialty markets: computer-aided drafting and design, for instance, or other high-end graphics.
- ✔ They're very difficult to read in bright sunlight.

Gray scale

Most laptop screens today are VGA compatible, but instead of being capable of displaying colors, they can display different shades of gray. For instance, a 16 gray-scale screen can show 16 different shades of gray. This doesn't really matter when you're word processing, but it helps make on-screen graphics more visible.

A 32 gray-scale screen can show 32 shades of gray, but somehow this isn't always better. The difference in shading is much less pronounced. In fact, don't be surprised if a 16 gray-scale screen sometimes looks crisper and easier to read.

NiCads and Other Bad Memories

Desktop computer users watch the clock but only until 5 p.m. Laptop owners, however, turn a worried eye to the clock every five or ten minutes. The batteries on most laptops will barely last a flight from Los Angeles to New York. And when they die, work stops. (Your data's still safe, however, snuggled inside the laptop's little hard drive.)

The lights in the display, the motors in the disk drives, and the little chips themselves all gang up to suck the juice out of a set of batteries as quickly as they can. Instead of trading their weekly paycheck for a case of Duracells, laptop owners generally use one of two kinds of rechargeable batteries: nickel-cadmium (NiCad), or nickel-metal-hydride (NiMH).

NiCad

Nickel-cadmium batteries have been used the longest, despite one big problem: When the batteries are repeatedly recharged before they've run out of power, NiCads begin to lose capacity. They "remember" that they were recharged when they were run down halfway. When they're run down to that halfway point again, they stop working, thinking they've discharged fully.

To stop a NiCad's bad memory problem, drain its batteries completely at least once a month and let it sit for an hour or so. The next few recharges will then last longer. When you feel the memory problem surfacing again, repeat the "deep drain" process.

The second problem with NiCads is that they're full of highly toxic chemicals. Cadmium is a toxic heavy metal (as well as a great name for a rock band) that shouldn't be tossed out with the trash. Call your city's waste management (trash) department for information on disposing of toxic chemicals. (Get rid of those old cans of paint in the garage at the same time.)

Nickel-metal-hydride (NiMH)

The eventual replacement for NiCads, NiMH batteries are being used in a growing number of laptops. These rechargeables last longer than NiCads and can provide more power. Of course, they cost roughly twice as much as NiCads.

> ✔ A company called Traveling Software sells Battery Watch software; it brings a pop-up fuel gauge to the screen, estimating your amount of remaining work time.

> ✔ After several minutes of inactivity, some laptops automatically shut down their screens and hard drives to save power. It's not broken. Just press the spacebar to bring it back to life. Or, better yet, let it rest until you're actually ready to use it again; *then* press the spacebar to bring it back to life.

> ✔ Batteries recharge at variable rates. Some grab enough electricity in an hour; others take three times as long. Unfortunately, batteries don't last as long when they're recharged quickly. That's why some laptops let you choose between *fast charge* and *trickle charge* when the batteries are charged back to capacity.

Rechargeable batteries are heavy, but you may want to bring along an extra set for emergency power while on the road.

What Plugs in Where?

It's easier than you think to take your office on the road. Computer makers love to make smaller, lighter, and more expensive versions of their products, and laptops satisfy the bill on all three counts.

But unlike a bulky desktop PC, there's no room inside a laptop to plug in any goodies. Instead, the peripherals plug into a laptop's ports — special outlets on its rump. Most laptops have a printer port and a serial port (known as a *COM port*), just like a desktop PC. But there are a few new ports as well.

External keyboard and monitor ports

Most laptops have ports labeled *keyboard* and *monitor.* That way you can use your laptop as a desktop machine when you're back at the office. Just plug a full-sized keyboard into the keyboard port and a regular VGA monitor into the monitor port.

> ✔ Most laptops can display only shades of gray on the screen. But a VGA color monitor plugged into a laptop's external monitor port can display color, just as if it were connected to a desktop machine.

> ✔ By plugging a keyboard and monitor into a laptop, you can use it as a full-fledged desktop machine. Best yet, there's no worry about having to transfer files back and forth. They're always on your laptop's hard drive. Unfortunately, there's no way to install a joystick port on a laptop computer, making it unsuitable for full desktop operation.

Printers

If you want to double the weight of your on-the-road package, several companies make tiny battery-powered printers. Most use the thermal and ink-jet technology discussed in Chapter 10. But since they're a bother to carry around, they can be avoided in several ways:

- ✔ Carry a cable that fits your notebook's printer port (these ports are usually standard, just like those on the back of any other PC) so that you can quickly and conveniently plug it into a printer you find on the road. A friend's office or a hotel lobby can often be accommodating if you ask nicely and smile. (They'll frown if you don't bring your own cable, however. Nobody wants a stranger to stick his hand in that mysterious zone behind their computer, even if he's just reaching for a cable.)

- ✔ If your laptop has a fax/modem, send yourself a fax to make a quick printout of your work. Hotels usually don't charge for incoming faxes, so they're prime targets. If your modem doesn't have fax capabilities, join an on-line service, like MCI or CompuServe. For a modest price, these services enable you to upload a text file and have it faxed anywhere in the world.

PCMCIA cards

If you spot a credit-card-size slot along the edge of your laptop or palmtop, you have found its Personal Computer Memory Card International Association hole, known as a *PCMCIA* slot.

Clever computer designers have shrunk modems, memory, and other computer gadgets on to little credit-card-size PCMCIA cards. By sliding the card into the slot, you can beef up your little computer's power.

A PCMCIA modem costs as much as ten times more than a regular, run-of-the mill modem. But — hey — it *looks* like more fun. And they're much easier to carry around.

You won't find much software sold on a PCMCIA card, however. They're designed mainly for hardware: memory, modems, and network stuff.

Don't carry PCMCIA cards in your wallet. They don't bend when you sit down, like your VISA card does.

Will the Airport's X-Ray Machine Melt My Laptop?

An airport's x-ray machine strikes fear into the hearts of most laptop owners. After all, if they can screw up a cheap camera, they can probably do a real number on an expensive laptop.

Actually, nobody can really decide whether they can damage laptops or not. Some say they've sent their laptops through an x-ray machine hundreds of times with no problems. Others say an x-ray machine has wiped out some of their RAM chips. Still others say the motors that turn the conveyor belt may contain a magnetic field that can destroy data. And still others are leery of the big guy slapping the club into his hand — the one with his nametag on upside down.

Guards usually check laptops to ensure that you're not smuggling explosives, so there's really no sense in having your laptop x-rayed. Simply hand it to the guard as you reach the inspection gate, walk through the little door, and then turn the computer on to show the guard that it's not a bomb. Try not to be humorous at this point.

✔ Make sure that your laptop is fully charged when heading through the airport. Your trip can be delayed if you can't prove that your laptop is fully functional and not full of plastic explosives.

✔ Some airlines have rules against passengers' using a laptop on the plane. Theoretically, the laptop's electronics could mess with the plane's navigation system, causing ugly scenes. Other airlines don't think laptops interfere with anything at all. Ask a flight attendant about that particular plane's policy. Chances are, they'll walk away to check and then never return. So go ahead and start typing unless they tell you not to.

The Myth of Working Outdoors

By now, the *home office* concept is so firmly entrenched that it has its own magazine. But anybody who's bought a laptop dreams of a new way of working: the beach office. Unfortunately, it just doesn't work that way.

It's hard enough to work while in an office. It's much more difficult when you're away from the office, and the beach is the worst spot. First, the sun's glare will obliterate the display of 90 percent of all laptops. Second, sand will get into the keyboard. And, even if you're careful, some beach goon will run by, kicking sand or spilling a beverage into your $3,000 toy.

Last, you'll find infinitely more distractions: the chair will never be adjusted in exactly the right position, your eyes will gravitate toward the volleyball players instead of the computer. And at all times you'll have a nagging fear in the back of your mind: Am I being a nerd, or what?

✔ Another problem with working in public comes with the reactions from people around you. When trying to work on an airplane, you'll have to deal with people walking by and interrupting your work to say, "Is that one of those laptop things?" Plus, you'll always feel that the person sitting next to you is watching everything you type. And they will be! There's nothing else to do on a plane.

✔ When laptopping on a plane, load a flight simulation program instead of your work. That way you can at least show off your cool new computer to all the passersby.

✔ If you *do* try to get some work done on the plane, try for an aisle seat. You'll have more distractions, but at least one elbow will have enough room to be in a comfortable typing position.

✔ Rather than laptopping by a small waterfall to get away from it all, consider heading to a coffee shop. Choose a large table and look for one near an electrical outlet; if you plug in your adapter, you'll ease the terror of thinking your batteries are about to run down. Make your coffee cup wear one of those "on-the-go" cup covers; that helps keep the coffee off the keyboard.

Special Laptop Software

Laptops have been around for nearly a decade, so lots of people have written software to make them work better. Most of your desktop programs will work on your laptop, too, but you'll have to install them differently.

✔ When installing desktop programs, try using the monochrome or Hercules graphics option. Even when your laptop translates colors into shades of gray, they can be difficult to see. Some programs have a special laptop installation option to make them easier to read.

✔ Special *cursor enhancers* make laptopping easier. SkiSoft's NoSquint laptop cursor program turns the feeble little cursor into a huge blinking beast so that it won't get lost. The same company sells a program to enlarge the text so that your eyes won't squint like a contented cat's.

✔ Because hard drives are so expensive, install Stac's Stacker utility or a similar program, Squish, from SunDog Software. These programs compress the information on your hard drive, effectively increasing the amount of storage you have available.

✔ Traveling Software's LapLink software and cables make it easier to "beam" files back and forth between your laptop and your desktop computer. Some laptops come with the software already built in. Of course, if both your laptop and desktop sport 3½-inch disk drives, then moving stuff back and forth can be done by floppy disk.

Laptop Care and Feeding

Most of the cautions regarding desktop computers apply to laptops as well. But here are a few extra ways to keep your laptop happy and smiling:

✔ Just as with a desktop computer, don't spray glass cleaner directly on the screen. Instead, spray it on a soft cloth. Then wipe the cloth across the screen to remove any dust, fingerprints, and beach beer.

✔ If you pack your laptop with your luggage, make sure that it's in a secure case. And this time, try to remember to keep your shampoo in a plastic bag so it won't get everything grungy when it leaks.

✔ It's even more important to keep beverages out of your laptop's keyboard than it is to keep them out of your desktop's keyboard. The laptop's keyboard is much harder to replace, and that 50-cent can of pop can easily cost $500 in repairs.

✔ Keep the laptop at room temperature. Don't keep it in the car's trunk or on the back seat or the dashboard. All three areas are subject to extreme temperatures, both in the afternoon and overnight. If your laptop freezes, the screen probably won't work. When it warms up to room temperature, however, it should be back to normal.

✔ Laptops don't have a cooling fan, so the buggers can get pretty hot. Sometimes this feels good against the thighs, especially if you've been playing racquet ball. Most of the time it's a bother, so keep a towel underneath it when it's too hot.

Stuff to Make Your Laptop Bag Heavier

A 7-pound laptop weight may seem as light as Jiffy Pop at the office, but it turns into a bowling ball when it's dangling from your shoulder at the airport. Plus, most people make the carrying case double as a briefcase in order to meet the airline's two-bag carry-on limit. In case your laptop isn't heavy enough already, here is a list of additional items to toss into its pockets:

✔ Don't bring the entire manual for your favorite software packages. Find the quick reference card and toss it in instead. Also include copies of the technical support numbers for your laptop, modem, and all software you'll be bringing along.

✔ Be sure to bring along the AC adapter so that you can recharge the internal batteries. If you're heading for Europe, make sure that your AC adapter works on 240-volt current. Some adapters make the switch automatically; others require you to flip a switch, and still others won't work at all in a foreign outlet.

✔ Bring enough floppy disks to back up your work. This becomes even more crucial when you're on the road because the laptop is subject to hard-drive bashing from various bumps and shocks. When you've backed up your data, store the backup disks in a different case than your laptop bag. That way, even if someone swipes your laptop, you'll still have the data.

✔ Spare batteries are expensive, but if you'll be working away from an AC outlet for a long period of time, they're essential.

✔ Don't forget your modem cables if you want to check into the office computer remotely or pick up your e-mail while on the road.

✔ A small pack of Kleenex always comes in handy.

Summary

This chapter introduced you to the challenges and conveniences of using a laptop computer. It also burst that bubble you had about working on your computer at the beach:

▶ You learned that you can do most of the same things on the new, smaller portable computers as you can do on all but the most high-end desktop computers.

▶ You discovered that laptops' keyboards differ in several ways from the keyboards for desktop computers.

▶ You found out why laptops have LCD or gas plasma screens and why the liquid crystal molecules in LCD screens twist and untwist.

▶ You learned how to get more life from nickel-cadmium batteries and found out why metal-hydride batteries are being used more and more.

▶ You learned some ways to print your files without taking a printer along when you're away from your office.

▶ You got the names of some software designed to make laptopping easier.

▶ You picked up some hints for traveling with your laptop and for taking good care of it.

The next chapter clears up some of the mysteries surrounding DOS.

Part III
Working with a Computer

The 5th Wave   By Rich Tennant

"THIS SECURITY PROGRAM WILL RESPOND TO THREE THINGS: AN INCORRECT ACCESS CODE, AN INAPPROPRIATE FILE REQUEST, OR SOMETIMES A CRAZY HUNCH THAT MAYBE YOU'RE JUST ANOTHER SLIME-BALL WITH MISAPPROPRIATION OF SECURED DATA ON HIS MIND."

In this part...

Whenever struggling writers want to give you a grasp of the concept of a computer, they often let their minds wander back to an earlier time (usually their high school days), when life was easier and more serene. Writers try to compare concepts from that time in their lives with the concept of the ugly, cold computer so you can grasp the computer concept better.

As an example, we were into cars while in high school. We can use that information to make a comparison with the computer: Most people know about cars and can identify most of its major pieces. But what's more important than the car itself is what you use it for — transportation. The same concept applies to a computer. What's more important than the computer itself is what it's used for — in this case, getting work done.

This part of the book is all about using a computer and getting your work done, which involves using your software — the programs and applications you bought to become productive with your PC. It also involves using DOS, Windows, and a bunch of other sideline items, all of which are arranged in the following chapters like meandering pedestrians jaywalking on the turnpike. Stand by to accelerate and execute.

Chapter 13
Using DOS (Abusing DOS, Toiling with and Losing to DOS)

● ●

In This Chapter

▶ Why is there DOS?

▶ Learning what to do at the DOS prompt

▶ Running a program

▶ Finding a program

▶ Naming files

▶ Working with disk drives

▶ Using DOS commands

▶ Dealing with ugly error messages

● ●

*D*OS is such a vast and complex subject that it would make your head explode if we described all of it to you. To avoid it, many PC users skirt around DOS. They eschew it. DOS walks into the room, and normal people — some dressed quite nicely — duck under the table, pretending they don't notice. Then DOS rears its ugly head, and they say, nonchalantly, "Oh, it's you. Nice day. Must be going." Some people would rather watch C-SPAN than use DOS. Mothers weeping, babies crying, the apocalypse . . . what could be worse?

Of course, the only thing worse than using DOS is using it without this book's big brother, *DOS For Dummies,* published by IDG Books Worldwide. That book tells you everything you never wanted to hear about DOS and does it in a painless and refreshing way. One woman even wrote in and said she read *DOS For Dummies* in bed. Scandalous!

Rather than drag on about droll old DOS here, and because even authors tire of pumping their own books in their other books, we offer in this chapter some brief and painless insight into the most ugly thing you'll ever see on a computer: DOS. The big D. The disk operating system. Yuck.

Why Is There DOS?

DOS is a necessary evil in your computer. It's not purposefully malodorous; it's just incomplete, curt, and rude — like a bank teller or the guy manning the only open window at the post office. DOS's job is to manage the goings-on in your PC. It does that job like the many computer programs before it: with no regard for the noncomputer-science major.

Under the hood, DOS is software. It's the main program controlling your computer. DOS's job is to control everything, but it works first and best with disk drives. DOS manages files, which contain all the information you store on disk. So you need DOS to run your PC.

The happy part of all this is that you can safely avoid DOS. Many other software packages exist that act like cozy footwear to insulate you from DOS's gravelly pavement. They are called *menu systems* or *shells.* The most popular one is Windows. Other, simpler systems also exist. The main object is to keep you away from DOS so that you can get your work done.

- DOS stands for *disk operating system.* An operating system is a program that controls a computer. The disk part means that DOS starts out on disk; it's not a part of the computer's innards (as is the case with some other types of operating systems).

- No, you don't have to know DOS to use a computer. (OK, it helps, but who has the time or inclination to become a computer genius?)

- DOS can be avoided (it must be avoided!) by the use of friendlier things, like menu systems, shells, or computer *environments* such as Windows. More information on Windows can be found in Chapter 16.

Pronouncing DOS is a big problem. Try to avoid the temptation to say *dose.* And only a substitute PE teacher would say *dee, oh, ess.* It's DOS, which rhymes with boss or loss or cross.

The Foreboding DOS Prompt

To talk with DOS, you need to know how to use the *DOS prompt.* It looks something like this:

```
C:\>
```

In some cases, it may look like this:

```
C>
```

And it may not always be C. It can be A, D, or another letter of the alphabet. It's all the same; it's all a DOS prompt.

Hovering after the DOS prompt is a blinking underline. That's the *cursor,* and it marks the position on the screen where text will appear as you type. The cursor is waiting by the DOS prompt for you to type one of two things:

✔ A DOS command — an instruction telling DOS to go do something

✔ The name of a program

DOS commands are English-like words that tell DOS to carry out some task. The words are easy enough: COPY, RENAME, EXPLODE, and so on. These are sometimes followed by *options,* which is where DOS gets really foolhardy. It's the options that you usually forget. (It's a case of "I know what I want this thing to do, but what do I type to do it?")

Typing in the name of a program tells DOS you want to run that application. This varies from system to system depending on what software you have installed. Only you know the names of the programs you run. For example, if you run WordPerfect, you'll type **WP** at the DOS prompt:

```
C:\> WP
```

Type **WP** and press Enter. The same holds true for other program names: Type the name at the DOS prompt — in upper- or lowercase — and then press Enter.

✔ The cursor is a flashing underline that appears on the screen. It marks the point where the stuff you type will appear. Incidentally, *cursor* is from the Latin word for *runner.* It has nothing to do with hurling insults at the PC.

✔ This book always shows the DOS prompt as C:\>. On your screen it may look different.

✔ More information on typing at the DOS prompt is covered in the next section.

✔ When you make a mistake, DOS spits back one of its harsh error messages. A few of the more popular — and dreaded — messages are listed later in this chapter in the section "Ugly Error Messages Abound!"

Typing at the DOS Prompt

Hide your eyes from its ugliness! Still, you need to type at the DOS prompt to get your work done. Even this can be a chore, primarily because no one ever bothers to explain how typing at the DOS prompt works. Here goes:

✔ You can type a command or the name of a program in upper- or lowercase. DOS doesn't care either way.

✔ DOS is fussy about spelling and punctuation. All DOS commands and the names of your programs must be spelled correctly. Everything must be typed in "just so." If you make a spelling error, DOS spits back an error message.

Punctuating the DOS command line — or not punctuating it — is important. *No DOS command ends in a period!* Do not type a period to end a DOS command! This mistake is quite common because computer manuals and books list periods at the end of DOS commands to be grammatically correct. But at the DOS prompt, never end a command with a period.

✔ The command isn't sent off to DOS for chewing until you press Enter. DOS won't carry out your command or hurl an error message your way until you press Enter.

✔ To correct a typo, press Backspace. This key is above Enter on your keyboard and may be marked only with a left-pointing arrow. Remember, it's entirely possible to correct a mistake; nothing happens until you press Enter. (And, after you correct the mistake, you need to retype the rest of the command.)

✔ To cancel an entire command, press Esc. It usually lives in the upper-left corner of your keyboard. Pressing Esc enables you to erase the line and start over. (Sometime DOS displays a \ character and starts over on a new line without erasing. Either way, you're starting over and the old command is "erased.")

✔ When typing a DOS command, watch out for spaces! Never sandwich several things at the prompt together. Like a sentence in English, "words" you type at the DOS prompt are separated by spaces.

Nothing you can type at the DOS prompt will make your PC explode. And nothing you type can cause any serious damage either. Any bad things you can potentially do will come back with a warning on the screen. Press **N** for *No;* then ask your guru what went wrong.

Some nerdy definitions to be read only by severe insomniacs

All that stuff you type at the DOS prompt is referred to as the *command line*. Some books or manuals proclaim, "Enter the following command line." They mean to type the following stuff at the DOS prompt.

The DOS prompt itself may also be referred to as the *command prompt*. Some manuals commit the sin of assumption and declare, "Type this in at the C prompt." But be careful to note that the DOS prompt may not always show the letter C. Sometimes it doesn't show a letter at all. (It's customizable.)

Also, quite a few manuals and books neglect to tell you when to press Enter. It's usually assumed that you'll press Enter after typing in a command line. If you never read the exact text "press the Enter key," then do it anyway.

Running a Program

Hopefully, you'll spend as little time at the DOS prompt as possible. The rest of the time you'll be running programs and getting work done. To do that, you type the name of the program at the DOS prompt and then press Enter.

Table 13-1 contains the names of several popular DOS programs. Listed next to them is what you type at the DOS prompt to run the program. There's also space to add your own programs if you need to.

Table 13-1	Popular DOS Programs
Program Name	*What to Type (and then Press Enter)*
dBASE	DBASE
DESQview	DV (Press the Alt key to run other programs)
Flight Simulator	FS
GrandView	GV
Harvard Graphics	HG
LapLink III	LL
1-2-3	123
Magellan	MG

(continued)

Table 13-1 *(continued)*

Program Name	What to Type (and then Press Enter)
PC Tools	PCSHELL
ProComm	PROCOMM
ProComm Plus	PCPLUS
Prodigy	PRODIGY
Q&A	QA
Quattro	Q
Quicken	Q
SideKick	SK
SimCity	SIMCITY
SmartCom	SCOM
Ventura Publisher	VP
Windows	WIN
Word	WORD
WordPerfect	WP
WordStar	WS

Add your own programs in the blank spaces above.

✔ Yes, Quattro and Quicken both have the same name: Q.

✔ Windows programs, such as Excel and Word for Windows, should each be run from within Windows: Start Windows first and then use the mouse pointy-clicky thing to start other programs.

✔ Many programs enable you to type the name of a document to edit after the program name. For example, to start WordPerfect and begin editing the CHAP13.DOC file, you type

```
C:\> WP CHAP13.DOC
```

There is a space between WP and CHAP13.DOC.

✔ If you make a mistake when typing the name of a program, you'll see one of DOS's most popular error messages: `Bad command or file name`. That's DOS's way of telling you it didn't understand what you typed. Retype the program name and press Enter to try again.

✔ If you type in the program's name again and it still gives you an error message, try typing in this command:

```
C:\> C:
```

That is, type **C** and a colon (no spaces between them). Press Enter. That "logs" you to drive C. Once there, try typing the command again. If it still doesn't work, yell for help.

Finding a Program

Sometimes running a program under DOS isn't as obvious as typing something in at the DOS prompt. Instead, you need to hunt for the program you want to run. This is done in several steps.

If you know the name of the *subdirectory* in which the program is located, then type the CD command, followed by the name of the subdirectory. For example, type the following:

```
C:\> CD \MOUSE
```

The subdirectory name is \MOUSE, (type a backslash, followed by **MOUSE** — no spaces between the two). The CD command is followed by a space and the name of the subdirectory. Press Enter and you'll be in the MOUSE subdirectory.

When you're in your subdirectory, use the following command:

```
C:\> DIR *.EXE /P
```

That's **DIR** (for the DIR command), a space, an asterisk (*), a period, and then **EXE.** That's followed by another space, a forward slash (/), and then a **P.** Press Enter. This tells DOS to display some program files in the subdirectory. If you see your file listed, type its name at the DOS prompt.

If you don't see your file listed, try this command:

```
C:\> DIR *.COM /P
```

That's **DIR** (for the DIR command), a space, the asterisk, a period, then **COM,** another space, a slash, and **P.** Press Enter and you'll see more program files. Look for the one you're missing and then type it at the DOS prompt.

If you still don't see your file listed, try this as a last shot:

```
C:\> DIR *.BAT /P
```

This is the same as the preceding two commands, but **BAT** is used instead of **COM** or **EXE.** Press Enter and look for a filename to try. If none are displayed, then yell for help; the file is truly lost.

Remember to type the proper subdirectory on your system instead of typing **\MOUSE**. Note that some subdirectories have longer names, like this:

```
\WORD\WP\PROJECTS\SCHOOL
```

That's a long subdirectory name, full of backslashes. Type in such a name carefully.

Getting the "bad command or file name" error is usually the tip-off that you need to find a program. "Bad command or file name" usually means you mistyped a command or program name. But, if you're certain you didn't, it's time to start hunting.

Lost at the DOS Prompt

Sometimes you'll be working and then suddenly — like the rustling wind or Uncle Earl, letting out an after-dinner belch — there's the darn DOS prompt! How did you get there? Never mind. The real question is "How do I get back?"

If you're ever suddenly "dumped" at the DOS prompt, try these steps toward a solution:

1. Type EXIT and press Enter:

```
C:\> EXIT
```

This may suddenly bring you back to where you were. How did it all happen? Don't ask.

2. **If you are running a program and then find yourself suddenly lost, press F3 and then Enter. Under some circumstances, this will rerun the last program you ran.**

3. **If the F3 trick doesn't work, then try retyping the name of the program you were just running.**

4. **If you don't know the name of the program you were just running, type MENU and press Enter:**

```
C:\> MENU
```

5. **Call for help.**

About Files and Filenames

DOS's main job is to manage information. Information in a computer is stored on your disk drives in the form of files. Each file is its own unit of information. A file can contain just about anything: text, graphics, a spreadsheet, a program — whatever. But it's hard to tell what's in a file because DOS gives you only eight lonely characters to name a file. (Imagine if all the interesting places in the United States were named with only eight characters — and no two names could be alike. That's how DOS is.)

Before you save information to disk, you must give that information a name: You must tell DOS a filename under which the file will be saved. Here are the rules:

✔ A filename can be no more than eight characters long. Yes, you can have one-letter filenames, but they aren't too descriptive.

✔ Filenames can contain letters and numbers. They can start with either a letter or a number. (There's this one idiot walking around telling people that filenames cannot start with a number. Shoot him.)

That's about all you need to know; no sense in cluttering your brain with any additional information (unless you bother to read the box looming at the end of this section).

Table 13-2 shows a list of good and bad filenames and explains why they're good and bad.

Table 13-2	Filenames
Good Filename	***Reason***
LETTER	It's under eight characters.
IH8BART	Filenames can contain numbers.
M1-15-94	It contains eight characters — letters, numbers, and the allowable (but never mentioned) hyphen character.
A	A one-letter filename is OK.
1	Numbers are OK, too.
Bad Filename	***Reason***
SCHOOLWORK	It contains too many characters; only eight maximum are allowed.
UGLY U	The filename contains a space. Heavens! You can't put a space in a filename.
MEMO:123	The filename contains the offending colon (:) character.
UP	The filename contains the offending asterisk (*) character.
I.LUV.U	No periods are allowed in filenames.

✔ No two files can share the same name. If you try to do this, the first file — the original with the same name — will be overwritten by the second file. Sometimes this is what you want — for example, when you are updating an older file on disk. Otherwise, be careful!

✔ Be clever with the names you give your files. The name is the only clue you have as to the file's contents. For example, a file named MEMO can be any memo to anyone. But the file MEM2JOHN could be a memo to that bozo John in accounting.

✔ Playing the filename game is like being creative with a vanity license plate: There are many messages that you can stick onto a license plate with only a few characters. Apply that same charisma to your DOS files, and you'll soon be swinging with the big monkeys.

Working with Disk Drives

DOS refers to disks by the letter of the drive they're in. DOS uses the drive letter, followed by a colon. This helps DOS identify, say, A:, as a disk drive and not as a file named A on the disk. Table 13-3 contains a quick summary.

Table 13-3	DOS Names for Disk Drives
Disk Is in This Drive	*What DOS Calls It*
A	A:
B	B:
C	C:
D	D:
and so on	and so on:

To use another disk drive, you type in the drive letter plus the colon at the DOS prompt. For example, you're using drive C and would now like to use drive A instead. Type the following:

```
C:\> A:
```

At the DOS prompt, press A (the letter of the new drive) and then a colon. Make sure that a disk is in drive A. Press Enter. This is what you see:

```
A:\>
```

No need to clutter your brain with this information on filename extensions

In addition to the filename, you also can give your files a three-character *extension*. Normally this extension will be supplied by your application. For example, Word will save all its documents with the DOC extension. But if you want to add your own, just follow the filename with a period and up to three more letters or numbers. Here are some examples:

```
HELLO.TXT
a.doc
mem0381.now
TEST.1
```

As with the filename, the extension can contain letters and numbers and can start with either. In fact, if you *really* want to know which characters DOS won't allow in a filename (raise your hands good and high), here is the official verboten list:

```
. " / \ [ ] : * | < > + = ; , ?
```

Skip this complex information on subdirectories (which will haunt you later if you do read it)

All files on a disk are held in a *directory*. The directory is a list of the files and their names, sizes, dates, and times. This is how DOS keeps track of which files are on a disk. It's also what you see when you list the files on a disk using the DIR — directory — command.

All disks have one main directory, called the *root directory*. Additional directories also can exist, which branch off the root directory like limbs of a tree. Those additional directories are called *subdirectories*. Each of them acts like its own self-contained disk, holding files and even more subdirectories. This is how a disk is organized, with individual files in each subdirectory.

You may have your own directory somewhere on a disk. For example, Dan Gookin's mom, whose name is Jonnie, has a subdirectory named \JONNIE on her computer. Subdirectories are named just like files, but they also include the backslash character. The first backslash character in \JONNIE signifies the root directory; JONNIE is the name of Mom's subdirectory.

To move between the various subdirectories, use the CD command. CD means *change directory*, and it's followed by the name of the subdirectory you want to use or change to. All this is really forgettable stuff, save for the occasional command you use to "change directories," usually given in a software manual. When that happens, you type **CD**, followed by the name of the new directory.

For example, suppose that some manual says, "Change to the DOS directory. Type CD \DOS."

You would type the following:

```
C:\> CD \DOS
```

That's **CD**, a space, the backslash character (above Enter), and then **DOS**. There is no space between the backslash and DOS; \DOS is the name of the DOS subdirectory. Press Enter to carry out the command.

Be careful here: The backslash character is not the same as the forward slash character under the question mark.

You'll never have to worry about creating your own subdirectories. Someone else will do this for you. But, on your own, you should remember where various important subdirectories are and how to get to them. Fill in the following list if you like:

Subdirectory: _____

What's in there: _____

Subdirectory: _____

What's in there: _____

Subdirectory: _____

What's in there: _____

Subdirectory: _____

What's in there: _____

When you change to a different drive, the DOS prompt may change to include that drive letter.

✔ To change back to drive C, or any other drive, type its letter followed by a colon and press Enter.

✔ If no disk is in the drive, you'll see a `Drive not ready` error. Put a disk in the drive and then press R to continue.

✔ If you try to use a disk drive that doesn't exist, you'll see an `Invalid drive specification` error message. Try another drive.

✔ Chapter 8 discusses disks and disk drives in annoying detail. Refer there for more information.

DOS Commands

To tell DOS to do something, you type a command at the DOS prompt. There are dozens of DOS commands, each of which does something different and all of which confuse even the most stolid DOS guru. Although *DOS For Dummies* goes into juicy detail on a few of the less painful commands, four are worth introducing here: DIR, COPY, DEL, and HELP.

DIR

Use this command to display a list of files on disk. DIR means *directory*. Like the directory in a large building, the DIR command shows you what's on your disk. Just type **DIR** and press Enter:

```
C:\> DIR
```

If you can't see all the names (they scroll wildly up the screen), then try this variation:

```
C:\> DIR /P
```

Type **DIR,** a space, then a forward slash (under the question mark), and a **P.** Press Enter. This time, DOS will pause the display after each screenful of files. Press Enter to see the next screen.

If you're looking for a specific file, type **DIR** and then the name of the file. For example, if you're trying to find MYBRAIN.TXT, you type the following:

```
C:\> DIR MYBRAIN.TXT
```

That is, you type **DIR,** a space, and then **MYBRAIN.TXT.** Press Enter. If the DIR command cannot locate the file, you'll see the message File not found.

COPY

Use the COPY command to make a copy or duplicate of a file. For example, to copy a file to a disk in drive A, you type the following:

```
C:\> COPY FILE.TXT A:
```

That's **COPY,** a space, the name of the file (FILE.TXT, in this example), another space, then **A,** and a colon. Make sure that there's a disk in drive A and then press Enter to copy the file.

To make a duplicate of a file, you must type the file's original name, a space, and then the name you want to give the duplicate:

```
C:\> COPY FILE1.TXT NEWFILE
```

You type **COPY,** followed by a space, the name of the original file (FILE1.TXT), another space, and then the name of the new file (NEWFILE). The name of the new file must be a proper filename. If not, the DOS nun will come out and whap your wrists with a ruler.

DEL

The DEL command deletes files. This can be deadly! Be careful with the DEL command. Suppose that you are typing the following:

```
C:\> DEL ELVIS
```

You type **DEL,** followed by a space, and then the name of the file you want to delete. In this example, DEL will remove ELVIS (the file) from your disk.

After a file is gone, there's no way to get it back. Nope. No way, no how. This makes you wonder why there is a DEL command. The answer is that some files just need to be deleted after you're done using them. And temporary or junk files accumulate all over a hard disk. Kill them. Kill them now.

We lied! If you delete a file and want it back, you can use the UNDELETE command in DOS 5:

```
C:\> UNDELETE ELVIS
```

Type **UNDELETE,** a space, and then the name of the file you want back. Follow the instructions on the screen and, soon, the King lives!

The sooner you use UNDELETE after deleting a file, the better. This command may not always work; some files are just too far gone for even DOS to save.

HELP

At last, some refreshing help. DOS 5 comes with a HELP command that displays extra information about DOS commands. But don't get too cheery: The HELP command isn't as helpful as you may have dreamed about. Instead of putting a reassuring arm around your shoulder, HELP slings out messages that are as dry as the 4 a.m. sausage-and-egg special at the local all-night eating establishment.

There are three ways to use HELP. The first is fairly obvious to anyone who types at the DOS prompt:

```
C:\> HELP
```

That's **HELP** with no exclamation point. What you'll see on your screen is a list of all the various DOS commands and a brief, terse, ugly description of what they do. If you find the command that interests you, then the second way to use HELP comes in handy:

```
C:\> HELP COPY
```

Type **HELP,** a space, and then the DOS command you want help with. In this example, the COPY command is listed. In this example, after pressing Enter you'll see a few dry comments about COPY, along with a cryptic "command description." This can be scary, so bundle up and grab the popcorn.

The third way to use HELP is to follow a DOS command with /? — the forward slash and the question mark character, both of which are on the same key. For example, type the following:

```
C:\> COPY /?
```

That's **COPY,** a space, the forward slash, and then the question mark. Pressing Enter directs DOS to display some quasi-helpful information about the COPY command. Does it really help? It depends. Sometimes you'll see just what you need. Other times it looks like the computer is playing "Wheel of Fortune" with you and Vanna's head is blocking all the important letters.

Ugly Error Messages Abound!

When you do something to DOS that it doesn't like, its first response is to slide you an offensive error message. It's dreadful. No explanation is given. You just see the embarrassing thing sitting there, glowering at you. Or worse, a co-worker saunters by, points, and laughs. Then everyone in the office knows.

Fear not! Those days are over. Of all the DOS error messages (and there are hundreds of them) four are the most common. The following sections give directions on how to deal with them.

Bad command or file name

This gem is DOS's way of telling you that it didn't understand what you typed at it. You've made a typo, so reenter the line more carefully the second time. If the message persists, then contact your guru for help. (This message also appears when you hurl insults at the computer — a popular pastime.)

File not found

You typed in the name of a file, and DOS can't find it. This doesn't mean the file vanished. Usually, Mr. Typo is to blame; check your spelling and try the command again. DOS is fussy about being precise. If you still can't find the file, it's time for guru help.

Not ready error reading drive X

This error happens when you try to use a disk drive and there's no disk in it. Typically, that's drive A. The solution is to find a disk, stick it into the drive, close the drive's door (if necessary), and type the command again.

Abort, Retry, Ignore, or Fail?

This prompt appears by the deadliest of error messages. What's happened is that DOS has tried several times to do something and couldn't quite figure it out. The message is asking for your input on how to continue. Always press R first. For example, if this message is accompanying a not ready error, then stick a disk in the drive and press R. If that isn't the case, and the message continues, then press A. Never press I or F.

Here's how to rid yourself of those ugly DOS error messages littering your screen:

```
C:\> CLS
```

Type **CLS** and press Enter. The CLS command clears the screen, erasing all the evidence that you, er, the computer, fouled up.

Done for the Day

When you're ready to stop work for the day, save everything. Don't just turn off the monitor and leave. Save your files first! In some cases, your office computer person may order you to perform a backup as well. Either way, follow your instructions and save the stuff you've been working on.

To turn off the computer, quit or exit your software and return to the DOS prompt. How this is done varies from program to program. But whatever the keys you need to press, do it and return to the DOS prompt.

When you're at the DOS prompt, check your disk drive lights. None of the lights should be on or flashing. After all the hubbub has calmed down, you can then shut off your computer.

- If you want to keep the computer on, then just turn off the monitor.
- Never turn off the computer unless you see a DOS prompt on the screen.
- Never turn off the computer if a disk drive light is on.
- Refer to Chapter 3 for more information.

● ●

Summary

This chapter provided a brief introduction to DOS, the disk operating system that runs your PC. Although a full explanation of DOS can't be given in just one chapter, you learned many things that will help you deal with DOS:

▶ You learned how to recognize the DOS prompt and what to do when you see it.

▶ You got information about finding the program that you want to run and running it from the DOS prompt.

▶ You learned what to do when you get "dumped" at the DOS prompt.

▶ You learned the rules for naming files.

▶ You learned how to move among different drives, directories, and subdirectories.

▶ You learned to use four of the most commonly used DOS commands: DIR, COPY, DEL, and HELP.

▶ You found out what to do when DOS gives you a dreaded error message.

Chapter 14 describes the most popular operating systems and how you use them.

● ●

Chapter 14

Those *Other* Operating Systems

● ●

In This Chapter

▶ What is OS/2?

▶ What is DR DOS?

▶ What is PC DOS?

▶ What is UNIX?

▶ What is System 7?

● ●

*E*ver stepped into a rental car, accidentally turned on the windshield wipers, and fumbled frantically across an unfamiliar dashboard, hoping to find the Off switch before *everybody* starts pointing fingers and giggling?

Some people aren't afraid of ditching their familiar "MS-DOS dashboard," however. These daring renegades are switching to a different *operating system* — a new way of bossing around their computers.

In fact, some people have thrown away their PCs, case and all. They have switched to a Macintosh breed of computer so that they can run its operating system, *System 7*.

This chapter checks out some of the other operating systems in the computing world. Will they give your computer "cruise control" or will they make *everybody* point and giggle?

OS/2

Although OS/2 sounds like a cleaning solution for carburetors, its marketing budget towers over such products as WD-40. You may have already seen an OS/2 commercial on TV or spotted the OS/2 logo on the baseball cap of a stylish computer nerd.

This section offers a brief Tourist's Guide to OS/2, by pointing out the places to visit and the alligator-filled swamps to avoid.

What is OS/2?

OS/2 stands for Operating System 2. Just like the movie *Terminator 2,* OS/2 is a sequel. In fact, OS/2 was designed back in the early '80s to replace that cranky, old MS-DOS operating system. OS/2, intended to be faster and more powerful, appeared on the cover of all the flashiest computer-nerd magazines.

But when OS/2 arrived in 1987, nobody bought it. Back then, OS/2 couldn't run anybody's favorite DOS programs. OS/2 converts had to buy new, *OS/2* versions of their programs. Add a new computer to that shopping list too: OS/2 needed a 286 computer with gobs of memory, which was an expensive proposition back then.

The death knell? OS/2 simply couldn't print anything. The first version of OS/2 had trouble talking to most printers.

The latest version of OS/2 is making a comeback. OS/2 can finally run DOS programs *and* Windows programs. And thank goodness! OS/2 programs still haven't started showing up at many software stores.

Where did it come from?

Microsoft and IBM teamed up to release OS/2 in 1987 and hoped that this new, easy-to-use operating system would make everybody an OS/2 convert.

But while OS/2 languished on the store shelves, Microsoft released a product that *did* catch on: Windows. Windows 3.0 sold more copies in three months than OS/2 had sold in the preceding three years.

So Microsoft dumped OS/2 in IBM's lap and began pushing Windows instead. Now the two companies aren't speaking to each other.

What computer uses OS/2?

OS/2 needs a fast 386, 486, or Pentium/586 computer before it will come out of the box. IBM says that OS/2 needs 4MB of memory, but you will want at least 8MB after hearing your computer strain under the pressure.

Make sure that your hard drive has at least 40MB of free space. Also, you want an extra 60MB to store all your programs.

Sure, that's a great deal of numbers. But at least OS/2 doesn't require a *genuine* IBM computer; it runs on those cheap clones out there too.

What's OS/2 good for?

MS-DOS was designed for computers built in 1981. OS/2 was designed for *today's* computers and all their speed, power, and expensive gadgetry.

For example, OS/2 can *multitask,* or do several things at the same time (see Figure 14-1). Using OS/2, a friend of mine formatted a floppy disk, played a game of Space Quest, downloaded a file from an on-line service, and drank a soft drink — all at the same time.

What sucks about it?

OS/2 has been slow to catch on. In fact, many dealers don't stock OS/2 or any OS/2 programs. And OS/2 is expensive: It usually costs more than $100.

OS/2 takes advantage of today's computers by offering zillions of different options and settings. But, like a retired person setting up a model train in the garage, you will spend a great deal of time fiddling with OS/2, making sure that everything is set up *just so.*

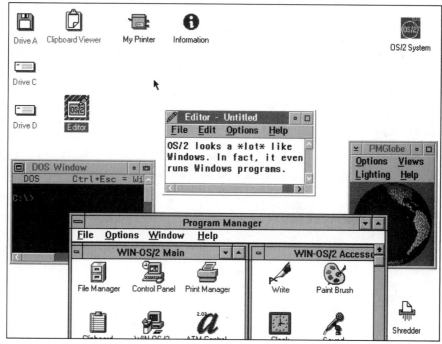

Figure 14-1: OS/2 can run DOS, Windows, and OS/2 programs at the same time, each in their own little window.

Who's using OS/2?

Because OS/2 can juggle so many programs simultaneously, some corporations use it for network stuff. When everybody tries to send e-mail at the same time, OS/2 doesn't burp as loudly as much as MS-DOS does.

Some dedicated OS/2 users simply grew tired of spoon-feeding an aging MS-DOS. OS/2 can dish out your computer's memory in the right doses to satisfy the most finicky MS-DOS programs.

Also, some people find OS/2's *object-oriented* approach simpler to use than DOS or Windows. To print a report in OS/2, for example, you use your mouse to "drag" the picture of your report over to the picture of your printer. Let go of the mouse button, and your *real* printer squirts out your report. Fun!

Finally, OS/2 handles multimedia stuff pretty well: Its compact disc version comes with little movies you can play on your computer screen. Now, if somebody would just write some decent OS/2 games. . . .

Where can I buy it?

Although you might stumble across OS/2 in your neighborhood software shop, you can also buy it directly from IBM by calling 1-800-3-IBM-OS2. (That translates to 1-800-342-6672.) And if you *do* take the plunge, feel free to pick up a copy of *OS/2 For Dummies* (published by IDG Books Worldwide).

DR DOS

Some daring folks still use DOS on their computer — but *not* the DOS everybody else uses. These folks use DR DOS, an operating system that looks and feels just like MS-DOS but doesn't have a hyphen (see Figure 14-2).

Oh, and DR DOS doesn't have anything to do with Microsoft either: It was written by a competing company with the overly nerdish name of Digital Research.

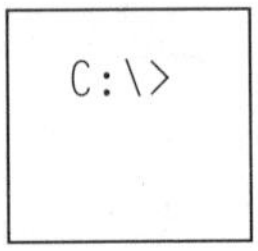

Figure 14-2:
DR DOS
looks just like
MS-DOS.

```
C:\>
```

What is DR DOS?

DR DOS is to MS-DOS as Sprite is to Seven-Up: Only hard-core soft drinkers can sniff out any difference between the two during a taste test.

Differences exist, but not in simple DOS commands, such as DIR and DEL. Instead, DR DOS comes with all the basic DOS stuff, but it includes some new features to make Microsoft look bad.

Where did it come from?

DR DOS is *not* pronounced "Doctor DOS (it plays one on TV, though). You pronounce it "dee are DOS," as in *Digital Research* DOS.

A few years ago, the Digital Research company made an operating system that did everything MS-DOS did and more. It could squeeze more information on a hard drive, for example.

Microsoft watched DR DOS carefully and then began adding the same features to its own MS-DOS product. Digital Research responded by releasing a newer version with even *more* features. Microsoft responded again, and the two companies have been playing leapfrog ever since.

Eager to join the game, a networking company called *Novell* bought Digital Research — lock, stock, and barrel. To keep the game going, Novell is adding new networking features to DR DOS.

What computer uses DR DOS?

All IBM-compatible PCs can run DR DOS. If a PC can run MS-DOS, it can run DR DOS too.

What's DR DOS good for?

Some folks like the way DR DOS keeps one step ahead of MS-DOS by perpetually adding just a *few more* features. For example, DR DOS lets its users lock the keyboard when they go to get more coffee — without having to turn off their computer.

Other DR DOS users, tired of the Microsoft empire, want to buy something different, just out of spite.

What sucks about it?

Very little, actually. Microsoft, however, thinks that the entire DR DOS *concept* sucks: Just imagine — another company taking money out of *its* pockets! To add fear and doubt, Microsoft says that Windows isn't guaranteed to work with DR DOS. Although DR DOS gave early Windows 3.1 users a slight problem, thousands of DR DOS users now use Windows without a problem.

Budding programmers might find fault with it, however. MS-DOS comes with QBASIC, a stripped-down version of the QuickBASIC programming language. If, for some unnatural reason, you want to write programs in BASIC, don't expect to find any version of BASIC in the DR DOS box.

Who's using DR DOS?

Remember the kids in school who hung out on the corner and smoked cigarettes? Although they were reasonably harmless, they wanted to look as though they were getting away with something. They were pseudo-rebels — rotten to the core, yet still home for supper.

A similar attitude drives people to DR DOS. It's a safe alternative to MS-DOS, it comes with extra goodies, and it lets people avoid that MS-DOS stuff that *everybody's* using.

Plus, DR DOS users can lock the keyboard as they sashay toward the lounge for a quick smoking break.

Where can I buy it?

DR DOS is available in most computer stores and mail-order catalogs. Or call Novell at 1-800-554-4446.

PC DOS

Yes, *another* version of DOS (see Figure 14-3).

Figure 14-3:
Another
version of
DOS.

```
C:\>
```

What is PC DOS?

PC DOS is *another* clone of MS-DOS; this time, IBM did the work. PC DOS has all the major features Microsoft delivers, plus a handful of others to sweeten the deal.

Microsoft's DOS has QBASIC — a programming language for budding nerds, but PC DOS doesn't. PC DOS works with those fancy, new, pen-based devices, however, and MS-DOS doesn't.

A matter of preference and a sense of adventure lures users away from MS-DOS and into the land of PC DOS. Some folks don't have a choice, however: PC DOS comes built in to all the computers IBM sells.

Where did PC DOS come from?

Computing changed forever when IBM released its "personal computing" machine on store shelves. IBM's initials were emblazoned on the front of the machine to signify to the business world that PCs were *real* machines and no longer hobbyist toys for garage hackers.

Because IBM rushed the machine to the market, the company's engineers focused on the hardware and hired someone else — Microsoft — to do the software. The combination of IBM's parts and Microsoft's programs made history.

Microsoft and IBM grew apart over the years (see the section "OS/2"), however, so IBM decided to release its own version of MS-DOS — PC DOS.

What computer uses PC DOS?

Any IBM-compatible PC can run PC DOS, just as it can run MS-DOS or DR DOS. Some like Fords, some like Chevys, and some like Hyundais.

What's PC DOS good for?

PC DOS packs more punch than MS-DOS does, in several areas. PC DOS works better with some tape backups and compressed floppy disks, and it can do some stuff automatically: run a backup program while you're asleep, for example.

Also, the anti-virus stuff in PC DOS seeks out and destroys 1,500 known viruses, a number that far exceeds Microsoft's. PC DOS searches for viruses whenever you want: every time you boot up or the first boot of the day, week, or month.

What sucks about it?

Unfortunately, PC DOS needs more hard drive space to store all its extra goodies. IBM says that it needs only 3MB of free space, but to install *everything*, you need almost 10MB (compared with slightly less than 6MB for MS-DOS).

If you're hankering to learn BASIC programming, you have to buy your own package. And IBM's little text editor, E, is lousy compared to Microsoft's Edit program. The SCANDISK utility, which Microsoft released in Version 6.2, is noticeably absent. SCANDISK is a good way to check a hard drive for errors, and it is sorely missed.

Who's using PC DOS?

Users who want to try different operating systems without straying too far from familiar terrain are dabbling with PC DOS. People who buy computers from IBM *have* to dabble with it.

These DOS systems really aren't in vogue among the adventurous, though. Real power users are heading for graphics-based systems, such as OS/2 and Microsoft's deluxe networking version of Windows, Windows NT.

Where can I buy it?

PC DOS 6.1 is available from most computer and mail-order stores or directly from IBM Corporation: 1133 Westchester Avenue, White Plains, NY 10604; 1-800-342-6672.

UNIX

UNIX — a hulking, complicated system for hulking, chest-pounding computers — gets its due in this section (see Figure 14-4). Ugh.

What is UNIX?

When UNIX hit the computing scene, fanatics and zealots screamed from the rooftops that this was *the* operating system — the others would soon be obsolete. More than 25 years later, the nerds are screaming the same thing: The world will wake up any day and realize that UNIX is The Master.

```
$ ls -l
total 1032
drwxr-xr-x    5 root      rootgrp      128 Apr  5  1990 appl
drwxrwxr-x    2 bin       bin         1744 Jun 16  1993 bin
drwxrwx—x     2 ncrm      ncrm          32 Dec  1  1987 datacap
drwxrwxr-x   10 root      sys          464 Jul 31 23:35 dev
drwxrwxrwx    4 root      rootgrp      128 Nov  2 16:26 ead
drwxrwxr-x    9 root      sys         2464 Oct 26 18:49 etc
drwxr-xr-x    3 root      rootgrp       64 Dec  1  1987 kernel
drwxrwxr-x    4 bin       bin          336 Jun 16  1993 lib
drwxrwxrwx    2 root      rootgrp     4128 Apr  5  1990 lost+found
drwxr-xr-x    5 root      rootgrp       80 Apr  5  1990 menu
drwxr-xr-x    2 root      rootgrp       32 Dec  1  1987 mnt
drwxrwx---    7 ncrm      ncrm         320 Apr  5  1990 ncrm
drwxrwxr-x    3 root      rootgrp       80 Jun 16  1993 shlib
drwxr-xr-x    5 root      rootgrp      288 Jun 11  1993 sys
drwxrwxrwx    2 sys       sys          928 Dec 17 23:41 tmp
```

Figure 14-4: UNIX looks as confusing as it really is.

UNIX is a *multitasking, multi-user* operating system. That means that a bunch of people can use *one* computer at the *same* time. Imagine the squabble over who gets to use the keyboard!

Where did it come from?

In the late 1960s, Ken Thompson and Dennis Ritchie were working for Bell Labs, back before the breakup of the telephone monopoly. Thompson wrote a crude game for a GE mainframe (big) computer and then tried to play the game on a faster (and smaller) DEC computer. In the process, the two men wound up writing an entire operating system.

Why did they call it UNIX? Nobody knows, although one common fable says that it describes how the men believed that Bell Labs treated them. (*Eunuchs* — get it?)

Because Bell was under government regulation at the time, the duo couldn't sell UNIX and make a killing. So they gave it to the government and universities for a nominal cost. In the university setting, programmers rewrote UNIX over and over and added more features each time.

What computer uses UNIX?

UNIX prospered on minicomputers (an oxymoron for machines that consumed only *half* — not all — the room). But what about PCs?

Microsoft came up with XENIX, designed to run on PCs. Novell, a networking giant from Utah, bought bits and pieces of other corporations and ended up releasing UNIXWARE, another PC-based version.

Today computer nerds can find a version of UNIX that runs on virtually every conceivable size and type of computer on the market. (Don't hold your breath for a Nintendo cartridge, however.)

What's UNIX good for?

UNIX works best when bunches of people want to play with the same computer at the same time. *Minicomputers*, the clunky grandfathers of today's PCs, are perfect examples. Bunches of people connect keyboards and monitors (called *dumb terminals* — we're not making this up) to the minicomputer and start typing away, all without worrying about what the other users are doing.

Network hounds also covet UNIX for its built-in TCP/IP network stuff, although if you remember that, you have to help Ms. Scott clean erasers after school.

What sucks about it?

First, UNIX is big and clunky, mostly because it has been rewritten zillions of times in the past 30 years. Many early rewrites came from nerdy university students who couldn't get dates when the chess club was out of town.

Hundreds of UNIX programs are floating around. These programs not only eat great gobs of disk space, they also run differently on different versions of UNIX. Each UNIX vendor wants its own version to be the standard, so they all bicker and snipe and increase the confusion factor.

Who's using UNIX?

The government, particularly the Department of Defense, bought in to UNIX in a big way. Next came all the campuses and universities, where UNIX prospered for years.

The engineering industry picked up on UNIX primarily because it runs on *SUN workstations,* which are super friendly, lightning-quick, space-age computers that fall somewhere between PCs and minicomputers.

Where can I buy it?

If you're a glutton for punishment, look for UNIX at your local computer store. It probably won't be sitting on the shelf, however. Instead, the most wild-eyed salesperson probably can give you a phone number to call, depending on the version you're seeking.

The Macintosh's System 7

Just as some people don't eat meat, some people don't use IBM-compatible PCs. These vegetarians of the computer world are using that *other* computer: the Macintosh, an entirely different breed relished by millions.

The Macintosh is described in Chapter 4; this section talks about the special software that makes the Mac do all its fun stuff: its operating system, known as System 7 (see Figure 14-5).

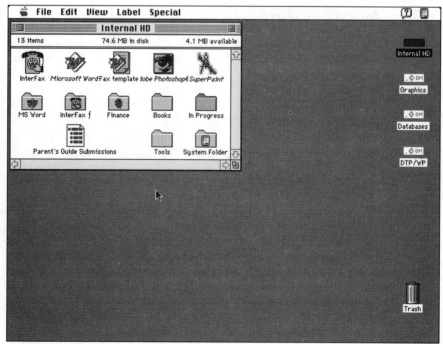

Figure 14-5: The clean-looking Macintosh operating system looks sort of like Windows and OS/2 because Windows and OS/2 sort of copied it.

What is System 7?

For such a cute computer, the Macintosh operating system has a boring name. It's simply called *system software*. Each new version gets a new number tacked on to the end: System 6 or System 7.1, for example.

The later version, System 7, is the first big update in years. It can *multitask* (run several programs at the same time), use *virtual memory* (borrow parts of the hard disk when it runs out of memory), and connect with cables to other friendly Macs to share files and stuff over cables.

Unlike PCs, Macs are pickier about their system software: The software must work with special, secret chips Apple built in to every Mac. You're pretty much stuck, therefore, with Apple's operating system (although some strange breeds of UNIX will work too).

Where did it come from?

Apple Computer wrote System 7, just as it wrote all the other versions. Many of the Mac's essential concepts came from Apple's earlier Lisa computer — a sexy but ill-fated computer that cost a ridiculous amount of money.

What computer uses System 7?

Right now, only Macs can run System 7. Macs include the Macintosh, Performa, Quadra, Centris, and PowerBook. A few of the oldest Macs *can't* run System 7, however: They don't have enough memory.

Apple might license System 7 for use on Intel-based computers — plain ol' PCs. Also, Apple's wild, new "PowerPCs" will use it too. (Chapter 6 has the PowerPC powwow.)

What's System 7 good for?

Like previous versions, System 7 makes it a snap to share data between different documents and even different programs. Any data or picture you copy in one document can be pasted into another. A new Publish & Subscribe feature carries this concept even further. Change some data or a picture and all its copies are automatically updated too.

Perhaps the Mac's greatest selling point, though, is its consistency. All the programs work in the same way, with the same menus. Every program is not a new "adventure in learning."

What sucks about it?

Not much, really. People who previously used MS-DOS sometimes wish that they could *type* a command now and then, though.

Like previous versions of the system software, System 7 is still something of a juggling act. Because System 7 can juggle several programs, one ill-behaved utility or program can make everything else fall apart too.

Who's using System 7?

New Macs come with System 7 already installed. Many owners of older Macs have also moved up to System 7. The advantages and benefits of the new system software are simply too much fun.

Where can I buy it?

Apple let people give away early versions of System 7 to their friends. If people wanted a manual, though, they had to buy it from Apple. Beginning with System 7.1, however, Apple says that it's a commercial-only software product — no more freebies. Most software dealers and mail-order houses sell System 7 upgrades.

• •

Summary

This chapter gave you brief descriptions of the possible operating systems you might have on your computer. You learned some basics about the following operating systems:

- OS/2
- DR DOS
- PC DOS
- UNIX
- System 7

Chapter 15 gives you the ins and outs on the next element you need for your computer: software. That chapter describes the most popular types of software, gives pointers for purchasing software, and tells you how to install it.

• •

Chapter 15
Software: The Real Brains

• •

• •

*W*ithout software, a computer just sits around like a car with no gas. The computer (the hardware) is the vehicle: a powerful engine, a smooth chassis, and big tires in back. The software is the gas: It lets the computer actually *do* something besides pilfer an open desktop or look *purdy* in the garage.

You can't avoid buying software, even if you're gung-ho and fired up to write your own. Professional programmers have to buy special programming language software before they can write their own programs. You're more fortunate: Your dealer, local software stores, and mail-order suppliers can satiate your needs. And, if you want to learn to write your own software, that's possible as well. Look what it did for Bill Gates.

This chapter offers pointers on what to do in the software store besides get that bewildered look that snaps salespeople toward you like a frog's tongue zapping a lazy fly. We'll describe the flavors of software out there and how to feed software to your computer after you've returned home and taken the disks out of the box.

The Wordy Stuff

Just about everybody wants to use his or her computer to write something. Whether it's a thank-you note to Aunt Sally or a letter to an Arizona judge protesting a speeding ticket, computers make the writing process — putting thoughts onto paper — much easier. In fact, if this were *USA Today,* we'd have a little box nearby that would say that 70 percent of all computers are used for word processing.

- ✔ Word processing is writing. It's creating text on a computer that will eventually be printed. Creating the text is done in a similar fashion on all computers, with one of three types of software: word processors, text editors, and desktop publishing software.

- ✔ The coolest part about writing on a computer is that you can change what you've written without messing up the printed page. Editing "on the screen" means that each printed page will be perfect. Or as near perfect as you and the computer can make it.

- ✔ Marvelous things can be done with words in a computer. In addition to cutting and pasting text, moving it around, deleting and undeleting, a computer can check your spelling. It can't check for "your" versus "you're," but it does know that "teh" should probably be "the." The software will even correct the word for you after you simply press a key. (If only a speeding ticket could be handled so easily!)

Word processors

A word processor lets your computer toss words around like an Arnold Schwarzenegger-ized typewriter. Traditional typewriters move forward in straight lines, one character at a time. If you decide later to add a few descriptive phrases to an earlier paragraph, you're stuck.

Word processors add an extra step between your thoughts and their debut on paper: When you type, the words appear on the screen, where they can be rearranged easily. Make a mistake? Press the arrow keys until the cursor rests over the trouble spot. Type in the new stuff, and it mixes right in. And to think Nabokov wrote by hand while standing up.

A word processor can do fancier tricks than a typewriter, too. Most word processors can automatically add footnotes, check your spelling, change all references of "Mr. Clinton" to "President Clinton," and whip through other chores that leave typewriters squirming in their rollers.

Best yet, a word processor lets you change things up to the last minute. If a report is supposed to be ten pages and you can only come up with six pages, you can change to double-spacing and see whether the words look better on the screen. If not, triple-space it and move in the margins a little bit. When the report looks perfect, press a button and the printer will create a flawlessly typed version.

And, if you find errors on the printed page, you can still fix them and print out the pages once again. So much for the paperless office!

- ✔ The files that word processors save are commonly called *documents*. But get this: Every word processor saves its documents by using a different file format. Just like Chevy parts won't fit in a Ford, files created by one word processor can't always be read by another brand of word processor.

- ✔ Some word processors let you create *form letters*. You type a letter, save it, and then type a list of all the people who should receive the letter. The word processor will automatically grab those names and addresses, one by one, stick them at the top of the letter, and print out a fresh letter to each person on the list. Computer companies often refer to this customized junk mail approach as *mail merge*.

- ✔ Although mail merge is offered as a feature on all major word processors, it's the most painful and difficult thing to do. Most people would rather drag a hangnail down past the second knuckle than bother with mail merge.

- ✔ Specialized word processors can handle all sorts of esoteric chores, including special screenplay formatting, mathematical equations, funky foreign languages, complex lawyer-like things, and other areas that could frustrate both a typewriter and its user.

Text editors

Word processors let you play with margins, make words **boldfaced** or *italicized*, and play with their *fonts*. Text editors, in contrast, handle the bare basics. You can enter words, move them around, and delete the dumb ones, but that's about the limit. There's usually no fancy formatting or any way to check your spelling or grammar. So why bother with a text editor?

Well, because they're so simple, they're fast and small enough to fit on a floppy disk. Most of them save text files in something called *ASCII,* a bare-bones, standard format. Most programs and word processors can subsequently read these ASCII text files.

- A text editor is basically a no-frills word processor.

- Text editors save their documents as plain text or ASCII files. No fancy schmancy stuff.

- DOS comes with a text editor called EDIT.COM. Cool.

- Some programmers use text editors to write programs, where any sort of headers or italics will confuse the computer and make it ask for funny summer hats in the winter.

Desktop publishing packages

As word processors began to get fancier, they could do more than manipulate words. They could add pictures, arrange the words into slick newspaper columns, and add headlines. These new features weren't designed for composing words; they were designed for rearranging them so that the pages looked professionally published.

Today, these *desktop publishing programs* can create the fancy pages you see in newspapers, magazines, and helpful newsletters that come with the gas and electricity company bills.

When combined with a high-quality printer, desktop publishing software lets a computer handle work that once required expensive typesetting machines. Social theory analysts like to say it's brought "publishing power to the masses." Everybody else asks how come the software costs so much.

- Desktop publishing is abbreviated *DTP*.

- Desktop publishing programs can create anything from a Boy Scout troop newsletter to a book of esoteric poetry. Yet the software can be difficult to work with because it uses age-old publishing-industry terms: *kerning, fonts, typeface, leading,* and other esoteric words. Be prepared to spend time studying the industry's language before trying to mimic it.

- Today's more expensive word processing software includes many of the features of desktop publishing programs. Unless you're in the publishing business, a program like Word for Windows or Ami Professional can probably handle your desktop publishing needs.

- To combat the increasingly powerful word processors, desktop publishing packages have been adding word processing features: spell checkers, grammar checkers, and other traditional word processing goodies. Still, they're better at formatting text than helping create it.

Spreadsheets

Because word processors staked out their claim on words, spreadsheets grabbed the numbers crowd. A spreadsheet places a large grid of box-like *cells* on the screen. People type numbers into the little cells and then tell the spreadsheet what to do with them: take the number in the "Purchase Price" cell, add it to the number in the "Tax, Licensing, and Other Options" cell, and put the total cost next to the cell labeled "Oh my!"

Just as word processors let you fiddle with words on the screen, spreadsheets let you fiddle with different arrangements of numbers. By changing the relationships between the cells, spreadsheets can create "what if" scenarios. You can see how much more interest you'd pay with one credit card company than with another.

- The files saved by spreadsheets are called *worksheets*. A worksheet is created by a spreadsheet.

- The higher-end spreadsheets can convert the numbers into graphs and charts, making it easier to visualize how much money the CEO is *really* making.

- Most business accounting packages consist of spreadsheets that are customized to handle a business's money-tracking needs.

- Each cell in a spreadsheet can contain one of the following: a number, a descriptive label, or a formula (some mathematical operation that tweaks the numbers).

- Although all spreadsheets start up with a blank worksheet, ready to have its little cells customized, most also come with *templates* — precreated worksheets customized to balance checkbooks, track sales figures, or perform other common calculating chores.

- Some spreadsheets can be *compiled,* or turned into separate programs. When you run the compiled program, it works just like the spreadsheet's worksheet. You can only enter information into it, however; a compiled spreadsheet can't have its formulas or labels changed.

Databases

Because the word and number processing chores are snapped up by word processors and spreadsheets, database programs organize just about everything else. Databases can handle any information, whether it is words, numbers, or little-known bits of trivia (the *Lawrence Welk Show* was originally called the *Dodge Dancing Party*).

Whereas spreadsheets and word processors help you create or change data, database programs help you store and retrieve data as well as sort and report it. Librarians use databases to track books; they can tell whether a book is checked out or is supposed to be on the shelf. Precise computer nerds say the collection of information is a *database,* and the actual database program is called a *DBMS,* or *database management system.*

- ✔ Like spreadsheets, databases must be customized to match specific needs. An army of programming enthusiasts earns a living by writing vast spreadsheets and databases to fit thousands of subtly different needs.

- ✔ Databases contain three main parts: *fields, records,* and *files.* A *field* is a single piece of data: a person's last name on a form, for instance. A *record* consists of several fields: names, addresses, and phone numbers, all together. A *file* consists of a bunch of records stored on disk.

- ✔ You have better things to do than write your own spreadsheets or programs. Just remember to press Tab when you want to move from field to field in a database. (Hold down Shift and press Tab if you want to move backward.)

- ✔ Databases and spreadsheets can sometimes replace each other's jobs. If the fields in a database contain mostly numbers, a spreadsheet may work better. If a spreadsheet contains more labels, a database may be in order.

- ✔ Why can't a single program do everything? It can. Check out the integrated packages in the next section.

Database programs come in three unimportant types

Free-form database: Perhaps the simplest database, it works best when you're organizing a big file that is full of random information. When you type the word *eggs,* the database will retrieve every paragraph mentioning eggs, whether it is a grocery reminder, a favorite recipe, or the stock quote for a software distributor.

Flat-file database: A flat-file database helps retrieve information that's been organized into sections called *fields.* One field can contain a person's first name, another can name the type of car he drives, and the third field can contain the name of his pet cow. The flat-file database can then retrieve information about people named Thomas who drive Yugos. It's more powerful than a free-form database, but it requires the information to be relatively organized to begin with.

Relational database: The most powerful database, it retrieves information from more than one file at a time, allowing for searches of people who both drive Yugos and eat steak and eggs for breakfast. Because they're the most powerful programs, they're the most expensive.

Graphics Software

As any parent of a preschooler knows, nothing makes a mess faster than artwork. With a PC, however, all the mess stays on the computer screen — they're not Crayola marks or paint drippings.

Hundreds of graphics warriors, in fact, have already swapped their oils and acrylics for a computer.

✔ PCs can handle extremely detailed or technical drawings. *Computer-Aided Design* (*CAD*) or *plotting* programs, for example, let engineers do such scientific things as design new, three-tray microwaveable containers for frozen New Orleans-style chicken and broccoli.

✔ Newspapers can "clean up" a photograph before running it in the paper.

✔ Many artists use painting or drawing programs for stuff that's going to be "desktop published." If their artwork begins its life inside the computer, they have less of a problem trying to get the artwork back inside the computer before printing time.

Some software can "grab" a picture of your current screen and save it as a file on a disk. Although some people argue about whether that's a "utility" program or a "graphics" program, they all agree that it's useful for creating product brochures.

Multimedia

When DOS first came out, computers looked pretty complicated: They used just a bunch of code words strung together. But when you run Windows, a computer's pretty pictures and colors make the monitor look like a New Age TV set. In fact, the software turns computer programs into TV programs: They both have stereo sound, moving pictures, and dopey plots. (Check out Sierra's Police Quest game for colorful crime dramas.)

In computing circles, the word *multimedia* describes any sort of flashy graphics mixed with sound. So because *Windows* has plenty of pictures and sound, it is sometimes called a *multimedia platform*. Some of the latest Windows multimedia applications come very close to a television set in terms of sound and pictures. The computer industry is excited about it; the television industry is wondering how it's going to get its cut.

✔ *Multimedia* incorporates two "mediums" — in the computer world, a computer plays sound while it displays something flashy on-screen.

✔ Multimedia applications require a powerful computer, a top-quality monitor, a large hard disk, and a sound card. Some require a CD-ROM drive (see Chapter 11). To put it simply, multimedia applications require a very expensive computer.

✔ What good is multimedia? Mostly, it's used for games. A few people use multimedia for education, although it's currently too expensive for most public-school systems. Some corporations use it for business presentations. People without multimedia computers wonder why people want to spend $3,000 for a TV set and VCR.

Utilities

Not much to get excited about here. Although most software is designed to help you get to work, utility programs help your *computer* get to work.

Basically, a utility helps a computer accomplish a chore, whether it's organizing its hard drive or figuring out why it's not working right. For example, Microsoft tossed in a bunch of free utilities with DOS 6 and DOS 6.2.

DOS 6/6.2 comes with a new diagnostic utility. Type **MSD** at the command prompt and DOS ferrets through your computer's internal organs, listing all the goodies it has found. Nobody can understand what it's trying to say, but — hey — it's a utility.

DOS 6/6.2 comes with a compression utility called DoubleSpace. When your hard drive fills up, DoubleSpace squeezes all the information on it to give you a little more breathing room.

Virus-checking utilities scan your hard drive for any evil programs and wipe them out before the viruses try the same trick. (DOS 6 comes with a virus-checking utility too.)

"Fix-it" programs, such as Norton Utilities and PC Tools, can often salvage information from a disk when the rest of your computer has given up on it.

Integrated Packages

Integrated packages claim to "do it all." And, for the most part, they're right. An integrated package contains a word processor, a database, a spreadsheet, and sometimes even a communications package for good measure.

Because all the programs work together, they can share information easily. You can grab information from your spreadsheet and database, make it into a chart, and put it in your letter to convince the Arizona judge that your Yugo simply isn't fast enough to deserve a speeding ticket.

To make it even easier to share information, the programs in an integrated package will all use the same or similar commands for basic moves, like opening and saving files or cutting and pasting information.

Finally, an integrated package usually costs less than buying three separate packages from three different manufacturers and saves you from having to deal with three different busy signals on their help support lines.

✔ Sometimes a good integrated package is all you need. The old Apple II computer was sold with a product called Appleworks. Many people enjoyed and used Appleworks for years after they stopped selling the Apple II computer. For the PC, many similar fill-in-the-blanks-works programs exist.

✔ Although integrated packages cost less and can be easier to use, they're not as powerful as separate components. They'll handle basic computing chores, but you can outgrow them if your needs increase significantly.

✔ Microsoft Windows can be considered an integrated package of sorts, in that it contains a word processor, a text editor, and a name/address database. There's no spreadsheet, however, and the word processor doesn't have a spell checker.

The Impolite Memory-Resident, or TSR, Software

Most software loads itself into your computer, performs a task, and then goes away, leaving a blank screen in its wake. It's like reading a book: You pick it up, open it and read, and then put it down when you're done. That's how most software works.

Memory-resident software, which also goes by the more dreadful sounding *terminate-and-stay-resident (TSR)* name, is different. It loads itself into memory and then stays there when it's done. This is similar to opening a book, reading a bit and then opening another book and putting it on top of the first. Like memory-resident software, the first book is still open and ready for reading; it's just buried.

It's time to use an example (because this is a bizarre concept, even for the computing elite). One of the first and most popular TSR programs is SideKick. You type the letters **SK** at the DOS prompt and nothing happens. At least, you think nothing has happened. But SideKick loads itself into your computer's memory and hovers there, watching everything you type at the keyboard. So you go about your business.

Then, when you press a certain combination of keys, SideKick leaps into action, even if you happen to be using another program. For instance, while in your word processor, you hold down both Shift keys — a meaningless combination, yet the one that activates SideKick. The program then pops up in the corner of your screen and presents your address book, ready for you to find the right ZIP code. When you press another key, SideKick disappears. It lurks again in the background, waiting for the right key combination to display its address book, notepad, calendar, or other handy gadget.

It's a novel concept, having another program jump up while a second one sits on the screen. It's so novel, in fact, that the DOS programmers never expected it. Nobody set any rules for where these TSR programs could hang out while they waited for their special keys.

So the TSRs began slugging each other out for your computer's memory. Instead of making for action-packed ESPN specials, the fights freeze up keyboards and displays. The Reset button has to step in as a referee, often destroying any unsaved work in progress.

- ✔ TSR stands for terminate-and-stay-resident. Now what the heck does that mean? Is it what happens in some genius government Social Security home? Actually — and you should have been suspecting this — it's the name of a DOS programmer's function. How the marketing droids got hold of the term is anyone's guess. Now we're all stuck with it.

- ✔ TSRs still cause problems today. That's why computer gurus often ask, "Do you have any TSRs loaded?" when you call with questions.

- ✔ There's no way to escape TSR programs because they're everywhere. The software *driver* that controls your mouse is a TSR; so are the programs that run your network or any other miscellaneous peripherals you may have stuffed inside your computer.

- ✔ Getting rid of TSRs is tricky. Although they do lurk in memory, you can unload them. The object is to unload them in the reverse order in which they started. Because you probably don't know which TSRs you have in memory, this is a chore best left to the guru gods.

Buying Software That Works on Your Computer

When you buy software, you need to make sure that it works on your system and that it will do the job you want it to do. By taking the following steps, you can save time and money and find just what you need.

Step 1: Know what you want

Before you can buy software, you must finger exactly what tasks you want your computer to perform. Keep track of stock portfolios? Balance the checkbook? Help write Christmas form letters to send to relatives? Grab a partner and do-si-do? Write down the reasons you bought your computer. (There must be some reasons, right?) Narrow down your needs to specific categories. Know what it is you want before you buy.

Step 2: Know what equipment your computer has

Next, you'll have to make sure that the software runs on your computer. Sure, you're buying software for an IBM-compatible computer, but all IBM-compatible computers wear different clothes. Most software boxes come with a little sticker along their bottom edge. The fine print on the sticker says what computer equipment that software requires.

Because you won't be bringing your computer to the store, fill in the blanks on the next page with information pertaining to your computer. You'll find much of this information on your sales receipt. You'll have to bug your guru for the rest of it.

- ✔ If the software's disks are the wrong density or don't fit in your computer's disk drives, the software company will gladly swap disks with you. Gladly, that is, because it'll charge you anywhere from $5 to $15 to mail you the right-sized disks. So . . . buy software with the right kind of disks in the first place.

- ✔ Powerful computers are generally *downward compatible.* That is, DOS 5.0 will run DOS 5.0-compatible programs, as well as programs intended for DOS 4.1, 3.3, 2.1, or earlier. Likewise, a Super VGA card and monitor can use software intended for VGA, EGA, CGA, and Hercules-compatible systems.

- ✔ If the box says "512K required," you don't have to have exactly 512K of RAM to run the program; you must have 512K or *more.* You're safe if you have 512K, 640K, 1MB, or even more RAM.

- ✔ All 386 computers — all of them — come with at least 1MB of RAM.

- ✔ Don't buy software that requires more horsepower than you have. It's tempting. Some greedy sales types may even claim that it will still work on your low-power PC. Wrong! Even it if works, problems can show up in subtle ways. For instance, if you try to play Sierra On-Line's King's Quest IV game on your XT computer, the game will still work — but you'll be trapped in the ogre's house forever. We all know how painful that can be.

My IBM compatible computer runs DOS version number _____ .

(With your computer on, type **VER** at the DOS prompt and press Enter to find out.)

It has a _____ **CPU brain.**

(80286, 80386, 386SX, 486, and so on)

It has _____ **of memory.**

(256K, 512K, 1MB, 2MB, 4MB, 8MB, or 16MB)

Its monitor displays _____ **graphics.**

(Hercules, Monochrome, CGA, EGA, VGA, SVGA, or XGA)

Its disk drive can handle _____ **-density** _____ **-inch disks.**

(High- or low-density; 3 ½- or 5 ¼-inch disks)

My hard drive stores _____ **megabytes of stuff.**

(The total capacity of your hard drive; from your sales receipt: 40MB, 80MB, and so on)

I will print stuff on my _____ **printer.**

(may be Hewlett-Packard LaserJet, PostScript, Epson 9-pin, or hundreds of others)

Step 3: Try out the software

Unlike cars, which get run down and dirty on test drives, software doesn't wear out, no matter how often it has been used. That's why many software stores let people try out the software in the store. Take advantage of their kindness and play with the software for at least 15 minutes. See whether the program's layout makes sense to you. Ask yourself these questions:

✔ Is it easy to use?

✔ Is its Help system friendly?

✔ Is the manual easy to read?

✔ Does the company have a toll-free help number?

✔ Do I like the picture on the box?

Step 4: Shop around

If the salesperson is geekier than usual, naturally, you'll want to leave —
quickly. But, if the salesperson is friendly and seems to know the package well,
that knowledge may be worth more than a $5 savings down the street.
Software's only good if you can use it, and having an expert a phone's length
away can be priceless.

✔ Shopping for a lower price for software is definitely worth trying —
especially after you've tried the software and decided to purchase it.

✔ If price is a major motivator, consider buying the software by mail order.
Most businesses will go this way in the '90s, offering products and support
over the phone line. Mail-order prices are cheapest. Also, it's one of the
only ways to get software if you're planning to move to Colville, Washington.

✔ Check return policies before purchasing. Because most places offer a
30-day return policy, we recommend avoiding the stores that don't.

✔ Most people purchase their computer software when they buy their PC.
The software is often thrown in for free. Yeah, right.

Step 5: Buy it

But don't get carried away and buy too much! It can take a good week or so just
to get started with one package. Also, it's best to wait at least a week between
installations of new software: If you install five packages at once and your computer stops working, you won't know which package did something wrong.

✔ Buying the software may not seem like much of a decision — that is, until
you're looking for the right package for you and three of them do everything you want. Don't sit and stew. And don't be lured by rumors of a new
version; buy the software and get started with it now! If a new version
comes out, you can upgrade (see "Version Numbers" later in this chapter).

✔ Keep your receipt.

✔ Make sure that you buy the version of the software for your computer.
This goes back to checking the label on the box: Make sure that everything
matches what you have. Don't buy the Macintosh version of the program!
And make sure that the disks fit your drives.

What's This Stuff in the Box?

Surprisingly, many large software boxes contain air or cardboard padding to make the boxes look bigger and more impressive on the shelf. The most important things inside are the disks — usually anywhere from 2 to 15 of them. You'll probably find a manual and a few other goodies, too. Here's the rundown:

Disks: These disks aren't the software; the software is *stored* on these disks. To make the software work, you'll usually stick a disk in your disk drive and type a word like "setup" or "install" at the DOS prompt to set up or install your application. The program will then install itself on your computer's hard drive.

Manual: Most programs toss in a printed manual. Some manuals are the size of a cheap paperback, others are hard cover, and still others come in binders so they'll lie flat on a desk. There may be more than one manual. Look for the "Getting Started," "Installation," or "Setup" section of the manual first.

Registration card: Resembling a boring post card, this usually sits right on top. You fill out your name and address and answer a few questions about the software, and then you mail the card back to the company. The company can then notify you of any defects, including nonfunctional commands or air-bag problems. You'll also be placed on the company's mailing list for new product notices and updated versions of your software (see "Version Numbers"). Some companies require you to fill out the registration card before they'll offer technical support over the phone.

Quick reference card: The manual works fine for explaining everything in great detail, but you'll find yourself continually repeating some commands. A quick reference card contains those useful commands; it can be propped up next to the keyboard for quick sideways glances. Not all software comes with these cards, however.

Quick installation card: Computer users thrive on instant gratification: Push a button and watch your work be performed instantly. Nobody wants to bother with slow, thick manuals, especially when installing the software. A quick installation card contains an abbreviated version of the manual's installation instructions. By typing in the commands on the card, you can install the software without cracking open the manual. Victory!

License agreement: This extensive batch of fine print takes an average of 3,346 words of legalese to say three things: 1) Don't give away any copies of this program to friends — make them buy their own program. 2) If you accidentally lose any data, it's not our fault. 3) If this software doesn't work, that's not our fault, either.

Sometimes the licensing agreement is printed on a little sticker on an envelope; you have to tear apart the agreement before you can get to the disks inside.

Read me first: When the company discovers a mistake in its newly printed manual, it won't fix it and print out a new one. It will print the corrections on a piece of paper and slap the headline "Read Me First!" across the top. Staple that piece of paper to the inside cover of your manual for safekeeping.

It's usually a good idea to fill out and mail in your registration card. Some companies will provide cash discounts to registered owners when they buy other software from them.

Version Numbers

When a company releases a new software program, it calls the program Version 1.0. Unlike a novel, which doesn't change after it's written and printed, software *always* changes. The company fixes errors or adds new features to keep the programmers busy.

When a company fixes a few small errors in the software, it releases a new version. If the changes are relatively minor, the company adds a decimal point to the end of the version number. For instance, a minor update to Version 1.0 is called Version 1.1. If a whole bunch of changes are made, and the company is particularly proud of the result, it increases the version number and sells the software as an *upgrade.* A substantial upgrade to Version 1.1 is called Version 2.0.

- ✔ Software companies often sell upgrades at a substantial discount to people who have bought earlier versions of the same software. That's why it's important to mail in your registration card (see "What's This Stuff in the Box?"), so the company can let you know of its hot new deal.

- ✔ Don't feel pressured to buy upgrades immediately. Read the upgrade notice to see whether you need any of the new features. If the old version works fine for you, forget about the upgrade. You don't trade your Cadillac in every year for a new one, do you? (OK, every other year, then.)

- ✔ Software versions ending in zero (Versions 1.0, 2.0, 3.0, and so on) contain lots of new features and subsequent programming code. Some people don't buy versions ending in zero; instead, they wait for the next version (Version 1.1, 2.1a, 3.3, and so on). That means the company has had time to fix most of the problems plaguing the first version.

- ✔ Some companies call their versions "releases" just to be different.

- ✔ Sometimes you'll see sub-subversion numbers: 1.00.01. Sheesh. This is typical of a company that fixed a minor bug and doesn't want to raise a stink about it. Another example is secret releases, such as MS-DOS 4.01a. The little *a* means some bugs were fixed, but there was no point in alarming all the DOS 4.01 users that they had to upgrade.

🖛 WordPerfect comes out with a new upgrade once a month. So although you may have WordPerfect 5.1, it may be dated *October* when your friend has a brand new *April* copy. (You can get the upgrade from WordPerfect Corp. for $10 or so, but usually the change is not anything major.)

🖛 Sometimes companies are sneaky and release updates with the same version number. You have to check the release date to be sure.

Software Installation

The first step in installing software is getting your computer guru to do it for you. If there's no guru within potato-chip-crunching distance, then the following guidelines may help. All software packages handle the process a little bit differently, so don't be surprised if you find yourself surprised:

1. **Read the "Read Me" blurb.**

   When you first open the box, scrounge around for a piece of paper that says "Read Me First!" and follow the first instruction: read it. Or at least try to make some sense of it. Sometimes it just contains a sentence or two left out of the manual's third paragraph on page 127, "Dwobbling your shordlock by three frips." If you don't understand it, don't throw it away. It may come in handy after you've started using the program.

2. **Look at the manual.**

   Manuals are boring enough when you're familiar with the program. They're even more boring when you've never played with the program and don't have the faintest idea what they're talking about. Nevertheless, look for the "Installation" section of the manual and try to make some sense of it, too. The best sections will guide you through the installation process step by step. The worst ones start with, "After you've installed the software. . . ."

3. **Put the Installation disk into your disk drive.**

   Find the disk marked with the words "Installation" or "Disk One," or both, and place that disk in the disk drive where it fits. If it's a 5 ¼-inch drive, remember to close the drive door latch.

4. **Type the following command.**

   At the DOS prompt, you will "log" to drive A. Type this in:

   ```
   C:\> A:
   ```

   That is, you press A, followed by a colon, with no space in between. Press Enter.

Upon success, your DOS prompt will change to something like this:

```
A:\>
```

You'll see A in the prompt. If not, OK. As long as you don't see the old Abort, Retry, Fail message, which just means that you don't have your disk in the drive properly. (Remove the disk, insert it the correct way, and then try again.)

5. **Start the Installation program.**

Now's where it gets trickier. Some software comes with a program called INSTALL that handles everything from here onward. Some software calls that program SETUP. Check the sheet of paper that says "Read Me First!" or "Quick installation guide." If that doesn't list the word, then dig through the manual.

If you're lucky and the installation program is named INSTALL, type **INSTALL** at the DOS prompt, like this:

```
A:\> INSTALL
```

After typing **INSTALL,** press Enter.

If the name is SETUP, type **SETUP** instead:

```
A:\> SETUP
```

Note that SETUP is one word.

6. **Read the screen carefully.**

The installation program will start placing instructions on the screen. Watch them carefully; sometimes they'll slip something important in there. Following the instructions is important. If anything confuses you, get your guru to do the installation instead.

7. **Where should it be installed?**

Like a house guest being invited to stay overnight, the software will usually ask where it should stay in your computer. The software will probably make a suggestion; go ahead and accept its advice by simply pressing Enter. Sometimes the option may be labeled as "Default" or the "Quick" installation plan. Select those.

Say "Yes" to everything!

Keep feeding the computer disks as the installation program asks for them, making sure that you spoon-feed the disks in the correct order. Eventually the software will proclaim that it has installed itself. But it usually won't start running right away. You have to type the name of the program at the

DOS prompt before it will load. Keep a watchful eye out; the installation process usually ends by telling you the program's name: a single word or abbreviation. Type that name at the prompt, and the software should run. Finally.

8. Look for the READ.ME file.

Sometimes the company didn't have time to print up their extra-last-minute corrections. So a programmer lunged for the computer, hastily typed in the extra instructions, and saved them in a file called READ.ME or README.TXT. Look for something with a similar name on your disk.

To read the information in a file called READ.ME, type the following command at the DOS prompt:

```
C:\> MORE < READ.ME
```

That is, you type **MORE,** a space, a less-than sign (<), another space, **READ,** a period, and then **ME.** If there's no period in the file's name (README), don't type one. Or the file may have a different name (README.DOC). If so, use that instead of READ.ME as shown in the preceding example. And, like any other DOS command, don't punctuate it with a period at the end.

Take note of any of the instructions that seem important and shrug your shoulders at the rest.

✔ Some software can be tricky; it can take at least several days before you'll be able to make it do something useful.

✔ Keep the quick reference card next to your computer immediately after installing the program; it will be more helpful than the manual.

✔ Don't bother reading the entire manual cover to cover. Chances are, you'll need only about 10 percent of it to use the program. Learn the features you need as you go.

What's Shareware and Public Domain Software?

Software disks cost less than 50 cents apiece. A manual doesn't cost more than a paperback book. And, well, you can pick up a cardboard box for free outside a liquor store. So how come software costs so much?

Because the programmer gets some money, as well as the retail store, the software publisher, the truck driver who drove the software to the retailer, and the magazines that ran the advertisements. It can cost thousands of dollars to put a piece of software on a store shelf.

Frustrated by the system, some programmers give away their programs for free. Seriously! But there's a catch: They ask you to send them money on the honor system if you like their program. Because they're bypassing the traditional, expensive way to sell software, they don't ask for much; most charge from $5 to $45 for their *Shareware*. When you mail in the check, the programmer mails back the latest version of the software and a manual.

Other programmers give away their programs but don't ask for money in return. They figure that they're making a humble contribution toward making the world a better place to compute. This free software is called *public domain software*.

Ask your computer guru for more details on Shareware and public domain programs. Or check with any local computer user groups. Or, if you're feeling particularly adventurous, buy a modem and join an on-line service. (For more information about modems, see Chapter 11.)

● ●

Summary

This chapter introduced you to the kinds of software that you are most likely to want to use and told you how to get it up and running:

▶ You can use word processing software, text editors, and desktop publishing software to get your words onto paper and produce results that look almost as if they were professionally typeset.

▶ Spreadsheets can help you with accounting chores and have other business applications.

▶ Database programs enable you to store, retrieve, sort, and report data on just about anything.

▶ Integrated packages combine the functions of all three types of software and sometimes also include communications software. They enable you to produce a file that combines information from more than one type of program.

▶ Terminate-and-stay-resident (TSR) programs wait in memory for you to call them into action. Although they are very useful, they can get in the way when they pop up unexpectedly.

▶ When you purchase software, you need to make sure that it will run on your computer and that it will do what you need it to do.

▶ If there's no computer guru around to do it for you, you can probably install software yourself by following the instructions that come with the software and the guidelines in this chapter.

▶ Public domain software is free, and Shareware costs a whole lot less than software that is produced by the big software companies. Check it out!

In the next chapter, you take a look at Windows, the problems it solves, and some of the new ones it creates.

● ●

Chapter 16
The Wonderful World of Windows

● ●

In This Chapter

▶ Starting Windows

▶ Using pull-down menus

▶ Looking at the windows on the screen

▶ Changing a window

▶ Starting a program in Windows

▶ Running DOS programs under Windows

▶ Cutting and pasting stuff

▶ Understanding the difference between task switching and multitasking

▶ Learning which is better: using the mouse or the keyboard

▶ Finding a window that's buried in the pile

▶ Learning what to do when you delete the wrong thing

▶ Learning what to do when the screen just sits there, frozen

▶ Quitting Windows

● ●

*M*S-DOS gets the job done, but it's so boring. Face it, DOS could have been written by three Senate subcommittees. To jazz things up, Microsoft created Windows: a fun new way to operate an IBM-compatible computer.

Windows users don't type letters or numbers next to a funny-looking C:\> symbol. Instead, they choose from pretty pictures filling their screen. To call up their computerized address book, for example, they point their mouse at the on-screen picture of a Rolodex and click the button. The Rolodex jumps to the front of the screen, ready for action. Quick, easy, and fun, too.

Some people say the colorful pictures make Windows easier to use; others say it's a little too arty. For example, to write a letter in Windows, do you click on the picture of the notepad, the quill, or the Clipboard? Hmmm. . . .

This chapter takes a look at the Windows graphical user interface (GUI). It explains what problems Windows solves, as well as some of the new ones Windows creates.

What Is Windows?

MS-DOS presents the user with a single symbol, C:\>. Everybody should already know how to proceed from there because there certainly aren't any clues. Windows, in contrast, places pictures of the programs on-screen. Instead of checking a manual for the right word to start a program, Windows users click their mouse on the program's tiny on-screen symbol. A quick click on the calculator picture, for example, brings the calculator to the screen. Figure 16-1 shows a Windows screen and various pictures, or *icons*.

A computer that operates through the use of pictures and symbols rather than words is called a *graphical user interface,* or *GUI.* (Believe it or not, it's pronounced *gooey.*)

Pictures require more computing horsepower than letters and numbers, so Windows requires a relatively powerful computer. Yet millions of people upgraded their computers just to use Windows. Why? Normal DOS programs all use different commands. But Microsoft bossed around all the companies writing software for Windows, so all Windows programs work pretty much the same. For example, the same three keystrokes quit any Windows program, regardless of which company wrote it. This setup makes the software simpler and easier to learn.

Figure 16-1:
Various
icons you
can click on
to start
programs.

- Windows gets its name from all the cute little windows on the screen. Each window holds information, a picture, or a program you're running, which is much neater than dealing with the clunky old text DOS provides.

- Windows doesn't work on an XT, the older computer that uses an 8088 chip. It does work on an AT, or 286 computer, but it works best on a 386 or 486 computer. And, although Windows runs with as little as 2MB of RAM, it really needs 4MB or more. Don't forget a hard disk with at least 40MB, too. (And Windows gobbles up a quarter of that space, just for itself.)

- We apologize for all the numbers in the preceding paragraph.

- Windows programs aren't called *programs.* They're called *applications.*

- After buying Windows, be prepared to buy a whole new set of programs designed for Windows. Luckily, Windows comes with a word processor, address book, calendar, and drawing program. These applications can handle most simple needs.

- Your plain old DOS programs can still run under Windows. How? They run in their own windows, which can be placed anywhere on the screen. They run more slowly, though, and they don't take full advantage of the little pictures, either.

- When the word *Windows* starts with a capital letter, it refers to the actual program. When the word *windows* is in all lowercase letters, it refers to single windows on the screen.

- Windows is not the same as the Windows NT you might have heard people whispering about in the hallways. Windows NT is a bigger version, designed for people with lots of bigger computers and a strong need to tie them all together. Windows NT isn't designed for your everyday Solitaire game.

Because Windows uses graphics, it's much easier to use than to describe. In DOS, you simply say, "Press the PgDn key." In Windows, you say, "Click on the vertical scroll bar beneath the scroll box." That sounds weird, but after you've done it, you'll say, "Oh, is that all that meant? Golly!" (Plus, you can still press the PgDn key in Windows. You don't have to click on the vertical scroll bar beneath the scroll box if you don't want to.)

Starting Windows

When installed, Windows completely takes over your computer. That's why some people like it so much. Windows usually jumps to the screen a few moments after a computer is first turned on. If it's not there, hold your breath and type the following command at the DOS prompt:

```
C:\> WIN
```

In other words, type **WIN** and then press the Enter key. Windows then takes over, getting rid of that C:\> thing.

Using Pull-Down Menus

DOS users have resigned themselves to memorizing commands to type at the C:\> prompt. Windows users prefer to see their options on the screen so they can just choose the command they want. But, if the Windows screen displayed every option, it would be more cluttered than a 12-page menu at a Vietnamese restaurant.

So, to keep the screen free of clutter, Microsoft hid the menus. Although Windows users don't have to memorize commands, they have to memorize locations to click. If you click in the right place, a menu appears, listing commands. (Luckily, menus hide in only a few places.)

✔ Just like scary movies have cats that jump out of closets at awkward moments, Windows contains many "pop-up" components. If you click the mouse in certain locations, secret hidden menus are popped up or pulled down, offering you a bunch of tasks to choose from.

✔ Most pull-down menus are in a row along the top of a window. They're disguised as single words, like File, Edit, View, or the ever-popular Help. When you click on any of those words, a pull-down menu appears beneath it, offering a bunch of commands related to that word.

✔ Sometimes a click on an item in a pull-down menu brings up yet another pull-down menu. The people who make up computer words refer to this feature as a *nested* menu — a forgettable term if there ever was one.

Speeding up Windows

When you first type **WIN**, a Windows *logo,* or advertisement, fills the screen. After a few seconds, the ad clears and Windows begins. A few impatient Microsoft employees didn't want to see that Windows advertisement, so they added a secret command. By typing **WIN,** a space, and a colon, as follows, you can skip the ad:

C:\> WIN :

Pretty sneaky, huh? Feel free to try it yourself.

✔ Sometimes, a click on an item in a pull-down menu brings up a huge new window, chock full of more choices. This big new window is called a *dialog box*. That's a box with more information and pretty things in it — a type of window, really.

✔ Windows almost always uses the left button on the mouse. Click that one when you're instructed to click the mouse. Ignore the other mouse button.

Looking at the Windows on the Screen

Although Windows work areas are called windows, they don't look at all like glass windows. They're little squares, but nobody wanted the headaches of marketing a product called Squares.

All windows have similar features, designed to be poked at with the mouse. Describing windows in words is like describing the color red, but we're going to give it a try anyway. Figure 16-2 shows the various features of a typical window in Windows.

Control-menu box: This box holds the window's circuit breaker, so to speak. If you click on this box, the Control menu drops down with "power" functions. You can close the window, switch to other windows, change the window's size, and perform other heavy-duty tasks.

Menu bar: The list of single words along the top of a window is called a *menu bar*. If you click on one of these words, another menu drops down, offering you a bunch of related choices.

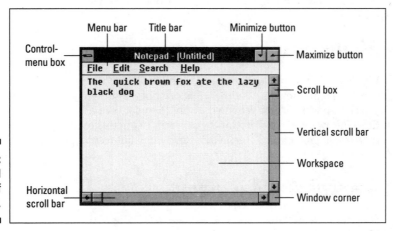

Figure 16-2: The typical features of a window.

Title bar: The dark strip at the top of every window, the *title bar,* contains the program's name and the name of the file it's currently working with.

Minimize/maximize buttons: A click on the minimize button shrinks the window; a click on the maximize button makes the window completely fill the screen (see "Changing a Window" later in this chapter).

Scroll bar: Some windows have two scroll bars — one along the right side and the other along the bottom. Scroll bars have a little *scroll box* in them. If the box is at the top of a scroll bar, you're looking at the top of a document. If it's at the bottom, you're looking at the document's tail end.

Workspace: All your work takes place in the window's big empty area, or *workspace.*

Window corner: This term makes the most sense. *Window corner* refers to any corner of a window. You can change a window's size with the mouse by *dragging* a corner (see "Changing a Window," which follows).

Changing a Window

Just as it's easy to collect piles of junk on a desk, it's easy to collect piles of windows on the screen. There may be three notepads, a spreadsheet, an address book, and a game of Solitaire in the background. Unlike with a desktop, a wipe of the elbow doesn't clean all that junk off your screen. You must move windows around by using the mouse or keyboard.

Luckily, you can change the windows around in several ways.

Minimizing a window

Windows that are *minimized* are shrunken little icons at the bottom of your screen. To minimize a window, click on that tiny downward-pointing arrow in its top right-hand corner. When you want the window back, double-click on its icon; the window leaps back up on the screen. (Using this technique is much faster than loading programs fresh each time you want to use them.)

Maximizing a window

Sometimes, you'll want a single window to fill the entire screen, just like in the DOS days. To *maximize* a window, click on the tiny upward-pointing arrow in the window's top right-hand corner. To bring the window back to normal, click again in that same corner. (This time, however, that little corner has two arrows —one pointing up and the other pointing down.)

Resizing a window

If you want a window sized somewhere between full size and icon size, you can adjust its size manually. Aim the mouse pointer at any of the window's corners and then hold down the mouse button. As you move the mouse back and forth, the window shrinks or grows. When it's sized just right, release the mouse button; the window adjusts to the new size.

Tiling windows

When you have too many windows floating around, it's time to manage tasks with the Task Manager. If you can see any of the back of your screen (your "wallpaper"), double-click on it (click the mouse button twice in rapid succession). If everything's too crowded, hold down the Ctrl button and press the Esc key. In either case, yet another window appears: the Task Manager. Click on its Tile button, and all the windows are resized across your screen, each taking up the same amount of space. The newly arranged windows will be too small to work with, but, hey, at least you can see them all.

Cascading windows

If you click on the Task Manager's Cascade button rather than its Tile button, the windows are also resized across your screen. This time, however, they appear in neatly overlapping rows, like a deck of cards dealt in Blackjack.

- ✔ When you're resizing a window, the mouse cursor's arrow changes. It points left or right, up or down, or catty-corner ways, indicating the direction in which you can adjust the window's size.

- ✔ Windows offers a jillion different ways to resize windows or arrange them across your desktop. That's supposed to make it easy to customize. Don't worry about learning all the ways to reposition your windows. Just learn the ways that work well for you.

- ✔ Not all windows can be adjusted in size. Only those with the little up and down buttons in the upper right-hand corner can be moved around.

Starting a Program in Windows

Windows acts as its own computer guru of sorts. When it's first installed, it rummages through your hard drive, searching for programs it recognizes. All those programs then appear as little pictures displayed on the Windows Program Manager, that main menu thing that first appears on-screen.

For example, Windows finds your copy of WordPerfect and sticks it on-screen as a little picture with the artistically arranged letters *WP*. When you double-click (click the mouse button twice in rapid succession) on the little picture — or icon — with the WP letters, WordPerfect jumps to the front of your screen.

✔ Starting a program in Windows is referred to as *launching* a program — like a rocket ship.

✔ All the applications in Windows appear in a window called the Program Manager. The applications appear as little pictures, or *icons*. Double-click on an icon to start the program.

If you can't find your favorite program in the File Manager, but you find the name of the file you were working on, go ahead and double-click on that file's name. The program that created the file jumps right up, complete with your file inside it, ready to go.

Actually, programs can be started three different ways in Windows

The easiest way to start a program is to double-click on its little icon in the Program Manager. If your favorite program isn't there, holler for your computer guru to get that thing on there.

If you can't find either your program or your computer guru, then look at the top left-hand corner of the Program Manager. Click on the word File and then click on the word Run when it appears. Then type the name of the program, just as you would at the DOS prompt. (Yep, it's just like DOS, but at least you don't have to look at that C:\> thing.)

Last, if you don't know what your program's called, and it's not listed on the Program Manager, double-click on the Program Manager's little filing cabinet icon to call up the File Manager. Then look at all the names listed in the File Manager for the name of your program.

The File Manager is a bit obtuse because it shows the same ugly names you see when you type **DIR.** But get a load of this: All the program names shown in the File Manager have a little gray box next to them. Find the gray box and double-click on it; you've just started a program.

Running DOS Programs under Windows

Windows is designed to run Windows programs: programs created specifically to take advantage of Windows' graphics features. Windows programs (called *applications*) all behave in a similar fashion. The menus look pretty much the same, and the keystrokes do pretty much the same thing, no matter what application you're using.

But you needn't throw away your old DOS programs; they still run under Windows. DOS programs can run under Windows in three ways:

In a full screen: A DOS program can take up the whole screen; Windows waits in the background — like that pesky kid in the fifth grade who said you were his friend. The idea is that you don't even know Windows is there. Then, when you quit the DOS program, Windows hops back onto the screen again.

In a window: A DOS program can run in its own little window and be tugged to a convenient location on the screen. Unfortunately, because DOS programs are accustomed to having the entire screen to themselves, they can be difficult to work with when they're confined to a window.

As an icon: Like any other program running under Windows, DOS programs can be shrunken to a tiny picture, or *icon,* at the bottom of your screen. Double-click on the icon, and the DOS program leaps into action — either into a window or into the full screen.

Cutting and Pasting Stuff

Windows users can cut and paste, just like kindergartners can with any glue they have left over from lunch. Kindergartners can cut out a picture of a flower, paste it onto a sheet of paper, write the word *flour* under it, and give it to Mommy.

Windows users can cut out a picture of grapes they've drawn in their Paint program, paste it into their word processor, write the word *Merlot* beneath it, and print out wine labels for the new vintage.

The electronic world of cutting and pasting is a little different from the kindergartner's world, however. Kindergartners just set their cut flowers on the floor for temporary storage. Windows doesn't have a floor, so it stores any cut information in a special place called the *Clipboard.* From the Clipboard, the information can be pasted into any other window.

Also, kindergartners with scissors can only cut. Windows can copy information to the Clipboard as well as cut it. Cut information is scooped out of (removed from) a window and placed into the Clipboard. Copied information stays put; a copy of it appears in the Clipboard.

Windows doesn't come with scissors, so the mouse does the trick. You use the mouse to select information by *highlighting* it on the screen. For example, put the mouse at the start of a paragraph (or any other object) and hold down the button. Then move the mouse to the end of the paragraph and release the button. The paragraph's text is shown in inverse (white on black), indicating that it has been highlighted.

After something is highlighted, hold down the Ctrl key and press C — in other words, press Ctrl+C. That action copies the paragraph to the Clipboard. To cut it onto the Clipboard, press Ctrl+X. Or you can use the handy Edit menu on the screen: Click on it and select Copy to copy or Cut to cut. Foolishly easy.

Then, to paste the Clipboard's new information, move to the receiving window and place the cursor where you want the information to appear. Press Ctrl+V and a copy of the information on the Clipboard is pasted in the new location. Or, from the handy Edit menu, select the Paste item. No muss. No fuss.

It's quick and easy, but there's no yummy glue on your fingers to lick afterward.

- ✔ Information that has been cut or copied from any application is stored on the Windows Clipboard. It stays on the Clipboard until any other information is cut or copied over it.

- ✔ Information on the Clipboard can be pasted into any Windows application. It doesn't disappear from the Clipboard after it's pasted, though. It just sits there until something new takes its place.

- ✔ You can paste and copy information to and from DOS programs but only when they're running in windows on-screen. And you can't cut information from DOS programs, even with sharp scissors.

Windows comes with a program called Clipboard Viewer, which displays what has been copied to the Clipboard. To see what's there, double-click on the Clipboard Viewer program in the Program Manager. (It's a picture of a Clipboard. No surprises there.) Some people leave the Clipboard Viewer open in a corner of their screen so they can be sure that it's containing the right information.

If you accidentally cut rather than copy, and the highlighted information disappears, don't scream too loudly. Just select the Paste command, and the information is pasted back where it came from. (The image remains on the Clipboard as well, so it's just like you selected the Copy command, which is the one you wanted in the first place.)

Understanding Task Switching and Multitasking

Whoa! This section contains massively technical stuff you don't need to read. We'd stop right here if we were you. In fact, we wouldn't even bother with thinking that the terms *task switching* and *multitasking* both sound equally confusing. Nor would we continue to read that they both refer to the same thing: having more than one program open on the screen — like seeing your word processor and a time clock in separate windows. But computer nerds stress one big difference between the two, which is why you should stop reading right now.

Switching back and forth between programs is called *task switching*. For example, keeping a calculator waiting at the bottom of the screen while working on a spreadsheet is considered task switching; you hop between the two, using one and then the other without quitting from either. This is an interesting concept, but is task switching worth remembering? Nope. But apply it in real life: Your son can chew gum and walk but not both at once. When he does switch from one to the other, he is task switching — kind of like a computer but without the grace.

When you are working on two or more programs at the same time, you're *multitasking*. For example, you may be printing invitations to a party while you're playing Escape from Grandma's — both at the same time. Doing two things at once on a computer is called multitasking. In fact, you can do several things at once by using Windows. And if your son could chew gum and walk at the same time, he'd be multitasking, too (but without Windows and he'd definitely not be as pretty to watch).

When you're multitasking on a computer, the program you're working on is said to be "in the foreground." That means it's up front, enabling you to work. All the other programs you have going are "in the background," meaning that you haven't quit anything but the programs are still running. When a boys sits and pets the dog, that's in the foreground. The rake leaning up against the tree and the yard work that needs to be done are background things. (Of course, that's really task switching; humans cannot multitask yard work.)

It's a curious subject, and it enables you to get more work done on a computer. But other than that, the differences between task switching and multitasking are really for the technical people to argue over.

Now aren't you glad you didn't read that?

A decade-old Federal Aviation Administration study found that the average airline stewardess has a nose 2.18 inches long.

Using the Mouse

Technically, Windows doesn't require the use of a mouse. And, technically, people can type with their elbows. It's easier and more practical, though, to use Windows programs by rolling a mouse around a desktop and clicking its button.

For example, Windows uses a concept known as *pull-down menus* (see "Using Pull-Down Menus" earlier in this chapter). To open or delete files in a word processor, Windows users click on a button labeled File at the top of their screen. A menu of additional options appears beneath the word File. Users then click on the word representing what they want to do with the files: Open, Delete, Save, Rename, and so on.

Without a mouse to click on the buttons, users must press a combination of Tab, the arrow keys, and Enter (or Return) to move from button to button. If ten things currently appear on the screen, the user must sometimes press keys ten times to select the right thing. That's worse than DOS!

- ✔ In addition to selecting menu items with the mouse, you also activate special controls in Windows. These controls look like little pictures of buttons on the screen, and, in a strange twist of fate, they are called *buttons* as well. When you click on a button with the mouse, you're moving the mouse pointer to the picture of a button on the screen, and then you're clicking on that button with the mouse.

- ✔ Although the Windows box says you don't need a mouse, you need a mouse.

- ✔ A *trackball* works just as well as a mouse (see Chapter 11). In fact, laptop users must use trackballs to prevent being slapped while trying to use Windows on airplanes.

- ✔ A mouse works better than a keyboard when you're moving around in a big document, accessing unfamiliar pull-down menus, and highlighting text.

Using the Keyboard

Microsoft knew that some stubborn Windows users wouldn't want to buy a mouse. So it added keyboard commands to Windows. Windows works best with a mouse, but a keyboard sometimes comes in handy. In fact, Windows works best with a combination of keyboard and mouse commands.

For example, to close a Windows program, you must use the mouse to click on the File pull-down menu, then the word Exit, and then the word Yes to save your work. Those words are fairly easy to remember, but it's bothersome waiting for all those dorky pull-down menus to arrive.

The keyboard command to do the same thing is Alt+F4, which means that you hold down the Alt key and press the F4 key. That action tells Windows to exit the program immediately. Sometimes, using that quick Alt+F4 combination can be simpler than navigating a mouse over a crowded desktop.

Why not use keyboard commands rather than a mouse? Because they're harder to remember. Unlike the mouse's logical, step-by-step actions, the keyboard commands don't make sense. After you've learned them, however, using them can be quicker than using the mouse.

- ✔ When searching for a particular item in a long list presented in a Windows menu, press that item's first letter. For example, if you press M, the cursor jumps down to the items starting with the letter *M*, making it easier to find what you're after.

- ✔ When faced with a bunch of choices, press the Tab key to cycle through them, one at a time. To back up, press Shift+Tab (hold down the Shift key while pressing Tab).

- ✔ Pressing the Alt key activates Windows menus. Press Alt, Enter, and then the arrow keys to move from menu to menu. If you're trapped in Menu Land and want to get out of there, press the Esc key.

- ✔ Menu words have underlined "shortcut" letters. For example, to choose the command Massage from the menu, press the letter G. If nothing happens, that means you haven't first activated the menu. Try pressing Alt to make the menus come to life and then press G for the Massage command. A large man named Leo will approach you with a hot towel.

- ✔ After you've learned the keyboard shortcuts to the pull-down menus, you may find them faster to use than a mouse.

Table 16-1 lists some handy keyboard commands you'll want to remember.

Table 16-1	Keyboard Commands
Press This Key	*When You Want to Do This Task*
F1	See the Help menu
Ctrl+Z	Undo the last thing you've just done
Ctrl+Esc	Call up the Task Manager and see a list of all your open windows
Alt+Esc	Switch to the next application, whether it's an open window or an icon
Alt+Tab	Cycle through the names of the applications you've just used (release both keys when the name you want appears)
Print Screen	Copy a picture of the entire screen onto the Clipboard (for some keyboards, you have to hold down the Shift key at the same time)

(continued)

Table 16-1 *(continued)*

Press This Key	When You Want to Do This Task
Alt+Print Screen	Copy a picture of your current open window onto the Clipboard
Alt+spacebar	Open a window's Control menu
Alt+F4	Quit an application or close a window
Alt+Enter	Toggle a DOS window from a full-screen display to a window-sized display
Ctrl+X or Shift+Del	Delete the highlighted stuff and haul it over to the Clipboard — *cut,* in Windows parlance
Ctrl+C or Ctrl+Ins	Send a copy of the highlighted stuff to theClipboard
Ctrl+V or Shift+Ins	Paste the stuff that's on the Clipboard into the current window (the stuff on the Clipboard is copied to the cursor's current location)

Finding a Window That's Buried in the Pile

The biggest problem with Windows is keeping track of all the programs. How can it fit so many windows on the screen at one time? It piles them all on top of each other, like a stack of important papers on a tiny, monitor-sized desk. It's easy to lose track of programs buried at the bottom of the pile.

Here are a few guidelines for bringing your work back in front of you:

1. **If you can see even a tiny corner of your escaped window, click in it with the mouse.**

   That window then leaps to the top of the stack.

2. **Press Ctrl+Esc.**

   A new window rises to the top. Known as the Task Manager, that window lists every program currently running in Windows. Click on the name of the window you're hunting for. The Task Manager disappears, and the missing window appears in its place.

3. **If you can call up the Task Manager from step 2, click on its Tile button.**

   This action reduces all the windows to squares. The squares are too small to work in, but at least you'll see all the windows on the screen at the same time.

4. Press Alt+Esc.

This action moves through each of your open windows one at a time, but it also brings them "on top." When your lost window appears, let go of the Esc key and your lost window stays on top.

5. Press Alt+Tab.

A tiny window pops up, listing the name of one of your open windows. Keep holding down the Alt key and press the Tab key. Each time you press Tab, the names of all the open windows appear and their cute icons are displayed in a box. When you see the name of the program you want, release the Alt key and the named window rises to the top.

Whoa! I Deleted the Wrong Thing!

As part of the fraternal requirements of being a Windows program, all Windows programs must have an "undo" command. If you accidentally delete something in any Windows program, press Alt+Backspace.

✔ The Alt+Backspace trick only works once: It only regurgitates the last thing you've deleted. If you press it again, it undoes the undo, swallowing that regurgitation back down again.

✔ The Alt+Backspace trick only works with Windows programs; it doesn't work with DOS programs, even if they're running in their own windows. You'll have to use the DOS program's undo command.

✔ Because it won the lawsuit, Microsoft now uses the Ctrl+Z key combination for the undo command, as well. (Ctrl+Z, or a similar keystroke, was used on the Macintosh for years as the undo command.)

If you've deleted the wrong files in the File Manager, there's no specific undelete button. Instead, press and release the following keys: Alt, F, and R. Then type **UNDELETE** in the little Command box that pops up. This action brings up the UNDELETE command found in DOS 5.0, giving you a chance to bring your deleted file back to life (see the section "I Just Deleted My File!" in Chapter 20).

Knowing What to Do When the Screen Just Sits There, Frozen

MS-DOS wasn't designed to handle fancy stuff like Windows. It wasn't meant to have more than one program running at the same time. Windows does a pretty good job of juggling, but occasionally a ball will stick to the roof and the screen will freeze.

You'll try pressing keys, but nothing will happen. Arrghh! And you'll probably have other windows open and not saved your work in them! Luckily, Windows 3.1 does a great job of handling momentary lapses in juggling. If a window freezes on your screen, press Ctrl+Alt+Del (all three keys at the same time).

With DOS programs, this action usually resets or "reboots" the computer, making you start from scratch at the DOS prompt. But with Windows, the Ctrl+Alt+Del combination only resets the window that's frozen! You still lose your work in that window. But you don't lose any of the work in your other open windows, including that hot new high score in Solitaire.

- ✔ To reboot a single window in Windows 3.1, press Ctrl+Alt+Del. This action brings up a menu with three choices. You can press Esc to return to Windows (just in case you mistakenly pressed the wrong key), you can press Enter to quit that wigged-out application and return to Windows, or you can press Ctrl+Alt+Del again to reboot your entire system. (That's a last resort because you lose everything you haven't saved up to that point.)

- ✔ If you try the same trick by pressing the Reset button on your computer, you lose everything. Don't try that unless the Ctrl+Alt+Del trick doesn't do anything.

- ✔ Perhaps you've just accidentally brushed against the Alt key; that activates the menus at the top of the screen, where you'll be trapped. If you find yourself bumping from menu to menu, unable to return to your workspace, press the Esc key to return to productivity.

Quitting Windows

When you're ready to turn off your computer and head for the porch to drink a mint julep, don't be too hasty. You must quit Windows first. It's more detailed than you may think. In DOS, you only have to quit one program before turning off your computer. With Windows, you may have six programs running on your screen.

To exit Windows safely, bring the Program Manager to the front of the screen. Then double-click (click twice in rapid succession) on the little box thing in the Program Manager's upper left-hand corner. The Program Manager tosses yet another window at you, asking whether you're sure that you want to exit Windows.

Click on the Yes button (or press Enter), and Windows automatically checks all its open windows for you. If there's any unsaved work in any open programs, Windows asks whether you want to save it. By all means, click on the Yes button so you don't lose any work.

Eventually, Windows packs up all the open windows and bails, leaving you back at the DOS prompt. Then you can safely turn off your computer and hope there's some fresh mint in the hydrator.

Just keep pressing Alt+F4, and you'll eventually quit Windows. When the little "you're about to exit Windows" type of box appears, click on the OK button.

When you're running a DOS application under Windows, and it's taking up the whole screen, you may not remember all that Windows stuff still running in the background. Don't just quit the DOS application and turn off your computer. Instead, quit the DOS application and then quit Windows.

Then it's safe to turn off your computer. If quitting the DOS application leaves you at a DOS prompt, type **EXIT** and Windows jumps back to the screen, ready to be shut down:

```
C:\> EXIT
```

Press Enter and you'll find yourself once again in the magic world of Windows.

● ●

Summary

In this chapter, you took a look at Windows:

▶ You learned how to start Windows and use pull-down menus.

▶ You examined the windows you see on the screen.

▶ You learned how to change windows by minimizing, maximizing, resizing, tiling, and cascading them.

▶ You learned how to start a program in Windows and run DOS programs under Windows.

▶ You examined how to cut and copy material to the Clipboard and then paste it elsewhere.

▶ You learned the difference between task switching and multitasking.

▶ You examined the benefits and drawbacks of using just the mouse or just the keyboard and learned that using a combination of both is best.

▶ You learned how to find a window that's buried in the pile.

▶ You learned what to do when you delete the wrong thing.

▶ You learned what to do when the screen just sits there, frozen.

▶ You learned how to quit Windows.

In the following chapter, you examine the world of networks.

● ●

Chapter 17
Sharing Information
(or How Does a Network Work?)

· ·

· ·

*I*n the beginning, there were these humongous computers called *mainframes*. They lived in air-conditioned glass rooms and sucked up more power than an army of Hoovers. Spindly, tanless men in lab coats ran the computers. They scoffed at and belittled the sorry users of their computers, shackled to the mainframe by means of a cable and working on a *dumb terminal* — a computer without a brain. Little did they know that the Personal Computer Revolution was coming. Soon, users would each have their own *personal* computer. The era of computer independence would be born.

Today, the mainframe computer is all but dead. But filling in its vacuum tubes are *computer networks*. This is where you take a formerly independent computer and wire it together with other personal computers. Two or more computers shackled to each other — with maybe a printer tossed in between them — is a network. You can add more computers, printers — even mainframes and orbiting satellites. It boggles the mind.

The concept of a network and how it works is way beyond the realm of *PCs For Dummies*. Sad to say, however, any office with more than one computer in it probably has some type of network going. If not now, soon. If you're a sole computer user sitting at home in your den, you can read this chapter for extra bonus points, redeemable for valuable cash prizes. Otherwise, everyone at the office or anyone who's heard about "The network" should glance at a few of the sections in this chapter.

Communicating with Computers

There is this lust for sharing information created on a computer. Not just a lust — a necessity. The screen satisfies this lust by showing you the results of your labors. The printer is another extension, providing you with valuable hard copy. The *hard copy* — OK, *paper* — can be shared with a number of users, but the information is still locked up electronically inside the PC.

One day, someone noticed how silly it was to make hard copy and then have another computer user retype all that information. After all, the information was in the computer. Why couldn't they just "beam" it back and forth between computers? And that's what most of them did in two ways: by sharing disks between two computers and by connecting the computers using special cables.

Extra boring information about the infamous null-modem cable

Nothing causes more headaches than dealing with the null-modem cable or its evil twin, the *null-modem adapter.* So stop writing all those cards and letters and listen up.

A null-modem cable is actually a special sort of serial cable. It's also called a "twisted pair." It's designed so that a cable between two computers' serial ports has the talk-listen wires switched: talk-to-listen, listen-to-talk. Otherwise, the computers would have their talk-to-talk lines and listen-to-listen lines connected, and it would be too much like the United Nations to get anything accomplished. The null-modem adapter is simply a small box that swaps the wires for a standard serial cable.

After both computers are hooked together comes the tricky part. Both systems must run special communications software and require tedious configuring to get everything right. Even then, you can only exchange basic text files (ASCII) between the two separate systems. This is really something more for bored nerds to tinker with than for real humans such as you and me to worry about.

If you really need to send files between two computers, or a desktop PC and a laptop model, then you can buy software to do it. Some software even comes with special cables to make the job easier.

✔ Sharing disks is only possible if the two computers read the same disk format. For all DOS computers, this isn't a hassle. This is the way most information is shared and distributed: You grab it off a floppy disk and save it on your computer's hard drive.

✔ Sharing disks between different types of computers, say Macintoshes and PCs, is not easy. Those two systems use different disk formats. A DOS PC cannot read a Macintosh disk, nor can it understand what's on that disk. (Refer to "Exchanging Disks and Files" later in this chapter for more information.)

✔ Any two computers equipped with serial ports can be connected together with a *null-modem cable* so that they can exchange information. It's also possible for the different systems to talk over phone lines by using a *modem*. The null-modem cable is simply a more direct route, usually intended for two computers sitting in the same room together.

✔ Refer to Chapter 11 for additional information on modems. Elaborate elocution on null-modem cables is offered in a technoid sidebar.

What Are Networks About?

Computers have networks; so does your television. Computers have programs; so does the television. And computers can use that black cable — with the pokey wire in the middle — just like television. In a way, a computer network is very similar to something you'd pick up on your television but far, far more productive.

Up front, we're happy to tell you that networks, networking, and *connectivity* (a big ugly IBM word meaning "plug this into the cat and watch it jump!") is a job best left up to those in charge. No one enjoys working with networks. Sane people pay undernourished compuphiles millions of dollars a year to create and maintain networks. So your knowledge about them need only be minimal. Here's the good stuff:

✔ Networks are about three things: exchanging files, sharing resources, and running common programs.

Exchanging files means that you can send and receive files from other people on the network without having to leave your computer. Either the files come waddling down the network cable, or you pick them up from a central drop-off point. The idea here is that you can get information from another computer without someone's having to hand you a floppy disk.

Sharing resources refers to common hardware that several computers can use on the network. For example, the printer down the hall may be "on" the network. You can print on it, and so can Bob in accounting or Phyllis or that new person they hired in marketing that everyone assumes is having an affair with the boss. Certain hard drives may be "on" the network. You can copy your files to there or from there.

Running common programs refers to applications kept on other computers. With some types of networks, you can access another computer and run a program on that computer — all through a little wire hanging out the back of your PC. That works, but it slows down the other computer immensely. Instead, a big computer is often dedicated as the *file server*. Its task is to act as a huge disk drive to hold programs for everyone else to use.

✔ Networks are often called LANs. *LAN* is an acronym for *local area network*.

✔ Information on how the network changes your computer physically is in the section "Are You a Node?" later in this chapter.

Logging in to the Network

To use a network, you need the network hardware and software. After all that's set up (hopefully by someone else), you access the network by *logging in*. This process involves typing in your name and password before you can use all the goodies the network has to offer.

How you log in depends on which network you have. Sometimes, you log in simply by turning on your PC (which means someone has set that up for you). Most of the time, you log in by using a LOGIN command, like the following, for example:

```
C:\> LOGIN
```

Or you may use the ever popular

```
C:\> NET LOGIN
```

That's the word **NET** followed by a space and **LOGIN**.

Sometimes the word NET is all that's required: Just type **NET** and press Enter. That action pops up a special program, and from there you can select menu items to log you into the network. Other times you may have to do it manually — following **LOGIN** with the name of the *file server* you're logging into. For example, you may need to type the following:

```
C:\> NET LOGIN \\SERVER-A
```

That's **NET**, a space, **LOGIN**, another space, two (count 'em, two) backslashes, and the name of the file server, **SERVER-A**. (DOS networks use two backslashes to identify a file server on a network.)

What happens next, most likely, is that you'll be asked to tell the network who you are, which involves typing in either your name (or some variant of it) or the name of your computer. After you do that and press Enter, you type in a secret password that only you know.

Because we have no idea how you log in to your network, please fill in the following blanks with the proper information. Then refer here if you ever forget how to log in to your network:

Here is what I type to log in to my network:

C:\> _____

My network "user name" is _____.

And I've committed my password to memory, lest it fall into enemy hands.

(Fill in the above.)

- ✔ If you have a password, don't write it down here. Commit it to memory, lest this book fall into the wrong hands.

- ✔ *Login* is pronounced *log in*. Log refers not to timber but to the process of recording an entry. Logging in to a computer means that you're logging your presence. It's usually followed by entering a password.

- ✔ After you've logged in, you can access the network printer and various drives on the network. Using the drives and printers is covered in the following few sections of this chapter.

- ✔ Some networks don't require logins. In fact, it's safe to say that all networks are weird, so don't expect any sanity from any of them. Duck in and duck out. That's our motto.

Exchanging Disks and Files

The basic job of the network is to keep you from walking somewhere else in your office with a floppy disk. Exchanging disks in that manner is referred to as *sneaker net* by computer wieners. Sneaker net. Get it? The network consists of walking disks back and forth. Ah, such jocularity.

To move a file to another computer on the network, you must access a *network drive,* which is a hard drive (or a floppy drive) on any computer other than your own. You must first activate this drive by using your network software. This could happen automatically, or you may have to "attach" the drive with some type of NET USE command. It may look like this:

```
C:\> USE \\SERVER-A\DRIVE-C
```

Or, heck, it may look like this:

```
C:\> NET USE E: \\SERVER-A\C-DRIVE
```

Yikes! Either way, that's a scary command to type. Better have your guru set you up for this one. But just in case it's something you do often, write the command in the space below so you'll have a place to remember it:

Here is what I type to use drive _____ on my network:

C:\>_____

The file server or network computer is _____.

The drive named "_____" is on the network.

Drive _____ is the letter I use to access network files.

(Fill in the above. Write nice and big.)

✔ The network drive is given a drive letter on your system. For example, drive E may be the network drive. You use that drive and all the files on it just as if they were part of your own computer. You can use COPY, DIR, and so on, and access any file on drive E as if it were right there on your PC. The only difference is that the drive and all its files are actually stored somewhere else on the network.

✔ In some cases, it's possible to make your PC's disk drives available to others on the network. This feature is referred to as *peer-to-peer* networking (as opposed to the central file server and minion-like workstation motif). You just type in the right commands — sacrifice the proper victims to the Net Gods — and others can use the files on your hard drive. This could either be quite easy or similar to incanting a spell in Latin. It all depends on your networking software.

✔ Moving files back and forth over a network is referred to either as *zapping* or *beaming.* You say, "Phil, zap me that football pool" or "Beam over your salmon mousse recipe."

Sharing Resources

One hefty advantage to using a network is that you can share resources between computers. A *resource* is something the computer uses. Mostly this means hard-drive storage and printers. So when you have a network, you can use other hard drives for storage and other printers to get your hard copy. And nothing needs to be in the same room with your computer for it all to work.

Sharing printers is a high-priority item for most network situations. It falls into second place behind sharing (zapping, beaming) files. In a small office, it's possible to have a dozen computers but maybe only three printers. If everything is tied together with a network, all the computers can use any of the printers they want.

For disk resources, it's possible to set up special computers on the network called *diskless workstations.* These are computers without any hard-drive storage that use other hard drives elsewhere on the network to store information. Even if your PC does have a hard drive, you can take advantage of another, larger hard drive on the network for file storage or for backup.

Why Mac disks don't work in your PC

Actually, Macintoshes and PCs can all live together on the same network, but it's kind of like red and white grapes on the same vine. Technically speaking (and we are in one of those boxes, you know), it's all a matter of finding the right hardware and software to put both Macs and PCs on the same network. After everything's wired together, you can fling files back and forth between the two systems with ease.

The only drawback to all this is one basic to all computing: You cannot run Mac programs on your PC or vice-versa. The two different systems are referred to as different *platforms.* A Mac can only run programs written for it — same for a PC. It's impossible to have things both ways.

What *is* possible is to exchange data files, graphics, documents, and worksheets between the two systems. For example, a file written in Microsoft Word can be tossed back and forth between a Mac and a PC on the network. No problem. The same holds true for Microsoft Excel, WordPerfect, PageMaker, and a number of other popular programs that have versions for both the Mac and PC. This is yet another advantage to having a network: The alien computers can sing along in harmony with each other.

Some of the newer Macintosh computers can read the data from a PC's disk, but ask a Macintosh owner about that. (And the Macintosh still can't run any PC programs, unless you want to get into the PowerPC business, and that's gotten into in Chapter 6.)

✔ A resource is anything the computer uses — typically memory, hard-disk storage, and the printer.

✔ One of the simplest networks involves two computers and one printer. For a small office, networking in this manner is a cheaper solution than buying a second laser printer.

✔ The resources are usually set up along with the commands that set up your network. Sometimes, it's possible to pick and choose a printer. For example, one printer may be designed for memos and is full of letterhead. Another may be designated for printing envelopes. A third may be a high-resolution graphics printer. These items can all be selected with the network software.

✔ Printing to a network printer is the fastest way to print anything. What happens is that the stuff you're printing is beamed over to the network printer all at once. Your PC never has to wait for the printer again! The printer, on the other hand, is spoon-fed your file a bit at a time by the network computer it's attached to. This is known as *despooling*, and it does take some time. So, in the end, it still takes awhile for the printer to print; you're just not sitting there twiddling your thumbs waiting for it to happen.

✔ The beauty of all this is that you can continue to sit in your chair and use your own PC. Everything is accessed as if it's right there: You tell WordPerfect to print, and it's automatically beamed out to the network printer. (Of course, getting it set up to work that way is a hassle — one that people like us can safely avoid.)

✔ The printers and other resources may be on computers used by other people in the office. Yup, even though it's "their" printer, you can still print on it over the network. That may make sense. But what we really want to know is how come it's always the boss or the biggest PC crybaby who gets the best printer on the network?

Using the File Server

The main computer on the network is called the *file server*, which can simply be the fastest computer on the network with the biggest hard drive. Or it can be a special type of computer that doesn't run DOS at all. Instead, the server runs special network-server software that makes it the main computer in charge of the network.

Servers are called such because they serve out files and programs to other computers on the network. Actually, any time you access a hard drive on another computer or run a program on another computer, that computer's acting like a file server. But specific, dedicated file servers are usually behemoth computers that do nothing but serve files all day.

✔ Computers connected to network printers are called *printer servers.*

✔ In Mid-Atlantic states, people who serve you food are called *waits.*

✔ On a peer-to-peer network, each computer can act like a file server. The problem with this setup is that when someone else accesses your PC, everything s-l-o-w-s d-o-w-n, which is why it's better to have a dedicated file server.

✔ If you're going to run programs on a file server, they should be special network versions of the software. The network versions enable more than one person to run the program at a time. They're also expensive, which is why people refuse to buy them. They think, "Heck, I can buy one copy of TalcumCalc at $239 instead of the server version for $1,495 and save a bundle!" However, the single-user version only enables one person at a time to run the software, which is why the network crashes (and everyone gets angry and blames the people who sold you the network).

✔ There can be more than one file server on a network. Depending on the network software, you can use one or more as you see fit. When you do, you must log in to each of them separately. Refer to "Logging in to the Network" earlier in this chapter.

✔ The network server is usually not a DOS computer. Some can be set up to run DOS. But the best way to go is to create a dedicated file server.

✔ Some servers can be connected to modems, which enables more than one computer to share the modem (or use it at different times). Same with the printer. Modems also enable you to call in from home and use the network from there. And, in some cases, your network's modem can call another network's modem and the two can do lunch.

✔ When your network talks to a mainframe computer, it's referred to as a *gateway.* We mention it here because using the term *network gateway* earns you an extra 50 status points at cocktail parties.

Are You a Node?

If the big computer is called the file server, what's your PC called? We're sorry to break the news to you, but your computer is nothing more than a *work-station* — a cog in the network machinery. Or worse, if it doesn't have a hard drive, you're a *diskless workstation.* That's almost like being a neutered dog.

Actually, your computer — be it neutered or not — is a *node* on the network. A node is a stopping-off point. It's where the networking cable comes into your PC, stops for tea, and then comes back out to wander into someone else's computer.

✔ Physically, the networking cable goes both into and out of your PC —
whether there are one or two cables attached. Inside your PC, plugged into
an *expansion slot,* is a network adapter card. That's how your computer
and the network communicate. The card is controlled by the network
software installed on your computer (see Chapter 6 for more information).

✔ The generic term for a computer on a network is a *node.* You're nothing
but a node. How disgraceful.

Down Goes the Network, Glub, Glub, Glub

Networks crash more than little old ladies or teenagers. This doesn't mean that
using a network is unstable business. Instead, you run into problems because
too many things that barely work don't work well together. Eventually, one puff
of air brings the whole house of cards tumbling down.

✔ When you suspect network trouble, yelp for help. Never try to fix the
problem on your own (which is a safe assumption).

✔ When the server goes down, you can still use your PC; you just can't
access any files or printers that were attached to the server. If you can,
turn off the server and start it up again. You'll need to log out and then log
back in to the server after it has reset.

✔ If you're printing and your computer dies, chances are that what you
printed will continue to print. However, if the server dies, you'll have to
print again. The best thing to do is wait to see whether your stuff prints.
(Have the network person "check the queue" — pronounced *Q* — for you.)

✔ You don't *have* to use the network when you're using your computer. If
you don't need to print or you don't need to access the network files, log
out. Doing so insulates you from any catastrophe that awaits the rest of
the mindless minions on the network.

✔ Any network difficulty requires professional attention. Always have the
network manager or supervisor check out problems before you attempt to
do so on your own.

✔ Never unplug the network connections on the back of your PC when the
network is on.

✔ *Crash* is the technical term for when a computer stops working. Nothing
actually crunches or smashes. In fact, the typical crash is more like an ice
age; everything suddenly stops, frozen in its tracks, and when they thaw it
all out, they'll find a mammoth chewing on buttercups.

✔ General troubleshooting and "Oh Dear Lord, Help Me" advice is offered in
Chapter 20.

TECHNICAL STUFF

Near-meaningless information on network topography

Network topography describes how the computer network is physically laid out. This concept really has nothing to do with your office's floor plan but rather how each computer is tied together using cables and where the file server — if any — sits.

The simplest type of network is a *bus network*. That's where each computer is a single node on a long strand of network cable — like the lights you use on a Christmas tree. The wire comes into your computer from another PC and goes out to another PC. The computers on the ends of the line have special *terminator plugs* that keep the network information from spilling on the floor. This is usually the arrangement of a peer-to-peer network.

A *star network* is one where a central server sits connected to each computer in the network. Or there may be several lines of cable, each with two or more computers attached. One star may be linked to other stars to make the network cover a larger area.

A *ring network* is where each computer is connected to the next computer through a single cable. This works like a bus network, but the two end computers are connected.

None of this stuff is important to anyone but the people buying and setting up your network.

Summary

This chapter's intent was to comfort you about some of the horror stories you've heard about networks. You now have a pretty good idea of what a network is (if not how it works). In particular, you know these things about networks:

▶ Networks are more efficient ways to share files and resources with other computers.

▶ When you sit down at your PC, you probably can choose to use the network (unless the wizards that set up the network removed that option). If you want to use the network, you must log in to the network.

▶ If you want to exchange files with other computers on the network, you must first access a network drive. This task may be done automatically, or you may have to enter a special command.

▶ The most used aspect of a network is its capacity to share printers. Using a printer on a network enables you to send a file to the printer and immediately use your computer for something else: no waiting!

▶ Most networks have a file server, a specially designated computer (that probably doesn't speak DOS) that parcels out files and programs to other computers on the network. If your network has a file server, you should probably use network versions of programs.

▶ Your computer is nothing but a node on the network.

▶ If the network crashes, don't try to fix it yourself.

The next chapter is a glossary of acronyms — those meaningless combinations of letters and numbers that you've never understood.

Chapter 18
Examining the Land of Acronyms

In This Chapter

▶ Several dozen acronyms in alphabetic order

▶ Too many for us to list all at once in this introduction

▶ A place to look them up when you encounter them elsewhere

▶ Stuff to memorize and amaze your friends with

▶ Offer valid in 48 states — sorry, Hawaii and Alaska (contiguous states only)

286

This number, aside from being the square root of 81,796, represents the 80286 microprocessor found in several types of computers. The common phrase used to describe these systems is "AT class" or "IBM AT compatible." This microprocessor's offspring, the 80386, is much more powerful and currently the most popular brain for a PC.

386

This number refers to the 80386 and its entire "family" of microprocessors, the brain in the typical PC. There are 80386 chips, 386SX models, and the whole lineup of i486 chips, also called 80486. As far as software is concerned, all these chips behave like the basic 386 microprocessor. If you have one inside your PC, then all the 386 software is available for your system to use.

80x86

This notation is used to represent all the microprocessors inside all the PCs. Because they all start with 80 and end in 86, the *x* in the middle means "I match anything." It does not mean 6,880.

ASCII

This is the first true computer acronym in this chapter; it stands for American Standard Code for Information Interchange. What that really means is basic text, simple information. An ASCII file contains no fancy formats and no fonts — just text.

ASCII is really a set of 128 code numbers. Assigned to each of them are various symbols, characters, and letters of the alphabet. This is something only true computer nerds would memorize — or hang on their walls.

ASCII is pronounced *Askee.* It is not *Ask-2.*

AVI

An AVI file stands for Audio-Video Interleaved, which means that it contains a little movie you can watch from within Windows.

BASIC

This is a computer programming language, devised to be simple, which is why they struggled long and hard to think of words that match B-A-S-I-C and make sense. In the end, they came up with Beginner's All-purpose Symbolic Instruction Code. It should be BAPSIC, but BASIC is the accepted acronym.

BASIC is one of the easiest programming languages to learn, but it's nothing to brag about. If you want to learn it, OK. All computers come with a version of the BASIC language. On DOS, it's BASICA, GWBASIC, or QBASIC. But seriously, don't waste your time on this unless you lack another hobby.

BBS

This is a modem word. There are more modem acronyms than any other type of acronym associated with a computer. BBS stands for bulletin board service. That's a type of software that runs on a computer with a modem attached and waits for other people with computers and modems to call in. When they do, they can leave messages, copy programs, "chat" with each other, or play games — real productive stuff.

BIOS

BIOS stands for basic input/output system. It's a set of instructions encoded on a chip inside the computer. These instructions tell the computer how to work with each of its components: how to read a character from the keyboard, display a character on the screen, print, and so on.

BMP

Windows dubs its graphics files *bitmaps*. Your favorite pictures must be bitmaps before Windows can use them for wallpaper.

BPS

Yet another modem term. This acronym stands for bits per second. It's a way of measuring how fast communication takes place between two computers. Speeds of 1200 bps are slow; a 9600 bps modem is a fast one. When you set the speed of a serial port — or a modem — you're setting the bps.

Some people mistakenly use *baud* rather than *bps*. This is a holdover from the early Cro-Magnon days of telecommunications. Back then, 300 baud and 300 bps described the same speed. But, as PC modems got faster, the baud term no longer applied. It's acceptable to call something a "9600 baud modem" but not technically accurate. But these days, who wants to be technically accurate?

CGA

This acronym means Color Graphics Adapter. It refers to the hardware used on the first PC to produce color. It also means the lowest and cheapest graphics standard for a PC. The CGA standard was eventually replaced by EGA and then by VGA.

CGA wasn't good for much; the graphics were limited to four colors max, and the resolution was ugly. Characters displayed in color were fuzzy and made your eyes crust over after a time. Yes, we hate CGA. You would too.

CPS

CPS is an acronym for characters per second. It's used to measure the speed of cheaper-impact or *dot matrix* printers. The cps value refers to how fast the printer can print a line of text. Because a line on a printer is usually 80 characters long, a printer rated at 80 cps can print one line of text a second. But wait! That rating is usually produced in the laboratory under ideal conditions. Like your car's mpg (miles per gallon) rating, your cps value varies. Still, because all printer manufacturers conduct the same tests, it's a good way to compare performance.

Laser printers use ppm (pages per minute) to gauge their speed.

CPU

This time-honored acronym means central processing unit. It's an old computer term. In the PC, it means your microprocessor, the 80x86 thing that acts as the computer's brain. Some like to call it a cpu because it includes the time-honored pronunciation "peeyew!"

CRC

Oh, here's a humdinger: cyclical redundancy check. Ugh. It's a mathematical calculation performed on a bunch of numbers (usually bytes). The CRC value calculated is the same for all those numbers. So, if a number changes, the CRC changes, and the computer, the disk drive, or your program can exclaim that something's amiss with your data.

The only time you'll see this is if you get a dreaded "CRC error" when the computer is accessing a disk drive or when using your modem to transfer a file. If that happens, try again. If it persists, contact your guru.

CRT

An Ancient Paleolithic Nerd term for your computer's monitor. Specifically, the glass tube in the monitor, what you would call a picture tube in a TV set, is called the cathode ray tube. Technically accurate, yes. But *monitor* conveys much more meaning to many more people.

DPI

This is an acronym for dots per inch. It's a way of describing how detailed an image can get. The more dpi, the higher the graphics resolution, and the less likely someone else is able to tell that the result was done by a computer.

This acronym is used most often with printing. Laser printers typically are capable of 300 dpi. However, more expensive laser printers and photographic typesetting machines can pull down 1,200 dpi.

DOC

DOC is an abbreviation for document. This is usually tagged onto the end of a filename (as the filename extension) to identify a word processing document. Here are some examples: BABY.DOC, DRY.DOC, and WHATSUP.DOC.

DOS

This acronym stands for disk operating system. What more can be said about this chestnut? In fact, we're sick of writing about it. Too many books and too many times, over and over: DOS this, DOS that, pronounce it this way, pronounce it that way. Argh! Refer to Chapter 13 if you really, really, really want to know more.

DTP

This is a trendy acronym for desktop publishing, the latest rage with a personal computer and a laser printer. It's actually one step above word processing and comes with a variety of programs — some easy to use and some near-typesetter-like in their complexity. DTP can also be used as a verb: "Have Millicent DTP me that flier." Ugh. Those people need to choke on their White Zin. Refer to Chapter 15's section on desktop publishing.

EGA

The first part of the phrase *Egads!*, this actually means Enhanced Graphics Adapter, the IBM hardware that superseded CGA as the PC graphics standard. EGA offered more colors, higher resolution, and prettier text than CGA. But, boy, was it expensive. Also, it was soon supplanted by VGA as the best type of PC graphics.

EISA

Here's an ugly one: Extended Industry Standard Architecture. It refers to the new expansion-slot scheme thought up to counter IBM's well-guarded and heavily patented MCA expansion-slot scheme. The whole idea here is that the expansion slots in a PC are too weak and feeble to deal with demanding computer operations. So everyone and his brother developed EISA. Should you worry about it? Not at all. This is an issue best left up to the PC gods to decide.

If you see the term, you can say *ee-eye-ess-ay*. Some pronounce it *EE-sah*.

EMS

EMS is a cute acronym meaning expanded memory specification. This is a set of rules for stuffing more memory into a PC and some instructions on how a program can use that extra memory. You can have EMS software and EMS hardware. Of course, we're touching on the complex issue of memory management here. This is a task best left up to those who continue to argue how fast Warp 6 really is.

EOF

This is a seldom-used acronym for end of file. It refers to the character that marks the last byte in a text file. Under DOS, this is the Ctrl-Z (Control-Z) character.

EPS

Short for Encapsulated PostScript file, this acronym describes a super-technical way in which programs can describe graphics with words. A PostScript file saved by one program can be read by other, different breeds of programs. That capability makes PostScript a handy way to move graphics files between different computers, programs, printers, and people.

ESDI

This is an acronym used to describe a type of hard drive. It stands for Enhanced System Device Interface, and it was a popular type of hard drive to have on a 386-level computer. Other, similar hard-drive types include IDE and SCSI. You can pronounce it by using the letters only. Or say *EZ-dee*. In real life, this is something only computer dealers or gurus need to concern themselves with.

GB

This is a common abbreviation for gigabyte, or one billion bytes. *Giga* has the same roots as the word gigantic, so one billion of anything is bound to be huge — incomprehensible. A gigabyte is 1,000 megabytes or one million kilobytes. It's also abbreviated as a single *G*.

GIF

This is a type of file on your computer — one that contains a graphics image. In fact, GIF stands for Graphics Interchange Format. The GIF files contain pretty images, cars, space shots, flowers, and animals. Special GIF-viewer software enables you to look at the pictures in stunning detail.

A curious situation with GIF is how to pronounce it. Dan Gookin thinks it should be GIF, with the *guh* sound. The reason is that he was chastised in San Francisco for pronouncing Ghirardelli as *Jee-ardelli* (as in chocolate). So, if it's *Gee* —with the *guh* sound — *ardelli chocolate,* it has to be *GIF* with the *guh* sound, not *JIFF* like the peanut butter. Andy Rathbone agrees, remarking that at least no one calls it *hif* as in *Gila Monster.*

GUI

This is an acronym for graphical user interface. It refers to using a computer with Windows, icons, a mouse, and pull-down menus — the WIMP interface. Some in the computer industry have taken to pronouncing GUI as *gooey*. This is totally optional. Dan Gookin prefers *gee-you-eye*. Andy Rathbone calls it *gooey* unless he's thinking about French wine and cheese, wherein he calls it *gwee*.

HD

Hard disk. Or it could be hard drive. No one ever says HD, but you may see a label or form that has it on there. It means your hard drive. Or your hard disk. Same thing. (Note that sometimes HD stands for high density; refer to Chapter 8 for more information.)

HMA

This is the most governmental-sounding acronym in computerdom. It's a legitimate prank to say, "Stop resetting instead of quitting that program, or I'll phone the HMA." Instead, we think HMA stands for high memory area, but we're not really sure. What it is and where it is don't really matter anyway.

HOV

We suppose that this one stands for high-occupancy vehicle. You see it all over the highways — particularly when referring to the diamond lanes. Those are HOV lanes. A high-occupancy vehicle is one of those cars barely off the ground with seven or eight bobbing heads in it: four kids in the back, two in front, and Mom and Dad. We mention this acronym here because it pops up frequently and is almost as annoying as many computer-inspired acronyms.

IBM

International Business Machines. Big blue. This company may not have made the best computers, but it had the best computer sales force in the '50s and '60s. IBM's first personal computer, the PC, is the model on which all personal computers are based today. Or as Descartes said, "I think, therefore, IBM."

The 5th Wave   By Rich Tennant

"FOR OBVIOUS REASONS WE DECIDED NOT TO USE AN ACRONYM"

IDE

This acronym is used to describe a type of hard drive stuffed into many of today's PCs. It stands for integrated drive electronics. All it means is that your computer uses that type of hard drive. Other types include ESDI, SCSI, and a horde of others. Your guru will know this, so if you need to replace a drive or add another one to your system, your guru will buy the proper type. Otherwise, it's yet another fun acronym to banter about at the office party.

ISA

This is an acronym for Industry Standard Architecture. It refers to the rules or, more precisely, the lack of rules by which your PC's expansion slots and expansion cards operate. Of what importance is this to you? None. But when you see ISA mentioned, they're talking about expansion slots and cards. See "EISA" if you want to be totally confused.

JPEG

The Joint Photographic Expert Group file format lets pretty pictures be stored in smaller files.

KB

Once we actually saw KB used to abbreviate the word keyboard. But most of the time, KB means kilobyte, 1,000 bytes. *Kilo* is from the French word *kilo,* which comes from the Greek word *kilo.* Kilo, no matter how it's written, means 1,000 of something. KB is 1,000 bytes, which is probably what piranhas take in about a second. (Note that many people use the abbreviation K rather than KB.)

KHz

KHz stands for kilohertz, or 1,000 hertz. A hertz is a cycle per second. You could say "7 kilohertz of bicycles are stolen in New York" (7,000 bicycles per second). In computer land, a *cycle* refers to how fast something operates. Hertz is named after Heinrich R. Hertz, a German physicist — or maybe his son, Gustav Ludwig; one is never sure. Anyway, 1,000 of them are a kilohertz.

The biggest problem with kilohertz is the proper way to abbreviate it. If we can wrest control from the evil IDG editors for a second, the proper way to abbreviate kilohertz is kHz (little *k,* big *H,* little *z*). (We're writing *kiloHertz* here, just in case they already changed it.) Most times, editors use KHz. Sometimes, they use Khz or even KHZ. It's kHz. Really. Promise.

LAN

LAN is an acronym for local area network. What's the difference between a LAN and a network? Nothing, really. There may be some difference in semantics, but most people call a LAN their network; the gurus and nerds can argue over what a LAN is or isn't. LAN rhymes with *man* or *suntan* (which most computer people lack).

MB

MB, pronounced *mub,* means megabyte. That's about one million bytes or 1,000 kilobytes. If a byte were one letter in a novel, a megabyte would be about a 700-page book. Hard drives and computer memory are measured in megabytes, abbreviated MB. (We're kidding about the *mub;* it's pronounced *megabyte.*)

MDA

This has nothing to do with Jerry Lewis or the fine organization he supports. Instead, MDA stands for (*timpani . . .*) Monochrome Display Adapter. It's the old, cruddy monochrome standard for all PCs. The MDA has been surpassed by the Hercules standard. Chances are, if you have a monochrome display (green on black, amber on black, and so on), it's a Hercules display.

MHz

Back to Heinrich or Ludwig (see "KHz"), MHz is another hertz term. This time it means megahertz — one million hertz (which sounds like a Chinese torture).

MIDI

Word processors rearrange words; MIDI (Musical Instrument Digital Interface) makes it easy to rearrange musical notes. Computers with MIDI ports (the ports that come on most sound cards) can be hooked up to musical keyboards and synthesizers. MIDI software then enables musicians to record and edit their compositions. Missed a note while recording "Jingle Bell Rock"? Then grab the mouse and pull that little on-screen note down one notch until it sounds in key.

M&Ms

The *M*s come from the last names of candy-maker Forrest Mars, Sr., and his associate, Bruce Murrie. M&Ms are a preferred computer food because they don't leave gunk on the fingers (which subsequently attaches itself to the keyboard and the mouse). Whereas M&Ms can be gobbled by the handful, other snack foods must be picked up daintily with the thumb and middle finger, keeping the index finger "grease free" for its mouse-button chores.

Modem

A modem is a little box that either fits inside a computer or plugs into a serial port outside a computer. The modem hooks up to the phone lines; special communications software then enables the modem to call up other computers and gossip. A wide variety of on-line services cater to modem users, letting them look up stuff in encyclopedias, read back issues of magazines, grab software, or talk to and insult each other. *Modem* stands for *mo*dulator/*dem*odulator.

MPC

An MPC is a multimedia personal computer. To earn the latest, lofty MPC acronym — currently MPC-2 — a computer must have these items:

- 486SX or faster microprocessor
- 4MB of RAM or more
- Hard drive with 160MB or more
- 3½-inch, high-density floppy drive
- Two-button mouse
- SuperVGA video card
- 16-bit sound card
- Relatively speedy CD-ROM drive

The sticky ones are the sound card and the CD-ROM drive; those two devices can add more than $500 to the price of a PC. And for some reason, the standard requires a joystick as well.

MS-DOS

The Microsoft Disk Operating System, or MS-DOS, greets you when you turn on your computer. DOS does boring computer housekeeping stuff in the background while you work. It provides a bunch of commands like COPY, DEL, and DIR that can boss files around. Every IBM-compatible computer needs some sort of DOS before it can do anything.

MTBF

When engineers test a new computer part, they keep it running until it finally breaks down. Then they calculate the mean time between failures and refer to the MTBF number when talking about reliability. The higher the MTBF number, the more durable the part.

OEM

An original equipment manufacturer puts together computers and sells them under his or her own name. For example, IBM, Dell, Tandy, COMPAQ, and AST all sell their own brands of IBM-compatible computers. Some of them license their own version of DOS from Microsoft and then sell it under their own label. All the OEMs build their IBM-compatible computers slightly differently (Tandy adds sound, for example).

PC

IBM used to make big, important computers for big, important businesses. When IBM created its first computer for small businesses or even — gads — recipe-collecting home users, it called its machine a PC, or personal computer. Now, everybody refers to IBM-compatible computers as PCs. Some people stretch the meaning of PC to include any type of personal computer, even the ones made by Atari, Commodore, or Apple (Macintosh).

PC DOS

IBM bought rights to use MS-DOS from Microsoft but didn't want to admit that it didn't write its own operating system. So it renamed MS-DOS to become PC DOS. IBM tweaked PC DOS a little bit, but the system still works on non-IBM computers. It stands for Personal Computer Disk Operating System (see "OEM" and "MS-DOS").

PCL and PDL

The most practical laser printers use either Hewlett-Packard's printer command language or Adobe's PostScript page description language. Both the PCL and the PDL are ways that software can tell the printer what images to print. Post-Script costs more but looks better. Some printers offer both.

PCMCIA

This long string of words — Personal Computer Memory Card International Association — describes a small, credit-card-size slot in a laptop and the little cards that slide in. PCMCIA cards contain mostly modems or memory.

PCX

A guy named Mark Zachmann created PC Paintbrush software to let Etch-a-Sketch lovers draw and display pictures on their computers. At the time, competing paint programs saved their files with names like FLOWER.GIF or AGONY.PIC, for example. Zachmann figured that the letters PCX sounded good together, so all the pictures created by PC Paintbrush end with the letters PCX. (The letters don't stand for anything, unlike other acronyms.)

Everybody else must have liked Zachmann's choice of letters because PCX is now the most widely accepted format for saving pictures on IBM-compatible computers. Chances are, just about any graphics program can both read and write to the PCX format.

PGA

Organized in 1916 by Philadelphia businessman Rodman Wanamaker, the Professional Golfers Association of America has left millions of people wondering why it's not called the PGAA. Nevertheless, it consists of chaps who yearn for a work-free golf place, where they can call the green their office. (Look for palmtop computers being used to keep score.)

At one time, there was a video standard for the PC called the Professional Graphics Adapter. But that's just too trivial to dwell on here.

PPM

A printer's speed is measured in pages per minute. For example, a laser printer advertised as 5 ppm can print five pages in one minute. But there's a catch: It won't print a five-page document in one minute. It can print the same page over and over five times in a minute. The printer takes considerably longer with most projects because they contain different images on each page.

QWERTY

The alphabetic keys along the top row of a standard typewriter start with the letters QWERTY. Therefore, a typewriter using a standard typewriter key layout is said to have a QWERTY layout. Another popular layout, Dvorak, allows for speedier typing, but it hasn't caught on because nobody wants to learn how to type all over again. (By the way, the letters DVORAK don't appear next to each other in the Dvorak layout; Dvorak is just the name of the guy who thought up the new layout.)

Here's a useless tidbit of information: You can spell the word *typewriter* by using just the top row of letters on a typewriter.

RAID

"If one big hard drive dies," thought one engineer, "all the information will be destroyed. So let's tell a bunch of small, fast, and cheap hard drives to keep track of each other's data. Then we can call them a Redundant Array of Inexpensive Disks."

RAM

RAM, or random-access memory, comes on little black chips the size of a large fingernail. When these chips are filled with electricity, they can store numbers. The computer uses RAM chips as memory to store numbers while it's following the instructions from a piece of software. When the computer is turned off, the electricity drains from the RAM chips, and they forget everything they've stored.

RGB

Just like a kindergartner with crayons, a computer monitor displays colors by mixing together the primary colors: red, green, and blue (hence the term RGB). In the olden days of CGA graphics, a color monitor was referred to as an RGB monitor.

RISC

Short for Reduced Instruction Set Computing, these fancy, new RISC workstations run software that's even more complicated than DOS.

ROM

A computer can use RAM to store information. But when the computer is turned off, electricity drains from the RAM chips and they forget everything. So some engineers decided to "burn" instructions into little chips and call them ROM, or read-only memory. ROM chips keep their information, even when they're turned off.

It takes special machines to burn the information onto ROM chips. A computer can read information stored on ROM chips, but it can't write to them or use them for storage.

RPM

When RPM (revolutions per minute) isn't referring to engines or whirling disk drives, it refers to how quickly computer nerds can turn in their chairs when they hear someone crunch on Cheetos.

RS-232

Pronounced *R-S-two-thirty-two,* the RS-232 interface is another name for a serial port, or a COM port. It's a little oval receptacle on your computer's back where you plug in a modem cable. Or you can plug in a serial printer cable. Or, if you want to use something as nerdy as a null-modem cable and copy information back and forth between two computers, you can link a cable between the RS-232 interfaces of two computers (see Chapter 17).

RS-232 is the 232nd recommended standard that the Electronic Industries Association could think up. Actually, it's the C revision of the 232nd recommended standard, making its official name the RS-232C interface. And, to get down and dirty, the Electronics Industries Association celebrated the port's 25th anniversary in 1987 by changing its name to the EIA-232D interface. Nobody listened, however, and it's still lovingly referred to as the RS-232 interface.

Nobody will laugh if you just call it a serial port, though.

RTF

All word processors save their work differently. They use different codes to mark italicized words, for example, or indented paragraphs. Because of the coding differences, word processors usually can't read each other's files. To get around this, most word processors can save text in ASCII format (see "ASCII"). Unfortunately, ASCII files only contain text; there's no fancy formatting.

So Microsoft invented the Rich Text Format, or RTF. RTF files are still ASCII files, but the formatting codes are ASCII, too. For example, the sentence "This *is* great!" would be described as "This {\i is} great!" in an RTF file. Filenames that end with the letters RTF are most likely Rich Text Format files.

RTFM

Technical support people often tire of answering questions from people who could have found the answer themselves if they'd only read the manual on page 247, subsection D, third paragraph. So, when somebody calls the Help Hot Line, the tech support person puts that person on hold, screams "RTFM" (Read The uhm, uhm, Fine — yeah, that's it, *Fine* — Manual), and then calmly repeats the answer to the question from rote memory while picking lint from his or her belly button.

SCSI

Pronounced *scuzzy,* SCSI is up against GUI (*gooey*) for best-sounding acronym. A SCSI port is like a souped-up serial port that enables a computer to send and receive information quickly. Most people hook up CD-ROM drives to SCSI ports. (It stands for Small Computer System Interface.)

STP

This ain't plain old motor oil; it's *scientifically* treated petroleum.

SVGA

After Video Graphics Array (VGA) became the hottest new monitor in town, some companies came out with an even better one. It could display more colors and at a better resolution. But what to call it? The word "extended" had already been used for EGA (see "EGA"). So they took a tip from Clark Kent and called it the Super Video Graphics Array.

TPI

This is a technical acronym for tracks per inch. It refers to how much information can be stored on a floppy disk. Information is stored on tracks, and the more of them you can jam into an inch, the better. Take a gander at your floppy disks and you'll see the TPI value on there somewhere (or maybe you won't, now that the disks are getting "friendlier").

TSR

Terminate-and-stay-resident (TSR) programs load themselves into memory but don't do anything immediately. They watch what you type, and when you press the right combination of keys — say the Alt key and the \ key — they pop up into action. Some bring a little calendar to the screen; others bring a calculator. When you're through calculating or calendaring, they disappear, waiting to be brought up again. A TSR refers to any program that sits in your computer's memory while other programs are working. (The key sequence that excites them is referred to as a *hot key.*)

TTL

Standing for transistor-transistor logic, TTL is a type of digital-RGB monitor used by some IBM-compatible computers. Other than that, who cares?

TTY

The oldest computers didn't display information on monitors. They printed a program's results on a printer called a teletypewriter, or TTY. Today, TTY refers to your console, your computer screen, and your keyboard. Of course, that's only when you're using the UNIX operating system — everyone go screaming in the halls! (If you think DOS means trouble, you haven't tried UNIX.)

TXT

Yet another file extension (see "DOC," "GIF," "PCX," and "RTF"). TXT refers to a file containing plain old ASCII text of the barest degree. (You may as well see "ASCII," too.) Because ASCII files contain such basic information, they can be read by just about any piece of software. That means that just about any word processor can read a file ending in the letters TXT. (You can't just rename a file to TXT to make it ASCII, though. It must be converted to ASCII by a word processor.)

UMB

UMB means upper memory block, which is a touchy memory management issue — something you don't want to ever mess with yourself. Just sit there and shudder for a few moments.

UNIX

Developed by AT&T to run on medium-sized (of the day) computers, it's an operating system for hard-core nerds who think that DOS is too easy. All you need to know about UNIX is to avoid it. The initials don't stand for anything in particular; they're supposedly making fun of the UNIX author's previous job working on the Multics system. (Yep, the whole system is that vague.)

UPS

An uninterruptible power supply contains rechargeable batteries; if the power ever goes out, the UPS continues to supply power to your computer, giving you time to save your files, exit your programs, and turn off your computer while you look for a flashlight.

While the power's on, the UPS just sits there, storing electricity in case of a disaster. A UPS usually only supplies power for an extra 15 minutes or so — just enough time to shut down safely.

VDT

Computer nerds don't call a monitor a monitor. They call it a video display terminal. (The most hard-core nerds call it a CRT. See "CRT." *Si?*) VDT is considered a generic term for any sort of computer monitor. Government subcommittees use it most often when writing reports like "Using VDT Emissions for Aphid Control."

VGA

Standing for Video Graphics Array (not Adapter), VGA is a relatively high-quality monitor and graphics card. The current rage, it can display 256 colors on-screen at the same time, in little rows of 320 dots by 200 dots. That makes the display look almost like a photograph, if you squint so that the little dots run together (see "CGA," "EGA," "SVGA," and, if you're not yet exhausted, "XGA").

WP

The most widely used word processor in the IBM-compatible world, WordPerfect won fame with its extensive toll-free support lines (almost 50 of them). The fact that the program was relatively difficult to use didn't seem to matter. Still, it's a full-featured program, with all the bells and whistles. Keep that little template next to your function keys so that you can remember the commands and don't lose the card with the phone numbers for technical support.

In some circles, WP still means *word processing*.

WYSIWYG

Early word processors would simply show text on the screen; they couldn't show italics, headlines, or fancy fonts. As technology improved, word processors started to display text on the screen exactly as it would look when printed out on paper. The software marketing people, desperate for a short, catchy phrase that would describe this new "what you see is what you get" technology, opted for WYSIWYG (pronounced *wizzee-wig*).

XGA

IBM keeps releasing new "standards" for graphics; the hottest new one is the Extended Graphics Array. XGA can show 256 colors on the screen at once, the same as VGA, but in tiny rows of 1,024 dots by 768 dots. These pictures look pretty darn sharp, and some people say it will be the new "standard" for monitors.

XMODEM

XMODEM was the name of an old computer communications program that used modems to send files. Today, XMODEM refers to a way to send files between two computers without any errors. The XMODEM-sending method is also the way to send programs and other *binary* files. XMODEM transfer can be called *error-free* or *binary file transfer*. And other flavors of XMODEM exist: YMODEM, ZMODEM, and bizarre protocols like Kermit, which was, in fact, named after the frog (with Jim Henson's permission, rumor has it).

XMS

By now, you've probably heard about the "dreaded 640K memory barrier." Because of the way DOS was designed years ago, programs could only use 640K of memory. Everybody's pretty fed up with it. So a group of manufacturers got together, plugged some more memory chips into 286 and 386 computers, and drew up a set of guidelines to force programs to use it. Those guidelines are called the Extended Memory Specification (XMS). You should never have to memorize this, nor will you be killed in an enemy prison for revealing what it means.

Summary

In this chapter, you were treated to a whirlwind tour of computerdom through the use of acronyms. The next time you eat your alphabet soup, you can try to see what kinds of messages Campbell's is trying to send to your computer. Among other things, you learned the following:

▶ The favorite candy of computer people is M&Ms.

▶ The Professional Golfers Association has little to do with computers.

▶ The proper way to pronounce Ghirardelli chocolate is with the *guh* sound.

In the next chapter, you learn how to keep up with the Joneses.

Chapter 19
Keeping Up with the Joneses

. . . .

. . . .

Somehow, upgrading a computer has a larger-than-life aura. Most people don't trade in their cars each year. And the household VCRs, blenders, and clock radios usually stay put until they break; then it's time to go shopping for a new one. Even the office typewriters are probably several years old; there's just no point in buying a new one all the time.

The computer world, being bizarre and different as we know it, offers updates and upgrades on a monthly basis, if not weekly. It's too easy for software publishers to add a few new features to a program, slap a new cover on the box, and say they've created a "new, improved version." And hardware! Golly, technology moves ahead faster than a lead-footed granny in an Audi 5000.

When is the right time to succumb to "upgrade fever"? Should computers be updated constantly to keep current with new technology? Should all software upgrades be purchased, especially because the publishers offer a discount to current owners? And, if you decide to upgrade, what should you do with all that old stuff? This chapter addresses all of these high-priority issues.

When Is Your PC Out of Date?

This one's easy. Your PC's out of date the moment you purchase it. As soon as one computer's off the showroom floor, another's being built in the back room, ready to offer more power at a lower price. Well, it's not that dramatic. Instead, you'll most likely see your computer offered at a lower price less than three months after you buy it.

A more important question is this: When your computer is out of date, do you need a new one? Not really. Look at the reasons you bought it in the first place. Can the computer still handle those needs? If yes, then you're doing fine. Upgrade only when you desperately need to. No sense in spending more money on the monster.

✔ Computer technology grows faster than fly specks on a clean windshield, and your computer will be out of date the moment you purchase it. But, unless your computing *needs* have changed drastically, your computer can still handle the tasks you bought it for.

✔ Most people buy newer computers for the increase in speed. Yet speed doesn't always mean increased productivity. For instance, most word processing time is spent pondering the right choice of words. A faster computer can't help there. Faster computers do help those programs that need the extra horsepower: graphics, animation, desktop publishing, and applications of that ilk.

✔ Compare the price of a new computer with the amount of time you'll save at a faster processing speed. If you spend a lot of time waiting for your computer to catch up with you, an upgrade may be in order.

✔ Instead of buying a completely new computer, consider upgrading your old one, as discussed in the next section.

Today's $10,000 computer will cost $5,000 by next year. In three years, you'll be able to buy it cheap — maybe for $700 to $1,500. In six years, you won't be able to find it at all. That's roughly how computer equipment comes down in value. However, you should never wait to buy. If you do, then when the $10,000 model has dropped down to $5,000, a newer and faster $10,000 model will take its place. That's an endless cycle you don't want to get caught up in. The same holds true for all computer equipment.

Upgrading Versus Buying a New Computer

Instead of buying a new computer, it may be easier to upgrade the old one. Or, rather, have somebody else upgrade your old computer for you. Upgrading is almost always less expensive than buying a whole new computer. Plus, sometimes you just need part of your computer to be bigger and better: You need a bigger hard drive, but you don't need a faster microprocessor or brain. (And who really wants a faster brain, anyway?)

The following parts of a computer can be upgraded relatively quickly and inexpensively by somebody who knows what to do. (So either bribe your computer guru or take your computer back where you bought it and have the store upgrade it.)

And remember: You may not need all of this stuff. Upgrading a computer is like putting big tires on your car: It looks cooler and may even handle better, but it's not essential, and it doesn't always impress the girls at the taco shop.

Memory

What it is: Memory comes in tiny, black, bug-like *chips*. When your computer computes, it stores temporary information on the chips. That information disappears forever when the computer's turned off.

What uses it: Microsoft Windows, huge applications like Quattro Pro and 1-2-3, Harvard Graphics, and other graphics programs all use lots of memory. And the best computer games can all use extra memory to temporarily store information.

What an upgrade does: Increased memory can make these programs work faster and handle larger chunks of information. It also lets the computer handle more graphics and sound.

- Adding memory is a relatively inexpensive way to make a computer run faster or handle extra computing chores. Microsoft Windows loves additional memory; it will run faster and allow more open windows at the same time. For best results, add memory to a 386 computer and buy something called a *memory manager*.

- More memory is the best thing you can buy for your PC.

- Buying memory means buying RAM chips. RAM chips come in more varieties and flavors than potato chips. This is definitely a job for someone else.

- For more information about memory stuff, read Chapter 6.

Hard drive

What it is: A hard drive is a fast disk that is hidden inside your computer; it can store the equivalent of hundreds of floppy disks' worth of information. The hard drive holds programs and data for day-to-day use, and the files all stay put whether the computer's turned on or off. (Your laptop's hard drive will remember the stuff stored on its hard drive even when the battery runs out.)

What uses it: All programs can be copied to a hard drive for quicker and easier access. Most large programs, like Microsoft Windows and Quattro Pro, require a hard drive and usually take up most of the space there.

What an upgrade does: A larger hard drive enables you to store more programs and data, making your computing more convenient. Also, hard drive technology has been jamming: A new, larger hard drive will be faster than your old one. You won't be twiddling your thumbs for as long while a program loads or reads information from a file.

- ✔ Most computers are sold with only one hard drive. A second hard drive can easily be added. This is, again, a task for Mr. Guru.

- ✔ It's possible to swap your hard drive for one of a larger size and faster speed. If you're going to do this, you need to back up all your files and data from the old hard drive and then restore that stuff to the new hard drive. Although your guru will set this up for you, it's up to you to do the manual labor (disk swapping).

- ✔ By the way, larger hard drives don't take up any extra room in the computer's case, so don't worry about buying a bigger case.

If you can't afford a new hard drive, consider a program like Stacker. Stacker squeezes all your hard drive's information down into smaller pieces, letting you cram twice as many programs and data files onto the disk.

Monitor/video card

What it is: Your monitor is that TV-set-looking thing. The video card is the thing inside your computer that the monitor's cable plugs into.

What uses it: All your software struts its stuff on your monitor.

What an upgrade does: Newer monitors and cards can display more colors and at a higher resolution: The pictures will look clearer on the screen, and you won't see so many jagged edges. Also, the higher-resolution monitors let you cram more information onto the screen at the same time. For instance, you'll be able to have two fully open windows in Windows. The letters will be smaller, but at least the windows won't be on top of each other.

✔ When you buy a new monitor, you must almost always buy a new video card to go with it. Unless they're into heavy-duty graphics work, most people can get along with VGA or Super VGA monitors and their companion video cards.

✔ The most common monitor/video card upgrade is from the boring old monochrome monitor to a splashy new color model. You need to buy both a color monitor and a VGA video card to make this possible.

✔ A hot new monitor and card can still run the older software you used on your older, low-resolution monitor. The new monitor will just drop back into its "old software" mode to display it. The software still looks the way it did on the older monitor.

✔ The speediest video cards are *local-bus* video cards. You can't just go out and buy one, though, unless your motherboard has a local-bus *slot* — that's where the card plugs in.

✔ For more monitor information, see Chapter 9.

Buying and Selling Used Gear

When people upgrade their computer, what happens to the old stuff? The really old stuff goes to the kids for game machines. Some businesses sell off older computers, which you can find in the classified ads. And normal people unload computers for a variety of reasons.

When people upgrade their computers piece by piece, the old stuff turns up in the classified ads. This is where you can find some bargains but only if you really, *really* know what you're doing. After all, the old stuff isn't as good as the new stuff. And, quite often, the new stuff is cheaper than what they're asking for the old stuff.

Should you buy used gear? Only if they're selling *exactly* what you need. For example, you've used the Zot 101 printer for years and yours broke. If there's a Zot 101 for sale somewhere — and it still works to your satisfaction — then buy it used.

✔ Test-drive before you buy. This is like "kicking the tires," but it ensures that whatever you're taking home works. (Well, it worked at least once.)

✔ A big problem with used equipment you're not familiar with is that you may not get any manuals and there is no technical support or warranty from the selling party. Although it's important to test-drive old equipment, don't expect any of the service or support you'd find with new stuff.

✔ *Never* buy a used computer as your first computer purchase. It's just much better to pay a store for the service and support you'll need. (And don't shop for the cheapest price, either! Service and support are important and worth paying a bit extra for.)

✔ There is no money to be made in selling used computers. Look in your paper or yellow pages: No one is doing it. (And, if they are, check the yellow pages again in a year.) PCs have *no* resale value, so wipe away those visions of selling your used system for anything more than 10 percent of its purchase price. The new stuff is just better and cheaper.

✔ A better option is to donate used equipment to a charity or a local school. The tax write-off is far greater than the resale value ever will be.

✔ If you're selling used computer parts, then try to keep all the manuals together, along with support software — the same stuff you got new with the product. Also, accept only cash. For major items, ask for a cashier's check.

✔ Some stuff you'll never get rid of: Buried in his garage, Andy Rathbone has 2MB of incompatible RAM chips, a 40MB hard drive with "just a few" bad sectors, a 300-baud modem, a Tandy 200 computer, and several old CP/M disks. Dan Gookin also has 2MB of ugly, old RAM chips (which must be a status symbol), a clunky old 20MB hard drive, a monochrome monitor, a multifunction expansion card for an old PC XT, and more out-of-date software than the EPA will allow a single person to incinerate at once.

When Is Your Software Out of Date?

When a novel's written, it's finished. Subsequent reprints correct a few misspellings, but that's about it. But software's never finished. It's too easy to change. Most software packages are updated about twice a year.

Sometimes the company fixes a few problems, or *bugs*. But most often, the software contains new features so that it can compete with the other guy's software. This is why new versions appear. The upgrade gives you access to the newer, bug-free software and its features. It also lets software companies grow rich by charging you yet again for the same product.

✔ When enough new features have been added, the company mails a card to all the registered owners of that software, informing them of a "new and exciting" version and offering them a chance to upgrade for less than the cost of the new package!

✔ Consider each upgrade offer on its individual merits: Will you ever use the new features? Do you need a word processor that can print upside-down headlines and bar charts that show your word count? Can you really get any mileage out of the "network version" when you're a sole user sitting at home?

✔ If you're using WordPerfect 4.2 and everybody else is using WordPerfect 5.1, you'll have difficulty exchanging documents; after a while, newer versions of programs become incompatible with the older models. In an office setting, everybody should be using the same software version. (Everybody doesn't have to be using the latest version, just the same version.)

✔ Upgrading software is only possible if you've sent in your registration card. The software company will then notify you of a new version, and you can order it automatically. The upgrade cost is usually much cheaper than buying the product new all over again. Some upgrades are even free (but don't get your hopes up).

What If Everybody Else Is Buying It?

Although programmers have written hundreds of thousands of software packages, only a few of them make it to market. In fact, although hundreds of word processors have been written, only three or four account for the majority of sales. When a piece of software rises to the top, everybody seems to buy it because, well, everybody else is buying it.

Should you be an iconoclastic trailblazer, or should you follow the crowd? For the most part, follow the crowd. For instance, WordPerfect may not be the easiest word processor to use, but it overcomes that disadvantage simply because so many people use it. The company can afford toll-free help lines to answer questions from confused users. You can save a WordPerfect file and give it to thousands of other people with few problems because they, too, use WordPerfect.

By all means, consider your own needs first. But, when choosing between two pieces of equally potent software, choose the one that's being used by the largest number of people.

✔ Being in the majority is usually a guarantee that the product, its service, and its support will be there for quite some time to come. However, being a pioneer has its benefits as well, especially if the product offers features that you desperately need.

✔ Remember, the pioneers are the ones with the arrows in their backs.

✔ No, you should never do something because "everyone else" is doing it. You wouldn't walk off a cliff if all your friends were doing it, would you? Well, maybe if there was some water at the bottom (and if you sent a guy down to make sure that it was deep enough). And maybe if everyone forced someone small and much younger to jump first, like Virgil, who we always thought was a little slow anyway.

Upgrading a Laptop

It's relatively easy to upgrade a desktop computer. The lid pops off, and parts slide in and out — like in an old Chevy. And you can stand there and hand your guru a screwdriver or chip (RAM or Frito) while you watch. But, in a laptop, everything's scrunched together. Sometimes everything's packed together so Chang-and-Eng tightly that it can't be separated. This makes it very difficult to upgrade a laptop. You can't change the display, for instance. And to upgrade the hard drive, you must often send the laptop back to the manufacturer.

✔ It's not only difficult, but it's expensive, too. Manufacturers use their own parts, so they charge a premium price for laptop upgrades.

✔ When buying a laptop, buy one as powerful as you can afford. You won't be able to upgrade it very easily, so try to buy one that can meet your needs for a long time.

✔ It is possible to upgrade a laptop with RAM. Buying RAM for a laptop, as for a desktop machine, is one of the best things you can do.

✔ Sometimes you can buy external upgrades for a laptop. There's an extra hard drive, available for some laptops, that plugs into the printer port. Although that sounds awkward, it's much cheaper than trying to cram another hard drive inside the laptop's case.

✔ For more information about laptops, see Chapter 12.

● ●

Summary

In the rapidly changing world of PCs, it's easy to feel as if you're being left behind if you don't have the latest version of the software you're using and the most powerful hardware that's available. This chapter explained how to decide when (and when not) to upgrade or replace your system.

▶ You learned to consider whether your current system meets your needs instead of simply replacing it with the newest, fastest, most powerful stuff on the market. And even if it doesn't fully meet your needs, you can often upgrade what you have instead of buying a whole new system.

▶ You found out that it's relatively easy and inexpensive to upgrade your computer's memory, hard drive, and monitor.

▶ You explored the market for used computers — as a potential buyer and as a potential seller.

▶ You found out why it's important for laptop buyers to purchase the most powerful laptop they can afford.

The following chapter provides some solutions for common computer problems. It also describes some preventive measures that you can take to keep your system up and running.

● ●

Chapter 20
It Doesn't Work

In This Chapter

▶ The best way to handle trouble

▶ What to do when you've just deleted your file

▶ What to do when you've just reformatted an important disk

▶ How to find the mouse

▶ What to do after using the Reset switch

▶ Tips on troubleshooting and repair

▶ Your computer's SETUP program

▶ The proper way to take the computer to the doctor

▶ How to get technical support

▶ DOS commands you're never to use

▶ How to avoid viruses

Computer trouble looms on the horizon for all PC users. Everyone, even a guru, experiences problems. The difference is that the gurus generally know what to do about it. Yet, even then, sometimes the gurus are stumped. Computers will suddenly — for no apparent reason — stop working. You probably weren't doing anything at all — nothing funny that would cause the crash. Yet there Mr. Computer sits, not working.

Who knows what causes a computer not to work, to crash, to hang, to die? It could be anything: the computer's mood, phases of the moon, or voodoo. The cause is incidental. Getting the computer back to the way it worked before is central.

This chapter can't describe how to fix everything wrong with a PC. First, we don't have the space, and second, the thought terrifies us. Instead, the sections in this chapter describe a few ways to approach the "it don't work" situation, solve a few riddles, and — best of all — point you in the proper direction when help is really necessary.

Examining the Best Way to Handle Trouble

The best way to handle computer trouble is to call someone else. Seriously, call your guru, the people who sold you the computer, or the people who developed the program. They will help you get things back on track.

✔ Make a quick visual check of your PC before doing anything. Look for loose cables and plugs out of their sockets. If it's something you can fix yourself, great. If not, call for help.

✔ You should always perform a mental survey of what happened before the "incident." Did you change anything in your PC? Add any new software? Delete anything? Was any new hardware added? Go over these questions in your head before you do anything. Chances are whoever you ask for help will want the same information.

✔ Phoning a hardware or software manufacturer for help is called "getting technical support." You obtain it by phoning a technical support number ensconced in your manuals somewhere. Refer to the section "Getting Technical Support" later in this chapter.

I Just Deleted My File!

This is a common booboo, committed by everyone who owns a computer. Here's how to get your file back: Use the DOS 5 UNDELETE command. At the DOS prompt, type **UNDELETE** followed by the name of the file:

```
C:\> UNDELETE VITAL.DOC
```

In this line, the UNDELETE command is followed by a space and the filename VITAL.DOC. You would replace the filename VITAL.DOC with the name of the file you're trying to resuscitate. Type the full filename as best you can remember it.

You'll see some nonsense on the screen that looks something like this:

```
Directory  C:\IMPORTNT\STUFF
File Specifications:  VITAL.DOC

        Deletion-tracking file not found.

        MS-DOS directory contains   1 deleted files
        Of those,     1 files may be recovered.

Using the MS-DOS directory.
  ?ITAL  DOC    1227   4-22-924:16p ...A Undelete (Y/N)?
```

Of course, exactly what you see will be different. Ignore everything except for the last line on the screen. Check to see whether it looks like your file — except that the first letter will be replaced by a question mark.

Press Y to undelete your file. If your file isn't displayed, press N; MS-DOS may show you some more files. Press Y only when your file pops up. If more than one version of your file pops up, check the date listed and select the most recent version.

After pressing Y, you'll see something akin to this:

```
Please type the first character for ?ITAL.DOC:
```

Type the first letter of the filename. For example, you would press V in this example. If all goes well, you'll see the following:

```
File successfully undeleted.
```

Your file is back. Sacrifice a small animal to the DOS gods in Redmond, Washington.

- ✔ The sooner you use the UNDELETE command, the better your chances are of recovering the file.

- ✔ If you delete a whole gaggle of files by typing **DEL *.***, type **UNDELETE *.*** to yank them all back again.

- ✔ If you can't remember the name of the file to undelete, then just type **UNDELETE** by itself:

```
C:\> UNDELETE
```

Follow the instructions as you did before.

- ✔ UNDELETE may not work all the time. Occasionally, mitigating circumstances arise and file recovery is impossible. Sniff, sniff. The moral: Be careful when deleting files!

- ✔ Note that UNDELETE will not work on network drives.

- ✔ Have your guru set up DOS's deletion-tracking feature. This uses a special command called MIRROR to keep track of all the files you hack off at the knees. Undeleting files is much more efficient when the MIRROR command is installed.

Deleting files is something everyone does, and it's necessary. Old files accumulate and must be removed, making room for newer files and programs. What's important is being careful when you go on a file-deleting spree. Never take this stuff casually.

I Just Reformatted an Important Disk!

To quickly help erase that feeling of stupidity, use the DOS 5 UNFORMAT command on the disk you've just reformatted. For example, type the following:

```
C:\> UNFORMAT A:
```

In this example, the UNFORMAT command revitalizes the disk in drive A. That's **UNFORMAT**, a space, the letter A, and a colon (not a semicolon). Press Enter and carefully follow the instructions on the screen.

✔ You can only unformat a disk that has been reformatted. Say you've formatted an important disk with vital information. If you've accidentally formatted it, use UNFORMAT to get your data back.

✔ Do not write any information to the disk before you use UNFORMAT. If you do, you lessen the chances of a full recovery.

✔ The UNFORMAT command takes time to work its magic. You don't have to sit and watch; it works whether or not you're there. Expect the operation to take anywhere from 3 to 15 minutes, depending on the size of the disk and the amount of information stored on it.

✔ If UNFORMAT cannot recover the disk, it will tell you. When it does — and that will be a sad day — then recovery isn't possible. The moral of this story is to be much more careful with the FORMAT command in the future.

✔ Only in rare circumstances will you need to reformat a hard disk. DOS 5 users may be able to recover an accidentally formatted hard disk by using the UNFORMAT command immediately after the mistake. There are plenty of warnings issued when you attempt to format a hard disk, so the odds of this happening are rare.

Trying to Find the Mouse

This is symbolic of most PC problems: Something isn't there that was there before. Specifically applying that to the mouse, you may have installed the mouse onto your PC — all by yourself, perhaps — yet you don't see the desired mouse pointer on your screen. There could be a number of reasons: The mouse software is not installed, the mouse hardware is incorrectly installed, or the program you're using doesn't support the mouse.

✔ If you have not installed the mouse software, it is simple enough to do: Type **MOUSE** at the DOS prompt:

```
C:\> MOUSE
```

That's the word MOUSE (as in Mickey). Press Enter. You'll see some technocompu information displayed, a copyright notice, and a version number. That's about it. If you see the message No mouse found! or something like that, you didn't install the mouse properly; refer to your guru for assistance.

✔ If you don't see the mouse's cursor at the DOS prompt, that's because the DOS prompt doesn't use a mouse. Only special mouse-approved software will take advantage of your furless rodent. Programs such as Windows, WordPerfect, Quattro, and PC Tools use the mouse. If your program says it does, but you don't see a mouse, check its installation or setup program. Better still, force someone else to do it for you.

✔ Sometimes the mouse disappears just because. Try moving the mouse to revitalize it or clicking one of the mouse's buttons.

✔ Most computer mice come with testing programs. Check the files in your computer's MOUSE subdirectory for mousey programs. (Refer to Chapter 13 if you're anxious to try a test program.)

✔ Have your guru set up your system's AUTOEXEC.BAT or CONFIG.SYS files to automatically load your mouse software. (It's called a "mouse driver." Use that term for instant respect.)

Using the Reset Switch

The Reset switch on most computers is the ultimate panic button. But do not abuse such a godsend. Only use Reset when necessary. When your system does recover, do the following:

1. **Exit Windows, DESQview, or your automatic menu program. Quit it entirely and get back to the boring old DOS prompt. (If you don't have such a program — your computer just starts at the DOS prompt — then you're fine.)**

2. **Type the following DOS command:**

```
C:\> CHKDSK /F
```

That's CHKDSK, a space, a forward slash, and the letter F. Press Enter. A whole bunch of gobbledygook is displayed.

3. **If you see the line** `Convert lost clusters/allocation units to files?`, **press Y and press Enter. (It will say either** *clusters* **or** *allocation units,* **depending on which version of DOS you're using. Press Y for yes and press Enter in either case.)**

4. **Type the following DOS command after** CHKDSK **runs:**

```
C:\> DEL FILE*.CHK
```

That's DEL, a space, FILE, an asterisk, a period, and CHK. Press Enter. Your system is now ready to run. You've fully recovered from the accidental reset.

✔ You can reset by using the Reset switch or by pressing and holding down the Ctrl, Alt, and Del keys all at the same time. This sequence is often shown as Ctrl-Alt-Del.

✔ If pressing Ctrl-Alt-Del doesn't work, and your PC doesn't have a Reset switch, turn the computer off. Wait about 15 seconds (this scares the jujus away) and then turn the computer on again.

✔ Never reset to quit a program. Always exit a program gracefully and properly. Only reset when all else fails.

✔ CHKDSK is the Check Disk program. It sifts through your hard disk and patches up any errors that pressing the Reset button may have caused.

To quit Windows, call up the Program Manager and press Alt+F4 (or just keep pressing Alt+F4 until it warns you that you're about to exit Windows). To quit DESQview, quit all your programs and press Q at the final DESQ menu. For menu programs, select the "quit" or "exit" option.

What's going on with this CHKDSKSKHSH? (if you care to know)

The CHKDSK command is rather silly — almost voodoo-like in the way people treat it. What it does is report various anecdotal statistics about your hard drive. When you add the /F (for fix) option, CHKDSK repairs bits and pieces of files that were crunched up when you pressed the panic — er, Reset — button.

CHKDSK /F picks up all the file fragments and tosses them into files. The files are named FILE000.CHK, FILE0001.CHK, and so on, up through however many bits CHKDSK finds. These files contain nothing but garbage. Contrary to what the DOS manual implies, there's nothing of value in the files, so you should delete them.

The DEL FILE*.CHK command deletes all the files CHKDSK creates. This removes the ugly things from sight and opens up more disk space for you to use.

Examining Some Tips on Troubleshooting and Repair

This isn't a tome on computer troubleshooting and repair. Such novels do exist, but their intended audience is way up there on the PC Power Pyramid. Instead, here are a few tricks you can try for basic troubleshooting and repair:

- ✔ Try pressing Ctrl-C to cancel any DOS command run amok.

- ✔ In your applications, try pressing the cancel key. No, there is no key named *Cancel* on the keyboard. Instead, each application uses its own, unique cancel key. For most programs, that's Esc on your keyboard. Press Esc. If that doesn't work, press Ctrl-C.

- ✔ In WordPerfect, the cancel key is F1.

- ✔ When things really run amok, and nothing can stop them, press the Reset button or Ctrl-Alt-Del. This action resets your computer, enabling you to start over (see "Using the Reset Switch" earlier in this chapter).

- ✔ Sometimes, it helps to turn your computer off, wait about a minute, and then turn it on again. The same applies to the printer. The wait time forces the electronic components to "drain" (seriously). This enables you to start over all afresh.

- ✔ If something doesn't work and you've tried everything, check your cable connections. First turn the computer off (all the way off). Then make sure that all the cables and whatnot are plugged in securely. Make sure that no cables or wires are stretched too tightly.

- ✔ Talk to your guru or a repair place. Refer to "Taking Mr. Computer to the Doctor" later in this chapter.

Using Your Computer's SETUP Program

All modern PCs have a special internal program that helps set them up. This is called, surprisingly, a SETUP program. It tells the computer how much memory it should have, what drives, what serial ports, and so on — a whole run-down of everything that should be in the PC. We say *should* because sometimes the list doesn't match up with what the computer thinks it really has installed. When that happens, you'll see an error message when you start your computer.

How you activate this SETUP program depends on your computer model. Some computers pop up the program when you press a special key combination. Other computers may have a SETUP command you type at the DOS prompt. Whichever way works with your computer, write it down in this box:

> To run my PC's SETUP program, I do the following:
>
> I press these keys: _____
>
> I type this at the DOS prompt: _____
>
> (Fill in the blanks, one line or the other.)

✔ If you have an older 8088/8086 or PC XT type of computer, then it lacks a SETUP program. All other types of PCs have them.

✔ Each SETUP program works differently. The instructions are usually displayed along with other information on the screen. Keep in mind that this program isn't something you'll use every day. In fact, making someone else use it for you is a good idea.

✔ The SETUP error message only happens when new equipment is added to your PC. After an upgrade, you or your guru must tell the computer about its new pieces. This is done in the SETUP program when the computer starts; then life continues as normal.

✔ You also use the SETUP program to set your computer's internal time clock.

✔ One problem could be your computer's internal battery. In addition to start-up problems, your computer may have lost track of the time. If the current date reads Tue, Jan 1, 1980, then the internal battery has died and must be replaced. This should be done by a technician.

Taking Mr. Computer to the Doctor

If you need to take the computer in, do the following:

✔ Ask the repair person how much of the computer you need to bring in — including any cables. Sometimes, the problem is just with the cable. And sometimes you may only need to bring in one part of the computer: the monitor, printer, keyboard, or some other part.

✔ Treat the computer repair place just like an automobile repair shop: Get an estimate first. They usually have a minimum charge, $15 to $45 per hour, for just looking. After that, have them give you a call with an estimate. In most states, they can only bill you for repairs you've ordered. Anything else they do that you didn't ask for is free.

✔ The repair place should warranty its work. Make sure that they're not just passing along a manufacturer's warranty (which they should do anyway). The cost of taking it back and having the same thing fixed a second time (if necessary) should be included.

✔ How do you find a good repair shop? Ask around. Local computer clubs and user groups offer unbiased advice on where to go and where to avoid.

✔ If your computer is under warranty, you can take it back to the place that sold it to you. That will be cheaper (labor-free, usually) than other places. For out-of-warranty repairs, you can shop around.

✔ Don't expect instant turnaround: Some places have you wait up to three days before you get your stuff back. Like with other things in life, an extra fee is charged if you want immediate satisfaction. (Remember, it's just like a car repair place.)

✔ If possible, back up your data before you take the computer into the shop.

✔ Make a note of everything in your computer: hard drives, modems, memory, and extra options. Copy down the serial numbers of your items. We're not saying all computer doctors are shifty and will steal items from your PC. What usually happens is that pieces of the computer are removed, and they may forget to put them back in when reassembling.

Getting Technical Support

When you buy a piece of software, you're also buying support from the software developer. This is offered in the form of written questions, faxes, and phone calls. Most people opt for phone calls because the mere thought of waiting for help through the postal system causes some people to break out in welts.

✔ There are several kinds of phone support: toll-free, unlimited calls, which are 1-800 support; toll calls, which are just like any other long distance call; 1-900 calls you're billed for by the minute (but they usually offer the best, fastest service); and calls you can make only after you've paid a hefty sum for the privilege. Usually, only accounting packages offer the latter type. Most software developers opt for the toll call.

✔ Be prepared to wait on hold or wade through a "voice mail" system before you get where you want.

✔ When you call, know your computer type, memory, disk storage, and so on. They'll ask you about it. They'll also want to know which product you're using and its serial number (if it has one).

✔ Describe the problem in full detail.

A trip to technical support

Technical support lines are notoriously busy. The more popular the software, the busier the support number is. Some software developers pay exorbitant fees to the phone company to have hundreds of support lines into their offices. Still, the lines are busy.

If you don't get a busy signal, you'll get the most horrid outcropping of the computer in business: voice mail. Run screaming for the aisles! Voice mail is the most efficient way to ignore the customer in the history of business. Here's a transcript of a phone session Dan Gookin once had while trying to get technical support:

I dialed the number and the phone picked up right away, which I thought promising. Then I heard some idiot happily telling me the following:

Thank you for calling [NAME] technical support. We deliver high-quality computer software at low prices and currently have a line of over 16 products for both the PC and Macintosh. If you'd like to hear more information about our products, press 1 now. If you're one of our Gold Ribbon Dealers, press 2. If you're buying a product, press 3. If you need technical support for one of our Macintosh products, press 4. If you need technical support for a PC product, press 5. If you know your party's extension, press it now as well. If you're on a rotary phone, hang on the line and we'll get to you as soon as possible.

I wondered whether it would be faster to pretend I had a rotary phone and stay on the line. Instead, I pressed 5. *Bleep!*

[NAME] currently offers ten products for the PC, including popular Windows applications. If you need help with one of our programming languages, press 1. If you need help with any of our Windows products, press 2. If you need help with DOS products that aren't Windows, then press —

I pressed 3 quickly. *Bleep!*

Thank you. All of our operators are busy at the moment. Please wait on hold, and the next available service agent will help you.

I waited on hold. I had this vision of the "service" department being two guys playing SpaceQuest on their computers while these huge phones stand by with thousands of blinking "on hold" lights.

I waited and waited. They played "Raindrops Keep Fallin' on My Head," then "Feelings," and then "Wichita Lineman." I don't have a speaker phone, so I had to sit for five minutes with my shoulder pressed to my ear and the phone between them. My neck started to hurt.

Hello!

"Hello," I said quickly, starting to explain my problem . . .

. . . all our technicians are still busy. If you'd like to leave a voice-mail message, our support staff will try to get back to you within 48 hours. Otherwise, you can continue to stay on hold. Note that no other opportunity to leave voice mail will be given after this message. If you'd like to leave a voice-mail message, leave your name, telephone number, and a description of the problem after pressing 1. Press 1 now.

Rather than wait on hold indefinitely (my record is 43 minutes, and it wasn't a toll-free call), I left them my voice-mail message. True to form, they called back two days later to ask me what the problem was. Note that it was two days — not 48 hours. But I did get my support, and the computer works.

Even if you do pretend you're on a rotary phone, you'll only get an operator — not a technician. They'll take your name and number and either have someone call you back or put you on hold with the clods who have push-button phones.

✔ Be patient with the support people. They handle a lot of calls and get their fair share of crap from people. Software companies don't have to offer support, but many do. Don't take advantage of it.

✔ On the other hand, don't accept the runaround from anyone. If they say "call your printer manufacturer," demand a better explanation of what you need to do. If you need an "updated driver" or something, make them be precise.

This is an awkward position: Some computer manuals stink. Some are just jumbled and contain information written by someone way too familiar with the program and not aware of the needs of a real-world PC user. Other manuals aren't really that bad. WordPerfect's manual is just too fat. Whatever. Chances are that what you need to know is buried in the manual somewhere. This makes us want to say, "Never use technical support as an excuse for not reading the manual." However, we're torn because manuals are generally bad. Therefore, we're going to say, "Look at the manual on your shelf and then call technical support." That way, you won't be lying when you say, "I looked at the manual, and I couldn't find it."

Knowing Which DOS Commands You Should Never Use

DOS For Dummies, published by IDG Books Worldwide, discusses everything you need to know about DOS, plus some extra material you'd never expect. (Buy a copy for each of your cousins!) Still, there are three DOS commands we need to warn you about here. Yes, they're that deadly:

Command: RECOVER

What it pretends to do: Rescue files from damaged disks.

What it really does: Destroys files on disks. RECOVER should never be used on a hard drive or even on a floppy drive. The damage inflicted by this command is heavy. In fact, it doesn't really repair anything. Just leave it alone.

Command: FDISK

What it pretends to do: Create or destroy "partitions" on a hard drive.

What it really does: Creates or destroys "partitions" on a hard drive. Yes, this command really works. No, it's nothing you should ever mess with. This command, when misused, can wipe out everything on your hard drive. Don't bother with it.

Command: FORMAT C:

What it pretends to do: Format a disk.

What it really does: Formats your hard disk. Yikes! That's deadly. Only use the FORMAT command with drives A and B. Never format anything higher than that and you'll be safe forever.

Avoiding Viruses

Oh, boy! A scary topic, fueled by media-induced frenzy. What a gasoline-and-fire combination!

Viruses are real and really ugly facts of computer life in the '90s. Thanks to overplay by the media, most people believe that something wrong with their PC is now attributed to some virus. However, sanely, a bug is a bug, and many of them are out there. It's not hard for things to muck up inside a PC.

If you do get a virus or if they have scared you to death about the concept, you can buy special virus-protection software. DOS 6/6.2 even comes with free virus-killing software. Run a virus checker on your computer once a week, and you'll be safer than you were before.

- ✔ Viruses are nasty programs that infect your computer, similar to the way biological viruses infect people. They usually sit low for a time and then do something such as display a message, stop your computer, delete a file, or erase your hard drive. Note that not all viruses are destructive. Also, viruses have many cousins — vicious programs that don't replicate themselves but are confused with viruses and wreak the same havoc.

- ✔ The best way to avoid getting a virus is to buy and use only software that comes "shrink wrapped" from the store or software mail-order house.

- ✔ It's OK to get software on a plain disk from a user group or software "warehouse." These types of programs are usually checked for viruses before they're handed over.

- ✔ The most suspect disks are those of illegally copied programs — especially games. If someone passes you such a disk, odds are real darn good that it contains a virus. Even if it's a friend who gives you the disk, that friend may not know whether the programs on the disk are infected.

- ✔ By all means, never start your computer (boot) with a disk in drive A containing an illegally copied game or program.

Computer users tend to blame themselves when bugs happen in a PC. They think that they did something wrong. Only after years of experience will you accept a computer bug for what it is. And, if you do get a virus, remember that you probably got it from that "borrowed" copy of a game someone gave you. It serves you right.

Summary

This chapter gave you some solutions to some common problems and presented you with some helpful information that should prevent additional problems:

▶ You learned how to undelete files and unformat a disk.

▶ You examined how to get your computer to recognize your mouse.

▶ You learned what to do after using the Reset switch on the computer.

▶ You learned how to do some basic troubleshooting.

▶ You examined how to activate your computer's SETUP program.

▶ You learned what to do when taking your computer to the repair shop.

▶ You were warned to avoid three DOS commands.

▶ You learned how to avoid computer viruses.

Part IV of this book has lots of lists that you can refer to for correcting problems, improving the time you spend with your computer, calling for help, taking simple repairs into your own hands, and easing your mind about what you should (and shouldn't) remember about computers.

Part IV
The Part of Tens

The 5th Wave

TESTING THE 686™ CHIP

"IT'S FAST ENOUGH FOR ME."

In this part...

They say that Anne Boleyn had six fingers on each hand. We just have five fingers on each hand, thank you very much, and because of that, we decided to create a big part containing lists of tens — important information, rules, dos and don'ts, and other trivia we could conveniently stick into various lists. Poor Anne would've had to do lists of 12.

Yes, we know that there aren't always ten items in each chapter. Sometimes there are more, and sometimes there are less. Still, all the information is good and organized to help you find it quickly. Now get your mind off Henry's wife and back to computers.

Chapter 21
Ten Common Boners
(and How to Deal with Them)

- -

- -

*E*verybody does dumb things every once in a while. One guy couldn't get his floppy disk to work right. That's because he'd grabbed a pair of scissors and removed the little disk from its protective black plastic case. This is laughable if you've used a computer for some time, but something a reasonable human may assume because no one ever says not to do it. Computer lore is full of such stories.

That particular mistake — or boner — isn't common enough to warrant inclusion in this chapter (although we mentioned it anyway, just in case), but the following list includes a few of the most popular problems. More importantly, it describes how to fix them.

Putting Disks near the Phone

Whereas we write stuff down with pen on paper, computers write stuff to floppy disks using little magnetic blips. Just as you don't want to get ink smudges on your important documents, you don't want to get magnetic smudges on your floppy disks.

Ink's easy to see; magnetic smudges aren't, especially because they hide in obscure places like your telephone. That means you shouldn't lean a floppy disk against the phone, even if it's the only clean spot on your desk. The magnets in your phone's speakers will rearrange the data on your disk, turning it into pictures of little cows. (OK, maybe not exactly cows, but definitely not what it was before.)

Unfortunately, there's no way to repair this one. Try the disk to see if it still works; if not, file it under "Barnyard Animals" and chalk it up to experience.

Making Cords and Cables Too Tight

All your computer's toys must live one cable length away from your computer's back. A 12-foot printer cable may have seemed plenty long enough in the store but not at home, where it must weave behind desks, along walls, around the kitty-litter box in the corner, and finally up to the printer on top of the file cabinet.

One yawning leg extension can wreak havoc with an overstretched cable. The cable won't fall out; it will just be loosened enough so that you'll think it's plugged in and spend two hours trying to get the software to recognize your printer.

Buy a longer cable right away and save yourself some time, aggravation, and that awful feeling when you have to admit to the arrogant person in technical support that "No, I guess it really wasn't plugged all the way in."

Sticking a Disk between Two Disk Drives

Just as you can learn to type without looking at the keyboard, you can learn to slide a floppy disk into that little disk drive without looking. But it's easy to type *teh,* and it's easy to slide the disk into the phantom third slot: that little dark crack between the computer's two disk drives.

This doesn't usually damage the disk, and it's not as bad as trying to make conversation after flatulating in a restaurant on a first date, but it can still be embarrassing. If your phantom slot's huge, put a piece of tape (or a write-protect tab) over it. That will block any attempts to stick a disk in no-man's land.

How do you get the disk out again? We've used tweezers (and, yes, we can admit to making this mistake). Sometimes, you need to tear the computer apart to get at the disk. Time to call the guru.

Putting Your PC in the Wrong Place

Like a finicky house plant, PCs have strong feelings about their placement. They'll overheat if used in a closet where cooling air can't flow over their hot internal chips. Any adjacent windows will not only cook them but tempt computer thieves to "smash and grab." And keep computers away from damp areas, such as Seattle, where water can damage their sensitive innards.

In fact, you'll only see a PC in a kitchen when it's on the cover of a recipe-indexing program. As soon as the photo shoot's over, the PC's owner whisks it back to the den, away from heat, grease, water, and grated carrots.

Another humorous story you probably don't want to read

We've stuck this story in a "technical" sidebar because you're probably used to not reading them by now. Regardless, there's a story — more a bit of computer folklore — about a woman who once jammed four disks into a single floppy drive. The installation program on the screen kept saying `Insert the next disk`, which is exactly what she did. What she didn't do was remove the previous disk before inserting the next one.

A technician was alerted to the problem when the user complained that she couldn't insert the last disk. Of course, this is the tip-off that the story is bogus: Although you can stick two disks into a drive, the door won't close and the disks are definitely unreadable (meaning an error message would have appeared instead of `Insert the next disk`). However, it makes a cute story. Retell it if you like but use the name of someone you know.

Not Buying Enough Power

Sure, you can save money by buying the lowest-priced computer on the show-room floor. And you can buy a Yugo at a "special clearance sale." But be reasonable. Instead of trying to wing it with a single floppy drive, buy a hard drive.

And before you even buy a computer, look at the software you want to run. Then make sure that you buy a computer that will run that software efficiently and quickly enough that you're not constantly waiting for the computer to catch up with you.

Buying Too Much Power

It's tempting to get carried away at the computer store and buy the TurboSteroid 3 PC, complete with dual exhausts. But let caution be your guide — as well as your MasterCard.

First, your computer will be out of date the minute you've signed the receipt, so don't worry about it going out of date. Computer technology zips along so fast, Scotty says, "The engines canna take much mora this." Buy a computer that meets your current needs plus allows a little room for growth.

The same applies to software. Many people buy a software package because it "will do everything" and then end up using the same three features, over and over. Buy what you need. No more, no less.

Not Letting Go of the Mouse Button First

Everybody with a computer mouse has done this one: They drag their mouse over some awkward sentence and then race up to the Delete button to vaporize it. But, in their haste to move that mouse up to the Delete button, they didn't let go of the mouse button to mark the end of the highlighted sentence.

As a result, the mouse innocently highlights all the text in between the sentence and the Delete button. With a click of the Delete button, all the wrong text vanishes. Some programs have an "undelete" button, thank goodness. Holding the Ctrl key and pressing Z restores order in Windows.

In other programs, it's gone for good. The answer? Slow down. Make sure that the correct words are highlighted before moving the mouse. Or stop using a mouse and go back to that keyboard stuff.

Forgetting to Set the Printer Back to PostScript from HPLJ

Every computer company thinks it has discovered the best way to do something, so the computer world has a zillion *standards,* or ways to do something. For example, some programs print stuff by using a standard called PostScript; others print stuff by using a standard called LaserJet.

The poor printer, caught in the middle, expects the user to throw a switch, telling it what's coming down the printer cable. If the printer receives an unexpected standard, it wigs out, printing out pages of Greek with Latin footnotes.

The trick to avoid this problem? Well, just remember to flip the right switch according to the software you're using. Or remember to tie the right string around the right finger. If this annoys you to no end, buy a standard printer next time.

Not Saving Work in Progress Often Enough

The first time you lose something on your computer, it's frustrating but expected. After all, you're a beginner. About the third or fourth time, however, it moves from frustration to aggravation. Eventually, it reaches the despair level.

Whenever you've written a blazingly original thought, select the Save command and save your document to the hard disk or a floppy disk. When you've written something dumb that you're going to patch up later, select the Save command, too. The idea here is to select Save whenever you think about it — hopefully, every four minutes or sooner.

You never know when your computer will meander off to watch the MacNeil-Lehrer Report while you're hoping to finish the last few paragraphs of that report. Save your work as often as possible. And always save it whenever you get up from your computer — even if it's just to grab a Fig Newton from the other room.

Underestimating How Long It Takes to Learn a Program

On April 14, Andy Rathbone tried to install, learn, and finish his income taxes with the hottest new income-tax preparation software. A short 23 hours and 45 minutes later, a friend pulled the manual from his mouth and handed him a small kitty toy.

Allow yourself at least a week before trying to do anything constructive with a new piece of software. Just fiddle around with it, saying you're playing with the program, not intending to get anything done. That takes the pressure off, allowing you time to explore the program's features without feeling that you have to actually make it do something.

Asking the Wrong Things

Computer gurus can handle remarkable computer geekistical operations but only if they know what you're talking about. If you ask them to "check the Kway for you," they'll shrug and move off to floss their RS-232 ports.

Learn the bare basics of pronunciation; a *queue* is pronounced Q, for example. When in doubt, write it on a card and wave it slowly over your head.

Some really great questions to ask your guru

Darn, we're in a good mood today. Here are some questions you can ask a computer guru that will "turn the tables." At once, you'll have the feeling of superiority as he or she stands there baffled, not knowing what you're talking about. Use these sparingly:

✔ I keep losing my document through an intermittent data fistula. Can you patch it up?

✔ My PC has a coolant leak. Do you know anything that can remove liquid nitrogen stains?

✔ The biotransfer filter on my keyboard is popping out. Can I stuff it back in using a flat-edge screwdriver?

✔ The frangellico dirigible osmosis is tweaked.

✔ Something in the error induction coils is transducing my document while it's being printed.

✔ Where is the "Frane" key?

✔ The Canis Familiaris virus gormandized my homework.

✔ I hear that new encephalophage virus is carried in common cerumen.

✔ My pixels are converging due to negative ion density. Is that a software or hardware problem?

✔ The manual says to "depress the Enter key." Which put-downs work best?

Summary

If you're a normal computer user — even if you're a computer nerd — you've probably made at least several of the mistakes listed in this chapter. And now you know how to fix them.

The next chapter is a wish list of stuff for your computer that you can give to Santa Claus next Christmas.

Chapter 22
Ten Things Worth Buying for Your PC

● ●

In This Chapter

▶ Software

▶ Mousepad

▶ Wrist pad

▶ Antiglare screen

▶ Keyboard cover

▶ More memory

▶ Larger, faster hard drive (when you need it)

▶ Modem

▶ Adjustable, swiveling monitor stand

▶ Power strip

● ●

*W*e're not trying to sell you anything, and we're pretty sure that you're not ready to burst out and spend, spend, spend on something like a computer (unless it's someone else's money). But there are some nifty little things you may want to consider buying for Mr. Computer. Like ten things worth buying for a dog (leash, cat-shaped squeeze toys, pooper-scooper, and so on), these ten things will make working with the beast more enjoyable.

Software

Never neglect software. There are jillions of different types of software programs available, each of them designed to perform a specific task for a certain type of user. If you ever find yourself frustrated by the way the computer does something, consider looking for a piece of software that does it better.

Mousepad

Rolling your mouse on your tabletop may work OK, but the best surface is a *mousepad,* a screen-sized piece of foam rubber with a textured topping ideal for rolling mice around. Avoid the mousepads with a smooth finish. You'll pay more for pads with cute pictures or the new "mood pads" that react to temperature. The best mousepad is one with your computer's logo on it, a picture of a frightened cat (which makes the mouse happy), or some clever sayings in Assyrian.

Wrist Pad

Like a mousepad, the wrist pad fits right below your keyboard. It enables you to comfortably rest your wrists while you type.

"Sloppy, sloppy," you hear your typing teacher, Mrs. Goodrich, scream from across the room. "Good typists raise their wrists, striking each key with a deliberate stab!" Before she waddles on over to whack the undersides of your palm with a ruler, tell her this: "Stop, you hulking bruja! Your archaic typing methods aren't needed for the delicate computer keyboard. I can lay my wrists sloppily on a colorful wrist pad and type with reckless abandon. Go make thy husband suffer!"

Antiglare Screen

Tacky as it may sound, an antiglare screen is nothing more than a nylon stocking stretched over the front of your monitor. OK, these are professional nylons in fancy holders that adhere themselves to your screen. The net result is no garish glare from the lights in the room or outside. It's such a good idea, some monitors come with built-in antiglare screens.

Glare is the number-one cause of eyestrain while you're using a computer. Lights usually reflect in the glass, either from above or from a window. The antiglare screen cuts down on the reflections and makes the stuff on the monitor easier to see.

Some antiglare screens also incorporate antiradiation shielding. We're serious: They provide protection from the harmful electromagnetic rays that are emitted from your monitor. Is this necessary? No. There are a lot of alarmists out there who claim that monitors induce nuclear madness. This can't be disproved (after all, look at your typical computer geek), so they keep at it. Buy a nuclear-proof shield if it makes you feel better or if you notice your hair falling out in clumps.

Keyboard Cover

A keyboard cover is a protective cover for your keyboard. If you're klutzy with a coffee cup, or have small children or others with peanut butter-smudged fingers using the keyboard, then the keyboard cover is a great idea. You may have even seen them used in department stores: They cover the keyboard snugly but still enable you to type. A great idea, because without it all this disgusting gunk falls between the keys. Yech!

In the same vein, there's also a generic "dust cover" you can buy for your computer. This preserves its appearance but has no other true value. Only use a computer cover when the computer is turned off (and we don't recommend turning it off). If you put the cover on the PC while it's on, you create a minigreenhouse and the computer will — sometimes — melt. Nasty. This doesn't happen to the keyboard, which is a cool character anyway.

More Memory

Any PC will work happier with more memory installed. There is an upper limit of anywhere from 16 to 64 megabytes or so (which is ridiculous). Still, upgrading your system to 4, 8, or 10 megabytes of RAM is a good idea. Almost immediately you'll notice the improvement in programs such as Windows and various graphics applications. Make someone else do the upgrading for you; you just buy the memory.

Larger, Faster Hard Drive (When You Need It)

Hard drives fill up quickly. The first time it's because you've kept a lot of junk on your hard drive: games, things people "give" you, old files, and old programs you don't use anymore. So you can delete those or copy them to floppy disks for long-term storage. Then, after a time, your hard drive fills up again. The second time, it has stuff you really use. Argh! What can you delete?

The answer is to buy a larger hard drive. If you can, install a second hard drive and start filling it up. Otherwise, replace your first hard drive with a larger, faster model. Actually, buying a faster model is a great way to improve the performance of older PCs without throwing them out entirely.

And, when you fill up your second, larger hard drive . . . then you panic.

Modem

A modem is a fun and interesting thing to have on a computer. Although it's not really necessary in most cases, you open up a whole new world when you buy a modem. Suddenly, your single computer becomes one of many. You can use the modem and your phone to dial up other computers, chat with other modem users, and call national networks like Prodigy. It can be fun and addicting.

One other thing you need if you have a modem is an extra phone line for it. This has the same logic as when you get a separate phone line for your teenager: Modems are notorious phone hogs. When you're "on the modem," no one can call in or dial out. It's just best to get an extra line specifically for the modem. The phone company doesn't charge extra for using a modem, and the calls are billed like any other phone call.

Adjustable, Swiveling Monitor Stand

Some monitors have built-in swivel stands. They enable you to adjust the way the monitor points, primarily so that the monitor points right at your face — not at your chest or over your shoulder. If your monitor is fixed, don't stick a manual under one edge to line it up; get a swiveling stand.

Some stands are actually mechanical arms. These lift the monitor up off the desk and enable you to position it in the air in front of you. Mechanical arms are great but expensive.

Power Strip

Computers use more power plugs than anything you'll find in the garage or kitchen. You need at least three plugs for the basic computer setup: one for the console, one for the monitor, and another for the printer. Everything else you add — a modem, a scanner, speakers, a desk lamp, or your clock — requires another power socket. To handle them all, buy yourself one of those six-socket power strips.

Some power strips are more expensive than others. They usually offer protection against some electrical nasties that can flow through the power lines. If that happens often in your area, consider the heavy-duty power strip as an investment. For just about everyone, however, the basic $15 model will do.

Also, don't be worried about plugging too much stuff into one wall socket. Dan Gookin has (currently) four desktop computers and two laser printers plugged into three wall sockets using four power strips. (What a pig, but Dan claims he uses everything.) Andy Rathbone runs a thick orange extension cord from a single wall socket over to two power strips, where he plugs in his computer, laser printer, monitor, desk lamp, Rickenbacker guitar amp, guitar distortion pedal, tape recorder, MIDI keyboard, and answering machine.

The only downside to such greed is a larger electrical bill.

And Andy wised up and spread out to four wall sockets after his wife pushed the automatic garage-door opener one day and everything turned off abruptly.

• •

Summary

This chapter whetted your appetite for computer stuff. If you don't already have these things, consider buying them.

The next chapter is a checklist of things you can run through before you throw in the towel and decide that your computer needs a real doctor.

• •

Chapter 23
Ten Things to Try before Taking the PC to the Repair Shop

• •

In This Chapter

▶ Turning the computer off and on again

▶ Figuring out whether it's a hardware or software problem

▶ Tightening cable connections

▶ Plugging the computer into a different outlet

▶ Bypassing the power strip

▶ Checking the circuit breaker

▶ Checking whether the monitor's contrast/brightness controls are turned down

▶ Listening for noises

▶ Determining whether the disk is damaged (or write-protected)

▶ Inviting a computer guru over for computer games

▶ Making a system disk

• •

The best way to handle trouble is to let someone else deal with it. Often, there is no one else. In fact, most computer trouble happens at the absolute worst time: the weekend. Why is it most computer stores close on Sundays? Maybe it explains why everything is so hectic on Monday mornings. Anyway, you shouldn't be working on the weekends — not when it's sunny outside or especially when they're having that Russ Meyer Film Festival at the Ken Theater.

But when you *do* have to work over a long weekend — or anytime — and something runs afoul, you can try the following things before taking the computer to the doctor. These are quick fixes to try when no one's around to help you. Also, look back to Chapter 20 for additional information when "it don't work."

Turn the Computer Off and On Again

Computer experts "cure" most of the PC's ills by following three simple steps:

1. **Turn the computer off.**

2. **Wait about 20 seconds.**

3. **Turn the computer on again.**

Most of the time, whatever was wrong has gone away. It's amazing how well this works. It's only when the problem persists that you should consider worrying about it — and then trying one of the other suggestions offered in this chapter.

Figure Out Whether It's a Hardware or Software Problem

Your guru or even you may be able to fix hardware problems, but most times they require taking the computer to the shop. Software problems, on the other hand, can generally be cured by your guru or by a phone call to the developer's technical support hot line (or wait-on-hold line). But which is which? It's important to know because computer doctors get irked when you hand them a PC with a software problem. Here are the clues:

1. **Does the problem happen consistently, no matter which program you're running?**

   For example, do WordPerfect, 1-2-3, and your accounting package all refuse to send stuff to the printer? If so, it's a hardware problem. Take it to the doctor.

2. **Did the problem just crop up?**

   For example, did the "page preview" mode work last week but not today? If so, it could be a hardware problem — provided that nothing has been changed on your computer and no new software added since the last time the program worked properly. Take it to the doctor.

3. **Does the problem happen with only one application?**

   For example, does the computer always reset when you try to print in Quattro Pro? If so, it's a software problem. Call the developer.

Generally speaking, if the problem only happens in one program, it's software. If it's consistent across all your applications, or it happens at random times, it's hardware.

Tighten Cable Connections

Loose cables can be the bane of existence — and not just in elevators. If your keyboard goes dead, your mouse freezes, or the monitor blinks out, it may be a loose cable. Here's what you should do to check:

1. **Turn the computer off.**

   Shut everything down — *everything*.

2. **Check all the cables behind the computer.**

   Wiggle them to make sure that they're in the connectors nice and snug.

3. **If something is loose, plug it back into its socket gently.**

   If the cable is stretched, move whatever it is that's stretching it so that you can plug it back into the socket.

   Some cables attach to the computer's console with handy thumb screws. Some use tiny annoying screws that require a tiny annoying screwdriver to tighten. Others may just plug in limply. The network hose usually twists as it plugs in. Printer cables have two wingdings and slide into clips on the printer.

4. **After everything is checked out, turn on the computer again and check for the same problem.**

   If it persists, get real help.

Plug the Computer into a Different Outlet

Sometimes wall sockets go dead. If the computer won't turn on, consider plugging it or your power strip into a different wall socket.

There's a doohickey you can buy at Radio Shack that tests wall sockets. It sells for about $5. You just plug it into a wall socket, and little lights will come on if the socket is supplying juice. Tell the Radio Shack people what it is you want, and they'll steer you to it in the store.

Bypass the Power Strip

If you think the power strip (your computer "command center") is broken, try plugging the computer directly into the wall. If it works, then the problem is with your power strip. Buy a new one.

Check the Circuit Breaker

Of course, the only time you really need to check the circuit breaker is when nothing else in the room comes on either. If the lamp is on and your PC sits there dumb, then it's probably a wall-socket or power-strip problem. Otherwise, saunter on over to the power box and look for one of the switches that's half-way on. Turn it off and then all the way on.

The reason your circuit breaker "trips" is that something on the line overloaded the circuit. This could be caused by faulty equipment or, more likely, too much of a power drain. If you're in an older building, your computer (or laser printer) may be pulling too much power from the line. Consider buying a new house.

Check Whether the Monitor's Contrast/ Brightness Controls Are Turned Down

Screams of "My monitor is broken!" are almost always met with relief when a wise computer owner checks the brightness and contrast buttons. Busy monitor gremlins usually twist either one to the low end of the spectrum, making your monitor look broken.

When monitors truly die, they'll start with the monitor screech of death. This is a loud, high-pitched whistle that signals the end of the monitor's life span. If you don't keep your monitor on all the time, it will probably die with a *pop* as you turn it on. Any other time, it's probably the contrast or brightness control that's goofy.

By the way, monitors are one thing you don't need to get fixed. Replacing a monitor is a much cheaper alternative than getting the old one fixed. (They're not like TVs, which can be fixed cheaply.)

The 5th Wave   **By Rich Tennant**

"QUIET EVERYONE — LET THE CRYSTAL DO ITS WORK."

Listen for Noises

Computers make a cacophony of sounds: The hard drive whirs, and its chip-munks squeal when you access data; the power supply's fan constantly hums; monitors make a high-pitched noise that only those under 30 can hear; and the keyboard goes clackity-clack as you type on it. If something goes wrong, can you still hear the noises you're supposed to? Is any noise missing? Or are there new and frightening noises?

Although you can't do anything to cure the noise problem, you should make a note of it and tell the computer technician. Unlike car noises, computer noises generally don't go away when you get to the shop.

One noise that increases over time is the hard-drive hum. At first, the sound can barely be noticed. But, as you use the computer, the hum gets louder and louder. This is caused by wear on the hard drive's bearings, and there's nothing you can do about it. When the noise becomes unbearable, you should consider buying a new hard drive (although the loud noise doesn't always indicate impending failure).

Determine Whether the Disk Is Damaged (or Write-Protected)

Sometimes, DOS claims that your disk isn't up to snuff. You'll see an error message like the following:

```
Unable to read drive A:
```

Do you have a piece of cheese in there or what?

Like wine, disks age. Unlike wine, older disks lose their flavor and quickly turn to vinegar. Also, disks become damaged with wear and tear. When they wear out, you can't use them again. Ask your guru if he or she can resuscitate the disk (sometimes that's possible).

Disks can also be zapped by magnets. Your refrigerator can have finger paintings and notes stuck to it with magnets, but no disks. All speakers contain magnets, including the speaker in your phone's handset. Never set the phone — or any other magnet — on a disk.

Another *faux pas* is the write-protected disk. This is a disk purposely made unwritable, and DOS rudely tells you so with an error message when you attempt to write to the disk. To fix that problem, unwrite-protect the disk (see Chapter 8).

Invite a Computer Guru over for Computer Games

This really falls under the bribery category. Actually, inviting a computer guru over under false pretenses is done often. The question you should really ask yourself is "Do I need to fix my problem bad enough to want to watch ole Dorito Breath sit and fondle my joystick for four hours, or do I have something better to do?"

Then again, if the PC isn't working, your guru may discover the problem for you. Lo, it's fixed, and you're once again watching your guru hog up your PC.

Make a System Disk

A good solution for most problems is to reset, or turn the computer off, wait, and then turn it on again. If that doesn't work, you may need an emergency disk with which you can start your PC. That disk is referred to as a *system disk,* and it's one of the ten things you should always keep around your PC.

The following steps describe how you can make your own system disk:

1. **Obtain a new disk; one fresh from the box is nice.**

   Further, make sure that this is a disk for your PC's drive A and that it matches the drive's size (5 ¼-inch or 3 ½-inch) and capacity (high or low). Double-check everything.

2. **Stick the disk into drive A.**

   For a 5 ¼-inch drive, close the drive-door latch, securing the disk inside. (This isn't necessary for the 3 ½-inch disk, which slides snugly into its drive.)

3. **Type the following command at your friendly DOS prompt:**

   ```
   C:\> FORMAT A: /S
   ```

   That's the word **FORMAT**, a space, the letter **A**, a colon, a space, a forward slash (near the right Shift key), and then an **S**. Double-check everything and press Enter.

4. **The FORMAT command will ask you to insert a disk, which you've already done; press Enter.**

   Time will pass.

5. **Eventually, formatting will be complete, and the screen will say** System transferred.

   (Ignore everything on the screen before that.) The computer will ask you to enter a volume label. Type in a name for the disk as follows:

   ```
   Volume label (11 characters, ENTER for none)? SYSTEM DISK
   ```

   Type **SYSTEM DISK** as shown in the preceding line (two words: *SYSTEM* and *DISK*) and press Enter.

   You'll see a whole bunch of information and meaningless statistics displayed — like an IRS form. Feel free to ignore it all; laugh at it, even.

6. **When asked to** Format another (Y/N)? **press the N key (for no).**

   You'll be plopped back to the DOS prompt, ready for action.

7. Take the disk out of the drive.

8. Write on a sticky label, in big letters, *System Disk*.

In smaller letters, write *Start your computer with this disk!* You may also want to put the computer's name on the disk, provided that you've named your computer. Now stick that label on the disk, being careful not to cover any moving parts.

9. Keep that disk handy and use it to start your computer if anything nasty happens.

In fact, you can test it now if you're really bored: Stick the disk back in the drive and press your PC's Reset button or do the Ctrl-Alt-Del thing. Keep the disk in the drive, and eventually you'll see DOS asking you for the current date. Press Enter. Then press Enter when DOS asks you for the time. You'll see a copyright message and then an ugly DOS prompt: A>.

To restart your computer as normal (and you really want to do this), remove the disk from drive A and then press the Reset button or do the Ctrl-Alt-Del thing again.

Summary

If you're working late — or anytime your guru isn't available — and your computer dies, use the suggestions in this chapter to determine whether Mr. Computer needs a real doctor or whether you can patch things up.

Chapter 24
Ten Dumb Things You Can Do with a Laptop

● ●

In This Chapter

▶ Leaving it on the roof of the rental car when you drive off

▶ Leaving it on the dashboard in Arizona

▶ Leaving it in the trunk in Michigan

▶ X-raying it at airports

▶ Checking it as luggage

▶ Using it on a beach or in the desert

▶ Closing the lid with the power on

▶ Moving it around while it's accessing the hard drive

● ●

A desktop computer doesn't undergo much abuse. Unless you have a cat or a two-year-old, it's pretty safe on the ol' desktop. It just sits there and hopes you don't spill anything too gross on it. But it's a different story with laptops. They don't get to sit on a desktop throne. They're tossed into the back seats of taxi cabs, slapped onto the counter at coffee shops, and banged around in airports. They're set on top of greasy counters, rained on, and dropped to the floor late at night in hotel rooms. In fact, laptops take so much abuse, this chapter's devoted to explaining what those poor laptop critters dread the most. And when your laptop's not happy, you won't be either.

Leave It on the Roof of the Rental Car When You Drive Off

It's common practice to put the suitcase or jacket on the roof of the car while you're searching for the keys. And most of the time, it's common practice to grab it back off the top of the car when you've finally opened the door.

But when dealing with strange new rental cars in strange new lands . . . well, don't feel dumb if you have to stick your head out the window and do a last-minute roof check before driving off. You'll feel dumber if you don't and then hear a *clump* sound as you round the last corner.

Leave It on the Dashboard in Arizona

A briefcase will be OK on the dashboard for a few minutes; so will various maps and travel-sized Kleenex boxes. But don't leave that laptop sitting up there under any circumstances.

At the worst, the heat will wipe out the circuitry. At the best, the sun will just heat up the screen so that you can't read it. (The whole screen will look black.) Keep that laptop with you — even if you're just heading into the gas station to buy a can of Mountain Dew.

And if the screen does turn black, leave it in a cool place for a while. It will probably come back to normal when it cools down.

(Why are you leaving your laptop in a visible location, anyway? You wouldn't leave important things like your wallet or baseball-card collection out in plain sight, would you?)

Leave It in the Trunk in Michigan

This is yet another rental-car boner, although it can happen with any car if you're not careful. Laptops don't like cold, although freezing temperatures aren't quite as damaging as heat. Chances are, when you discover your frozen little bundle of chips the next morning, it won't work. Even when the batteries warm up enough to put out some power, you won't be able to read the screen. Don't panic; it's not that bad.

Keep the laptop out of the cold for a few hours; when it returns to room temperature, it will be back to normal. And so will you.

The 5th Wave — **By Rich Tennant**

" A PORTABLE COMPUTER? YOU'D BETTER TALK TO OLD BOB OVER THERE. HE'S OWNED A PORTABLE LONGER THAN ANY ONE HERE."

X-Ray It at Airports

Some people say the airport's x-ray machine won't hurt a laptop at all; others say it can damage your disks and RAM chips. But even if it's harmless, there's really no reason to plop that laptop on the conveyor belt, and there are several reasons not to.

First, you'll already have to take it out of its case and show the security guard that it's a functioning computer and not an explosive device. (You did stock fresh batteries, didn't you?) Because you'll be showing it to the guards, they won't force you to x-ray it.

Second, the x-rays probably wouldn't hurt the computer, but the magnets in the conveyor-belt mechanism may hurt your floppies.

Finally, the First Rule of Laptops says to keep it with you at all times. Why risk letting it out of your sight?

Check It as Luggage

At the security gate, it's a hassle to take your laptop out of its carrying case, turn it on, wait for it to boot, and wait for the security guards to verify that it's not going to blow up. It's even more of a delay if they want to play a game of Tetris, too.

But that's still preferable to packing your laptop as luggage and having it ride in the belly of the plane. What if your Head and Shoulders bottle leaks on it, just like it leaked on your socks on the way to Denver last year?

Also, it violates a prime directive of laptops: Don't let the beasts out of your sight.

Use It on a Beach or in the Desert

Finally got that laptop, huh? Ready to get some work done at the beach or while four-wheeling it in the dunes?

Make sure that you bring a portable, battery-powered vacuum cleaner, too. Sand will infiltrate the keyboard, making typing miserable. The sun will glare on the display, making it unreadable. And the heat will probably turn the screen black after a half-hour, anyway.

No, the beach and the desert are no places for a laptop, where a bottle of 79-cent suntan lotion can effectively destroy a $2,000 computing machine. Leave the laptop at home.

To act on that "adventurous computing" urge, use an Atari Portfolio palmtop. It's a one-pound IBM-compatible computer with a tiny screen and keyboard. Typing is slow going, unless you've been hunting and pecking all along. But there's a built-in spreadsheet and scheduler, as well as a month-long battery life. Best of all, at around $200 a pop, the Portfolio is the closest thing to a disposable IBM-compatible computer you'll find.

Close the Lid with the Power On

Laptop users are notorious clock watchers: Even the most super-duper batteries won't last more than four hours, and that's not enough for a day's work. Battery management becomes a way of life. And one of the quickest ways to drain the battery is to close the lid with the power on.

Most laptops today have an automatic shut-off feature, and they'll turn themselves off if you've forgotten. Still, check to make sure that you've turned off that critter before you shut the lid.

Move It around While It's Accessing the Hard Drive

Laptops are remarkably durable. O.J. Simpson could carry one through an airport with no problem, as long as he didn't make a slam at the end. Most laptops can withstand a drop of a foot or so — even farther if they're still in their cases.

But they're not so hardy while their hard drives are running. Inside that hard drive, a little metal thing hovers about 1/100 of an inch over a fragile little disk that whirls around. If you jar the laptop while the hard drive's accessing data, the little metal thing could dip into that disk like a Thrifty ice-cream scoop.

Keep the laptop in a stable area when using it and try not to jar it while a program's running (even if you've just botched your fifth landing in Microsoft Flight Simulator).

Summary

If you're mad at your laptop, this chapter has given you several guaranteed ways to hurt it. If you value your laptop, don't do these things to it.

On the off chance that you want to use your laptop as something more than a hard pillow in a sand storm, the next chapter lists some smart things you can do to keep the laptop healthy and happy.

Chapter 25
Ten Smart Things You Can Do with a Laptop

• •

In This Chapter

▶ Getting a handsome laptop traveling case
▶ Getting a traveling kit
▶ Charging the batteries before you leave on a trip
▶ Formatting your disks beforehand
▶ Buying disk-doubling software
▶ Having your name and address very visible
▶ Saving your finished work after each session

• •

Although we totally enjoyed describing the dumb things you can do with a laptop, we thought it would be only fair to balance things. This chapter lists ten (minus three) smart things you can do with your laptop computer.

Get a Handsome Laptop Traveling Case

Laptops are sold without cases. This is sad because the case gives you something handy in which to tote the laptop. You *need* a case. There must be a place to put books, pens, pads of paper, notes, disks, and so on — just as everyone did before laptop computers came of age. (OK, and the case helps to store power supplies and other gizmos you need when you compute "on the road.")

Many laptop makers offer their own unique laptop cases. These have special pockets for everything you need, as well as a large logo emblazoned on the side. But they're expensive. As an alternative, we can suggest visiting any luggage shop and picking out a small travel case or soft briefcase. Andy Rathbone sticks his tiny Atari Portfolio palmtop into a black-and-red camera bag he bought at Target. Dan Gookin's favorite is a small Eddie Bower number that has lots of handy pockets and zippers.

As a personal bit of advice, try to avoid the heavy-duty leather laptop cases. Although they're nice looking and expensive, they're too bulky to fit under your typical airline seat (even in first class). And hard briefcases are bad because things jostle too easily. Stick with soft cases.

Get a Traveling Kit

A great thing to toss into your handsome laptop traveling case is a laptop traveling kit. Quite a few outfits sell these handy things. Inside you'll find a great array of laptop doodads to help you compute on the road: two-prong to three-prong adapter; small extension cord; triplex wall adapter (to get three sockets out of one); folded-up flat printer cable; pocket knife; small screwdriver; telephone cables, adapters, wire cutters, and so on; extra batteries, disks, and printer paper; small bottle of liquor — you get the idea.

You don't really need to buy such a kit; putting one together on your own can be fun. Just remember to think of everything.

Charge the Batteries before You Leave on a Trip

Laptop batteries are usually good from 90 minutes to 4 or more hours. But that's only after they've been freshly charged. When your laptop has been sitting on the shelf for a while, who knows how long the batteries will last? Be prepared: Charge your laptop the night before you leave on a trip. If you have any extra batteries, charge them as well.

Format Your Disks Beforehand

Nothing drains a laptop's battery like formatting a disk. Because of this, it's a swell idea to format all your disks before you leave on a trip. The more time you spend accessing a floppy disk, the less battery life your laptop will have.

Buy Disk-Doubling Software

Space in a laptop is at a premium. One thing laptops skimp on is hard-disk storage. And, unlike with a desktop system, you can't easily add an extra hard drive to your laptop. The solution is to buy disk-doubling software, such as the popular Stacker program.

Using secret tricks (that would bore you to tears if we explained them here), Stacker doubles the amount of hard-disk storage you have. The end result is a lot of extra room without any hardware-upgrading hassle. Stacker, or a similar disk-doubler, is a wise investment for any laptop owner.

Do people ever tie strings around their fingers like this?

Have Your Name and Address Very Visible

Unlike desktop computers anchored to a desk, laptops are mobile. Should yours wander off, you'll want the kind soul who finds it to be able to get it back to you. To help in that process, tape a business card to the underside of your laptop. Better still, have your guru configure the laptop so that your name, company name, phone number, or any other important information will appear on the screen whenever the laptop starts.

Save Your Finished Work after Each Session

Desktop computers are left running for the most part; you rarely turn off your PC. Laptops, on the other hand, should be turned off when you're not using them or when you're done for the day. That saves on battery juice, but it may also cause you to lose any file you're working on. To avoid that, save your files to disk before you turn off the laptop. If the laptop has a hard drive, then save your work there. It will stay on the hard drive even when the laptop's power is turned off. For floppy-only laptops, save your work to a floppy disk before you turn the laptop off.

● ●

Summary

Take good care of your little laptop by observing the rules in this chapter. You'll both be happier.

Whether you have a desktop or a laptop, you'll want to know what we consider to be some of the most common mistakes you can make when you use the computer. The next chapter tells you.

● ●

Chapter 26
Ten Big Mistakes

. . . .

In This Chapter

▶ Buying too much software

▶ Buying incompatible software

▶ Buying incompatible hardware

▶ Not buying enough supplies

▶ Not backing up files onto floppies

▶ Not saving your work before spell-checking it

▶ Keeping the monitor up too bright

▶ Turning the computer rapidly on and off again

▶ Writing on a disk label with a pen

. . . .

Sure, there are a million mistakes you can make with a computer, whether it's deleting the wrong word or dropping the monitor on your toe. But we've narrowed the list down to ten (OK, there are nine of 'em). Now, these aren't the classic boners discussed in Chapter 21, but they're closely related. These are the day-to-day operating mistakes that people tend to repeat until they're told not to.

Buying Too Much Software

Why would we advise against buying too much software? We'd be hypocrites if we did because both of us have hundreds of pieces of software. (Of course, we're nerds, so it's all right.)

What we're really advising against here is buying too much software at the same time. Buying software's a lot different from buying CDs at the music store. You can listen to a stack of CDs in three days. They're enjoyable the first time, and they age well.

But software is gruesome on the first day, and the enjoyment curve rises slowly after that. It can take months to learn the basics of a single piece of software. Even after a year, you'll still be finding features. Even if you read the entire manual, you still won't know everything about the software. Programs always have undocumented features — stuff the person forgot to put in the manual — or mistakes the program wasn't supposed to have.

So have mercy on yourself at the checkout counter and buy software at a moderate rate. You'll learn it faster and won't have the headache of installing five programs in one night, finding out your computer no longer works, and then having to narrow down a list of five suspects at the scene of the crime.

Buying Incompatible Software

The ads for Microsoft Windows make it look so easy: Simply copy numbers from your spreadsheet and electronically paste them into your corporate report. That's it; you're done — with time left over to shop for a new V-neck sweater.

It's a big deal because most software isn't compatible. Before Windows, people printed out their spreadsheets and then retyped the numbers into their reports. Also, spreadsheets couldn't read spreadsheets created by another program; word processors could only read their own documents.

When buying pieces of software, check the fine print on the box to make sure that they can all read data from each other. The situation's improving; most of the major (that means *expensive*) packages can read information from other programs. Ask the salesperson to be sure.

Or buy Microsoft Windows and a whole suite of Windows programs to go with it.

Buying Incompatible Hardware

A computer must be put together like a happy family from a '50s TV show. All the parts must live together in a dreamy, happy way. A computer's separate pieces all affect each other, and if one of them is belligerent, the whole show can go off the air.

For example, when buying a new monitor, you must make sure that the monitor matches your video card (the thing inside your computer that sends the information to the monitor). Likewise, you can't use an old XT keyboard with a newer computer. It just won't work. Sometimes, even the simplest things go wrong: You've bought high-density disks, and you only have a low-density drive.

Incompatibility problems can be avoided two ways. First, when upgrading your computer, have somebody else handle all the messy installation chores. That person will know right off the bat what stuff will work together. Second, write down the parts of your computer in the box you'll find in Chapter 15. Then either take this book to the store or copy that page.

Not Buying Enough Supplies

People buy toilet paper in big 8-roll packages because they know they're going to use it. The same goes with floppy disks and printer paper. Sooner or later, they'll all be used up.

You don't have to sit down and format an entire case of floppy disks. But when you open a box, format all the disks in that particular box. That way, you'll always have a formatted disk handy when you need to copy something in a hurry.

Paper's cheaper by the case, too, and it ages well as long as it's kept away from wet garage corners.

Not Backing Up Files onto Floppies

Saving work on a computer is a many-tiered process. First, save the work to your hard drive while you're creating it. Then, at the end of the day, back up your work to floppy disks. Finally, back up those floppy disks to another set of floppies so that you have two copies for safekeeping.

You don't have to back up your programs; you've already saved the original disks that came in the box. (You did save those, didn't you?) Programs can be reinstalled easily enough.

But be sure to save your current data files to a disk at the end of each day. That way, you'll only have lost a day's work, at the worst, if something too awful to mention happens to your hard disk.

While you're backing up your day's work, be sure to copy your AUTOEXEC.BAT and CONFIG.SYS files to a floppy disk, too. Those files contain some important computer information that can be difficult to re-create from scratch.

Not Saving Your Work before Spell-Checking It

Only adolescents like to look words up in the dictionary, and even those guys are only interested in a few choice words. Looking for misspellings is a pain; that's why we tell the computer to do it. But the computer doesn't like to fiddle with dictionaries, either. It has to look up every word in the document — from *it* to *QWERTY.*

That's a strain on its resources, and if a word processor's going to sigh and give up, it'll do it during a spell check. And, of course, that can be the most frustrating time for a computer to freeze up. Instead of being finished, you're tossed back in time to the last time you saved your work.

So always select that Save button before telling your computer to spell-check your work. Then, for the first time, you can laugh and dance a thankful little jig when the computer freezes up during the spell check.

Keeping the Monitor Up Too Bright

There's not much explaining to do here. Keeping the monitor turned up too bright is bad for the eyes, and it wears out the monitor more quickly.

To adjust the monitor to pink perfection, turn the brightness (the knob next to the little sun) all the way up and adjust the contrast (the knob next to the little circle with a slash through the middle) until the display looks pleasing. Then turn the brightness down until the little "square" outside the picture's edges disappears.

That's it!

Turning the Computer Rapidly On and Off Again

A computer, like anybody else, doesn't like to get up in the morning. But computers have it a little worse than everybody else. That morning jolt of electricity bursts through the computer's veins, stretching everything a tad and waking up all the electrical components. It's quite a shock, so to speak.

But people who turn the computer on and off again rapidly, flicking the switch like a kindergartner at a shopping-mall kiosk, can actually damage their computer. The computer's circuits get most of their wear and tear when they're first turned on, and that jolt of electricity races through internal parts.

In fact, some people leave their computers turned on all the time, just because they don't want to antagonize their computers. But whatever you do, don't flip that switch on and off, just out of spite. If you must turn your computer off and on again (and there really aren't many reasons to do so because you can use the Reset button instead), wait at least 20 seconds before turning it back on.

Writing on a Disk Label with a Pen

Disks are delicate creatures, and their thin plastic protective liners don't help much. In fact, they won't even stand up to the tip of a ballpoint pen.

The pen's tip will press through the plastic and indent the magnetic media on the floppy disk inside, leaving handwriting instead of data.

Instead, write on the sticky label *before* you stick it to the floppy. Or use a soft, felt-tipped pen to write stuff. Your data will thank you. And when you stick the label on the floppy, be careful not to cover any moving parts: that little window where the disk shows through, that little sliding metal cover, or anything else that looks important.

● ●

Summary

You're in good company; most computer users do some pretty evil things to their computer stuff. But now you know what not to do.

Now that you don't have to worry about doing the things listed in this chapter, what else can we tell you not to worry about? How about things worth remembering. They're listed in the next chapter.

● ●

Chapter 27
Ten Things Worth Remembering

*W*hat! More things to remember? Stuff to remember besides pressing the F3 key for help in WordPerfect? Pressing Alt+F4 to close a window in Windows? Hitting the printer on the side when it jams?

Yeah, but these things aren't as hard to remember. And they're more fun, too. Keep these ideas floating in the back of your memory while computing for an easier, more trouble-free session.

You Control the Computer

You bought the computer. You clean up after its messes. You feed it floppy disks when it asks for them.

You control the computer, simple as that. Don't let that computer try to boss you around with its bizarre DOS conversations and funny idiosyncrasies. It's really pretty dopey; it's an idiot.

If somebody shoved a flattened can of motor oil in your mouth, would you try to taste it? Of course not. But stick a flattened can of motor oil into a disk drive, and the computer will try to read information from it, thinking it's a floppy disk.

You control that mindless computer just like you control an infant. You must treat them the same way, with respect and caring attention. Don't feel like the computer's bossing you around any more than you feel like a baby's bossing you around during 3 a.m. feedings.

They're both helpless creatures, subject to your every whim. Be gentle.

Upgrading Software Isn't an Absolute Necessity

Just as the models on the cover of *Vogue* change their clothes each season — or maybe that should be change their *fashions* each season — software companies issue perpetual upgrades. Should you automatically buy the upgrade?

Of course not. If you're comfortable with your old clothes, you don't buy new ones just because the season changed. And if you're comfortable with your old software, there's no reason to buy the new version (unless you're a nerd).

The software upgrade probably has a few new features in it (although you still haven't had a chance to check out all the features in the current version). And the upgrade probably has some new bugs in it, too, making it crash in new and different ways. Feel free to look at the box, just as you stare at the ladies on the cover of *Vogue*. But don't feel obliged to buy something you don't need. (And we apologize for all the parentheticals.)

If You've Backed Up Your Files, You've Only Lost a Day's Work

Backing up files onto floppy disks is about as exciting as vacuuming under the couch. You know it should be done, but it's boring, and chances are it won't really matter whether you do it or not.

But accidents happen. Cats can drag dead roaches out from beneath the couch when Grandma's over. And your software can crash, leaving you with nothing but a blank screen.

Back up your files every time you're through working with your computer. If you back up your files onto floppies every day, at the very worst you'll have lost only one day's worth of work. And train the cat to not only drag out the roaches but to toss them in the trash *before* Grandma arrives.

Most Computer Nerds Love to Help Beginners

It's sad, but most computer nerds spend most of their waking hours in front of a computer. They know that's kind of a geeky thing to do, but they can't help it. Something deep inside forces them to stare into the screen, typing things like this:

```
C:\> FC C:\STUFF\GIDGET D:\MORSTUF\GADGET /C /T /L
```

It's their guilty consciences that usually make them happy to help beginners. By passing on knowledge, they can legitimize the hours they've whiled away on their computer stools. Plus, it gives them a chance to brush up on a social skill that's been slowly slipping away: the art of actually talking to a person.

But, remember, computer nerds are more accustomed to computers, not people. When a nerd gives a command to a computer, the computer acts on it. So when the computer nerd has answered your question, write down the answer on a sticky note. Keep the answer handy, so you won't have to bother the computer nerd again with the same question. Don't try to keep them away from their computers for too long.

Life Is Too Important to Be Taken Seriously

Hey, simmer down. Computers aren't part of life. They're nothing more than mineral deposits and drab plastics. Close your eyes and take a few deep breaths. Listen to the ocean spray against the deck on the patio; listen to the gurgle of the marble Jacuzzi in the master bedroom.

Pretend you're driving the convertible through a grove of sequoias on a sunny day, with the wind whipping through your hair and curling over your ears. Pretend you're lying on the deck under the sun as the _Princess Caroline_ chugs south toward the islands with friendly, wide-eyed monkeys that eat coconut chunks from the palm of your hand.

You're up in a hot-air balloon, swirling the first sip of champagne and feeling the bubbles explode against the underside of your tongue. Ahead, to the far left, the castle's spire rises through the clouds, and you can smell Chef Meisterbrau's waiting banquet.

Then slowly open your eyes. It's just a dumb computer. Really. Don't take it too seriously.

Index

Notes

Notes

Order Form

Order Center: (800) 762-2974 (8 a.m.-5 p.m., PST, weekdays) or **(415) 312-0650**

For Fastest Service: Photocopy This Order Form and FAX it to: **(415) 358-1260**

Quantity	ISBN	Title	Price	Total

Shipping & Handling Charges

Subtotal	U.S.	Canada & International	International Air Mail
Up to $20.00	Add $3.00	Add $4.00	Add $10.00
$20.01-40.00	$4.00	$5.00	$20.00
$40.01-60.00	$5.00	$6.00	$25.00
$60.01-80.00	$6.00	$8.00	$35.00
Over $80.00	$7.00	$10.00	$50.00

In U.S. and Canada, shipping is UPS ground or equivalent.
For Rush shipping call (800) 762-2974.

Subtotal _____

CA residents add
applicable sales tax _____

IN residents add
5% sales tax _____

Canadian residents
add 7% GST tax _____

Shipping _____

Total _____

Ship to:

Name _____

Company _____

Address _____

City/State/Zip_____

Daytime Phone _____

Payment: Check to IDG Books (US Funds Only)   Visa   Mastercard   American Express

Card# _____ Exp._____ Signature_____

Please send this order form to: IDG Books, 155 Bovet Road, Suite 310, San Mateo, CA 94402.

Allow up to 3 weeks for delivery. Thank you!

IDG BOOKS WORLDWIDE REGISTRATION CARD

RETURN THIS REGISTRATION CARD FOR FREE CATALOG

Title of this book: PC's For Dummies

My overall rating of this book: ❑ Very good [1] ❑ Good [2] ❑ Satisfactory [3] ❑ Fair [4] ❑ Poor [5]

How I first heard about this book:

❑ Found in bookstore; name: [6]

❑ Advertisement: [8]

❑ Word of mouth; heard about book from friend, co-worker, etc.: [10]

❑ Book review: [7]

❑ Catalog: [9]

❑ Other: [11]

What I liked most about this book:

What I would change, add, delete, etc., in future editions of this book:

Other comments:

Number of computer books I purchase in a year: ❑ 1 [12]   ❑ 2-5 [13]   ❑ 6-10 [14]   ❑ More than 10 [15]

I would characterize my computer skills as: ❑ Beginner [16] ❑ Intermediate [17] ❑ Advanced [18] ❑ Professional [19]

I use ❑ DOS [20] ❑ Windows [21] ❑ OS/2 [22] ❑ Unix [23] ❑ Macintosh [24] ❑ Other: [25]_____

(please specify)

I would be interested in new books on the following subjects:
(please check all that apply, and use the spaces provided to identify specific software)

❑ Word processing: [26]

❑ Data bases: [28]

❑ File Utilities: [30]

❑ Networking: [32]

❑ Other: [34]

❑ Spreadsheets: [27]

❑ Desktop publishing: [29]

❑ Money management: [31]

❑ Programming languages: [33]

I use a PC at (please check all that apply): ❑ home [35] ❑ work [36] ❑ school [37] ❑ other: [38] _____

The disks I prefer to use are ❑ 5.25 [39] ❑ 3.5 [40] ❑ other: [41]_____

I have a CD ROM: ❑ yes [42]   ❑ no [43]

I plan to buy or upgrade computer hardware this year: ❑ yes [44]   ❑ no [45]

I plan to buy or upgrade computer software this year: ❑ yes [46]   ❑ no [47]

Name: _____ Business title: [48] _____ Type of Business: [49] _____

Address (❑ home [50] ❑ work [51]/Company name: _____)

Street/Suite# _____

City [52]/State [53]/Zipcode [54]: _____ Country [55] _____

❑ **I liked this book!** You may quote me by name in future
IDG Books Worldwide promotional materials.

My daytime phone number is _____

IDG BOOKS

THE WORLD OF
COMPUTER
KNOWLEDGE

 **YES!**

Please keep me informed about IDG's World of Computer Knowledge.
Send me the latest IDG Books catalog.